REVISE ENGLISH

A COMPLETE REVISION COURSE FOR
GCSE

Stephen Tunnicliffe MA
Frances Glendenning BA
Denys Thompson MA

Charles Letts & Co Ltd
London Edinburgh & New York

First published 1979
by Charles Letts & Co Ltd
Diary House, Borough Road, London SE1 1DW

Revised 1981, 1983
This edition first published 1987

Illustrations: Kate Charlesworth, Philip Bannister

British Library Cataloguing in Publication Data
Tunnicliffe, Stephen
    Revise English: a complete revision course
    for GCSE. – 3rd ed. – Letts study aids
    1. English language – Grammar – 1950-
    I. Title   II. Glendenning, Frances
    III. Thompson, Denys
    428 PE1112

    ISBN-0-85097-780-0

Printed and bound in Great Britain by
Charles Letts (Scotland) Ltd

PREFACE

This book is a comprehensive revision guide for students of all ages preparing for the new GCSE examination and the standard grade of the SCE. It has been written after detailed and thorough analysis of the requirements of all six GCSE Examining Groups and those of the Scottish Examination Board for SCE. The book includes a summary of syllabus requirements and incorporates quotations and sample questions from the actual syllabuses.

The two biggest changes in GCSE English as compared with GCE and CSE are the increased use of *coursework* and the introduction of a compulsory *oral* element into the examination. These are both given due attention in this book as are the many other detailed changes of emphasis in the new syllabuses. Students, parents and teachers welcomed the first edition of *Revise English* in 1979 as a genuine organized revision course, not a mere 'crammer'. This new book maintains the concept, while being in no sense a mere revision of the original but a full-scale re-writing in the light of the new examination, which we welcome as incorporating changes that are in line with enlightened English teaching today.

As the book is designed to be used directly by students, it includes a substantial amount of self-testing material, mainly supplied with answers so that the student can check her or his own progress. No book can promise to get you through an examination; that depends on the effort and dedication a student puts into the preparation. We can say, categorically, that if this book is used fully, along the lines of advice given, particularly in the opening pages, the student will gain skill and assurance in the control of English and will be able to enter the examination with confidence.

This is a book to be used frequently and continually. It embodies a new approach to revision, aimed directly at the student. Because proficiency in English depends so much on varied and discriminating reading we have included samples of many kinds for study and enjoyment. Many of the passages should tempt students to seek out the books they come from and thus enhance their own enjoyment of literature as well as providing models which will increase their mastery of English. Because we believe that cheerfulness achieves more than gloom, we have included material that is light-hearted and humorous. We hope it will therefore prove to be entertaining as well as instructive.

We aim to maintain the usefulness of this book as an up-to-date revision aid. Any changes in syllabus will be included as they occur in future editions of *Revise English*.

Stephen Tunnicliffe 1987

Acknowledgements

Every effort has been made to trace copyright holders and to obtain their permission for the use of copyright material. The authors and publishers wish to make the following acknowledgements, and will gladly receive information enabling them to rectify any reference or credit in subsequent editions:

Text

pp. 22–3 reprinted by permission of Faber and Faber Ltd from *The Bog People* by P V Glob;

pp. 23–5 reprinted by permission of Associated Book Publishers (UK) Ltd from *Fenwomen: a Portrait of Women in an English Village* ed. Mary Chamberlain (Routledge and Kegan Paul);

pp. 25-6 reprinted by permission of David Higham Associates Limited from *The Countryside Explained* by John Seymour (Faber and Faber);

p. 26 reprinted by permission of the authors from *Country Bazaar* by A Pittaway and B Scofield (Architectural Press);

p. 28 reprinted by permission of Constable & Company Limited from *Heath Robinson, Artist and Comic Genius* by John Lewis;

pp. 29-30 'Care and Feeding of Mothers' reprinted from *Outrageous Opinions* by Helen Gurley Brown (NEL);

pp. 30-2 reprinted by permission of the Estate of the late Sonia Brownell Orwell and Martin Secker & Warburg from *Collected Essays, Journalism and Letters* by George Orwell;

pp. 34-5 'Are we feeding ourselves to death?' *The Times*, by Philippa Pullar reprinted by permission of Times Newspapers Limited;

pp. 36-7 reprinted by permission of BBC Enterprises Ltd from *A Guide to Alternative Medicine* by Robert Eagle (BBC Publications);

pp. 37-8 reprinted by permission of Martin Secker & Warburg Limited from *To Jerusalem and Back* by Saul Bellow;

pp. 38-9 reprinted by permission of Hodder and Stoughton Limited from *The Fearful Void* by Geoffrey Moorhouse;

pp. 47-9 reprinted by permission of Aitken Stone from *The Old Patagonian Express* by Paul Theroux (Hamish Hamilton);

pp. 49-51 reprinted by permission of Faber and Faber Ltd from *The Bell Jar* by Sylvia Plath;

pp. 54-5 reprinted by permission of Allison & Busby Publishers Ltd from *Absolute Beginners* by Colin MacInnes;

pp. 56-7 reprinted by permission of Virago Press Ltd from *I Know Why the Caged Bird Sings* by Maya Angelou;

p. 61 reprinted by permission of the author from *The Shocking History of Advertising* by E S Turner (Michael Joseph);

pp. 64-6 reprinted by permission of Michael Joseph Ltd from *A Kestrel for a Knave* by Barry Hines;

p. 67 reprinted by permission of Holt, Rinehart and Winston, Inc. from *Introduction to Anthropology* by Roger Pearson;

pp. 70-1 reprinted by permission of BBC Enterprises Ltd from *The Ascent of Man* by Jacob Bronowski (BBC Publications);

p. 73 reprinted by permission of the Office of Population Censuses and Surveys;

pp. 78-9 reprinted by permission of Oxford University Press from *'Master Harold'… and the Boys* by Athol Fugard;

p. 81 'Cathedral Builders' reprinted by permission of Christopher Davies (Publishers) Ltd from *Requiem and Celebration* by John Ormond;

pp. 85-6 reprinted by permission of the author from 'Cane is Bitter' in *Ways of Sunlight* by Sam Selvon (Longman);

pp. 88-9 'Moorings' reprinted by permission of Chatto & Windus Ltd from *A Round of Applause* by Norman MacCaig;

pp. 89-92 reprinted by permission of A D Peters & Co Ltd from *Sword of Honour* by Evelyn Waugh (Chapman & Hall);

p. 98 reprinted by permission of Peter Owen, London from *Advice to a Young Critic* by G B Shaw;

p. 106 reprinted by permission of Wolfe Publishing Limited from *The Awful Handyman's Book* by J. Wheeler;

pp. 106-7 'Additives Ban in Children's Food Urged', *The Times*, reprinted by permission of Times Newspapers Limited;

pp. 107-8 'School of Red Herrings' by Nicholas Blake reprinted from *Diversion*, ed. John Sutro (Macdonald and Jane's);

pp. 111-12 reprinted by permission of Her Majesty's Stationery Office from *Roadcraft: Police Drivers' Manual*;

p. 125 reprinted by permission of Heinemann Educational Books Ltd from the *Heinemann English Dictionary* ed. Harber and Payton;

p. 125 reprinted by permission of Oxford University Press from the *Pocket Oxford Dictionary* (Seventh Edition);

p. 145 'Chairman's Statement' reprinted by permission of Marks and Spencer Plc;

p. 146 'The Planster's Vision' reprinted by permission of John Murray (Publishers) Ltd from *Collected Poems* by John Betjeman;

pp. 146-7 reprinted by permission of Routledge and Kegan Paul from *Wellington Road* by Margaret Lassell;

p. 147 reprinted by permission of David Higham Associates Limited from *Watership Down* by Richard Adams (Rex Collings);

p. 148 'A Bird's Cold Comfort', *The Times* by Bill Boroughs, reprinted by permission of Times Newspapers Limited;

p. 150 article on alcoholism, *The Times*, reprinted by permission of Times Newspapers Limited;

pp. 150-1 reprinted by permission of Faber and Faber Ltd from *The Mouse and his Child* by Russell Hoban;

p. 152 reprinted by permission of the British Broadcasting Association from *The Listener*;

p. 154 reprinted from *Across the Barricades* by Joan Lingard (Hamish Hamilton);

pp. 155-6 reprinted by permission of The Bodley Head from *The Cay* by Theodore Taylor;

p. 164 poem by Kenneth Slessor reprinted from *Australian Writers and their Work* (Oxford University Press).

For use of specimen examination questions and syllabuses, we are grateful to the seven examining groups.

Photographs and Illustrations

Picturepoint pp. 22, 35, 69, 78;
J & W Collins and The University of Reading, Institute of Agricultural History and Museum of English Rural Life p. 25;
By permission of Gerald Duckworth & Co and the estate of W. Heath Robinson p. 27;
All-Sport/Dave Cannon pp. 31, 65;
W. Foulsham & Co Ltd p. 36;
Natural Science Photos p. 38;
Ian Beames/Ardea London p. 39, Valerie Taylor/Ardea London p. 103;
BBC Hulton Picture Library p. 53;
Press Association p. 53;
Virago Press p. 57;
Woodmansterne/Jeremy Marks p. 80;
Frank Lane Picture Agency p. 102;
Science Photo Library/Martin Bond p. 143.

CONTENTS

INTRODUCTION

How this Book is Organized

Our first aim has been to make the book a useful learning and revision tool for you, the student preparing for GCSE or SCE English. It is planned so that you can work directly from it and to a large extent check your work as well, by referring to the 'Answers' unit. As you see from the Contents page, there are *five* parts to this book.

WRITING AND READING: UNITS W1–W5

Writing and reading English will always be of the first importance for anyone trying to improve his or her understanding and control of the language, whether in the form of books and literature or of one's own writing attempts. The two go hand in hand, as you will see all through this section. The ability to find the right words, to write accurately, to relate your tone and style to your audience, to adapt your writing to particular circumstances (setting out a report, telling a story, writing a set of notes etc.) – all these depend to a great extent on your personal *experience* of English in use and much of that is bound to come from the printed word, whether in books, magazines, newspapers, even advertisements.

Nowadays, with so many electronic screens and ways of transmitting language, we need to extend the idea of 'print' to include writing displayed electronically. The work units in this section are identified by the letter 'W' (writing). All five units include practice material, for most of which you will find further guidelines or model answers in the section at the end of the book entitled Answers.

Unit W1

In this unit we are concerned with the most common forms of writing. For convenience and in line with GCSE thinking, we have divided it into three parts.

- **1.1** concentrates on facts and information and how to communicate these effectively in writing.
- **1.2** looks at the way ideas and opinions are incorporated in writing and at forms of writing used to develop a particular argument or point of view, and to persuade.
- **1.3** comes closer to the individual and examines writing out of your own personal feelings and experience and from your imagination.

Unit W2

Here we provide instructions, advice and practice in interpreting writing, drawing out relevant facts, summarizing the main points and so on. In the GCE written examination this kind of writing was often called 'comprehension' because it tested your ability to understand or 'comprehend' written material.

Unit W3

This unit brings together writing practice related to things read, in particular what is usually called 'literature' – fictional stories, plays and poetry. All GCSE syllabuses stress the importance of including such reading in the course and much coursework for the examination is likely to be derived from such writing. As it requires you to exercise and express your appreciation as well as your understanding of what you read this is often referred to as 'Appreciation' in English courses. You will find examples of first-rate literature for close study in this unit. But in fact that is true of many other parts of the book, because we want to show you that reading good literature is not always the hard work it is sometimes made out to be, but one of the world's cheapest and most satisfying sources of pleasure.

Unit W4

A convenient name for the kind of writing dealt with in this unit is 'utility writing'. Probably the most common form of this is the letter and the unit gives you clear guidance and practice in various forms of letter-writing. There are also reports to write, notes to compile and step-by-step advice on how to set about it, with practice of a kind appropriate to the new examinations.

Unit W5

In this unit we have brought together essential technical information needed to write accurate English–topics such as spelling, punctuation and points of grammar and syntax (which is the way words are combined to express meanings).

HOW TO USE UNITS W1–W5

We have set out this section so that it takes account of the new syllabus requirements. It is not necessary for you to work through it in the same order.

- Find a piece of writing that interests you, read it and follow up the suggested work.
- Use W3 as a guide to the way you write about any recommended books, poems etc. in your course.
- Use W4 as a reminder of the best way to set out letters and notes.
- Use W5 as a source of basic information on technical matters, especially spelling and punctuation.

We have deliberately avoided confronting you with long lists of 'books to read'. This does not mean we expect you to do well without reading. There is one complete short story in this section.

Find collections of short stories in your library and make a list of ones you particularly like. Use our notes on structure (p. 17) to help you assess how well-written other stories are.

If your attention or interest is particularly caught by any of the other pieces of writing, note the author and book title, and look for other books by him/her, or for the complete book to read.

Use our answers and further hints in unit 12 'Answers' (page references are given after each piece of work) to check your work *after you've done it*. Don't cheat!

If you want more practice in any particular type of work, look through the Tests checklist (p. 157) and see if there's one in unit 10 that suits your needs.

LISTENING AND TALKING: O6–O9

This section focuses on English that is spoken and heard (oral and aural English). One of the most important changes in the GCSE and SCE standard syllabuses is the greater importance given to the spoken language. Some boards set a special listening (aural) test with written responses (see syllabus summary on p. xi). *All* the syllabuses follow the Secondary Examination Council (SEC) guidelines in insisting on a grade in oral English forming part of the GCSE certificate. Although we recognize that the *written* word is not the best way to provide practical guidance in this aspect of English, we hope you will benefit from the points we are making here, following our suggestions for practice in oral and aural English.

We identify the four units in this section by the letter O (for 'oral).

Unit O6

This unit covers the communication of ideas and opinions, making accurate spoken reports and conveying sincere emotions–similar ground to unit W1 in the previous section.

Unit O7

In this unit we include help on that other aspect of spoken English, the skill of listening, and its interconnectedness with talking. If you are to be an effective speaker you need to be able to listen accurately and with attention and to respond to instructions or other spoken messages. This can be compared with unit W2 in which we concentrate on being able to read accurately and to draw out or infer information from what we read.

Unit O8

As in unit W3, this unit includes oral responses to literature and the spoken element in imaginative literature. Poetry, for instance, was a spoken art long before it became 'literature' and drama only becomes complete when spoken by actors and actresses and heard by an audience. Much of your oral work during the GCSE course will be connected with these oral art forms; often group work–discussion, role-play, improvization etc.–is directly stimulated by literature.

Unit O9

This unit brings together the technical points for the spoken language that are equivalent to those grouped in unit W5 for written English. It is particularly concerned with the second and fifth of the criteria we pin-pointed in the memory-aid *Cougars and Leopards Are Giant Cats* i.e. *language* and *clarity*.

HOW TO USE UNITS O6–O9

Use a tape recorder! We shall be saying more about this. Apart from your voice it is the most valuable tool you can have for oral and aural English.

● Memorize the five criteria for measuring and assessing what makes for good oral English. You should get plenty of oral practice during your GCSE course, much of it in groups. Use our ideas to help make it more effective. If you are not getting enough practice, find one or two good friends to work with. It will help if he, she or they each have a cassette recorder like yours, so that you can exchange tapes and criticize one another's efforts.

● Think about our five points (CLAGC) in relation to any of the exercises suggested and try to decide, or discuss with a friend, which are the most important in the particular piece of work being done.

● Take all the opportunities that are open to you to practise the oral and aural skills outlined. Some typical situations might be:

at home

● with younger brother or sister (explanation, persuasion, instruction)

● with parents or older friends/relations (descriptions, conversation and discussion)

● with people working or helping in your home, e.g. a painter, joiner, cleaner, coal delivery (passing on information, asking for specialist information)

in school

● on sports field as player or spectator (advice, encouragement)

● in practical lessons, e.g. sciences, handicraft, domestic science (relating spoken instructions to action, asking for instructions, passing messages, giving logical accounts and explanations of experiments).

SELF-TEST UNIT

The self-test unit is self-explanatory. As you will see from the check-list (p. 157), the questions have been devised to give you extra practice related to units W1 to W5. For most of them we have provided a mark scheme and a model answer or hints towards answering, so that you can check your progress. You will find it helps a lot if you can persuade a friend to do the test as you do, then exchange and mark each other's work.

THE EXAMINATIONS

This short section gives you some idea of the type of question you may expect in written examinations for GCSE and SCE Standard. No actual papers have been taken yet (1987), so we cannot give you many questions here. Because by the time you take a written examination at the end of your course you will already have earned a good proportion of your final grades (perhaps more than half), questions of 'exam room techniques' and last-minute nerves will not loom so large.

ANSWERS

Here we have brought together all the worked answers and advice relating to exercises set throughout the book.

The GCSE Examination

In England the GCSE examination replaces two former ones, GCE and CSE, and makes use of experience gained from a third examination, known as the 16+, which included coursework and introduced oral work to the English syllabus. Scotland, Northern Ireland and Wales have also revised their examinations for the 16+ age group and there are seven examining bodies: three national ones, and four regional ones in England. (These are listed on p. xv.)

In order to rationalize the idea of a common secondary leaving examination, an idea widely supported by the teaching profession, the Department of Education and Science (DES) through the SEC and in association with teachers developed the GCSE, incorporating the experience gained by the 16+ experiments, as well as changes in the various subject syllabuses since GCE and CSE were first introduced. For the 16+ the 24 different examining boards had to some extent amalgamated; for the GCSE this process was continued, grouping the boards into four regional and three national organizations. Meanwhile the equivalent examining body in Scotland, the SEB, was introducing a thorough revision of its own examinations.

THE NEW ENGLISH EXAMINATIONS

Detailed syllabuses have now been approved from all seven examining groups. For the purpose of this outline the aims and scope of the SCE Standard English examinations are sufficiently in line with GCSE for the two to be considered together.

For many years English teaching has been moving away from a mainly literary and academic view of the subject towards a more wide-ranging approach that takes account of the increased emphasis on the English language as it is actually used in today's world. Speaking and listening to English are now recognized to be central skills and form a compulsory part of the new examinations. Because the past emphasis on a single written examination has been found to leave out many important activities central to the use of English, the new examination has also given more prominence to work done *during* the GCSE or SCE course. Some boards in fact provide an optional syllabus in which the assessment is determined entirely or largely on the basis of coursework.

The effect of this is to reduce that 'exam day' pressure and to help your teacher and examiner get a truer picture of what you are capable of. We have written the book with this in mind; you will find few references to 'the exam' as a single strictly-timed written test, many references to coursework, and we emphasize the *variety* of kinds and lengths of written and spoken English that you can practise in your GCSE course. These changes will mean that schools and other places where GCSE English courses are offered will have a greater responsibility for assessing the achievement of their students and more control over the way they plan their courses.

For this book we have followed the national GCSE criteria for English published by the DES and its various interpretations by the different examining groups. These are summarized in the Syllabus Summary which follows, so that you can see at a glance what particular emphasis your own examining group places on the syllabus. As a sort of 'running guide' to the new exams we have also distributed quotations from the actual English syllabuses throughout the text. These quotations are set out in boxes, like this:

> Drafting and re-drafting is seen as an essential aspect of the creative process of writing in . . . coursework.
>
> (NEA & SCE)

so as to catch your eye and help you to relate our material to the examination requirements.

The names and addresses of the seven Examining Groups (four English regions, Scotland, Wales, Northern Ireland) are given on p. xv. Below we have set out briefly the main syllabus requirements for all of them. The purpose of this summary table is not to give a comprehensive list but to indicate clearly any special emphases or any unique features. The information here can be supplemented by the quotations in boxes throughout the book. As the whole structure and content of this revision course has been planned to prepare you for the new examination, you do not need any more detailed information on the separate Group syllabuses.

▮ Syllabus Summary ▮

The main requirements of the seven Examining Groups are outlined in the table on the opposite page. Numbers in brackets and in bold ink (e.g. **(2)**) refer to the notes following the table, which give fuller details.

THE ORAL TEST

All syllabuses set a separate oral test, which is graded 1 to 5. This grade appears on the Certificate. Candidates have to achieve at least Grade 5 to receive a GCSE certificate and the Oral grade will not be recorded unless at least Grade G is achieved in English. Any special features of the oral test of specific syllabuses are described on pp. xiii and xiv, after the notes on syllabuses.

Table of Analysis

Group	%	Papers	length (hrs)	%	Coursework	No. of pieces	Special features
LEAG*	50	'Paper 2' Understanding and Response	2¼	50	Expression (1)	5	Passages in exam thematically related at least one whole text (i.e. book, play) read during course.
				50	Understanding and Response (2)	5	
MEG (1) Syllabus A Scheme 1	50	'Paper 2' Directed 20% and continuous 30% writing (2)	1¾	30	folder (3)	4	Special aural test 20% (see note (1))
Scheme 2 Scheme 3				80	folder (4)	8	Special aural test 20% (see note (1))
				100	folder (5)	10	
Syllabus B Scheme 1 (6)	35	Paper 1 Argumentative and Informative writing	2	30	(folder) (7)	4	Syllabus B Scheme 2 is same as Syllabus A
	35	Paper 2 Personal and expressive writing	2				Scheme 3 (see note 5)
NEA A	50	Section A (30) response to set lit. texts (1) Section B (20) writing based on texts in A(2)	2	50	folder (3)	5	All exam questions related to given lit. extracts Folder to include non-lit. work Both syllabuses insist on at least one whole work of lit. during course
B				100	folder (4)	10	
SEG A	25	Paper 1 (1) Lit. passage for understanding and appreciation	1½	50	folder (3)	6	Total min. 2500 words in folder
	25	Paper 2 (2) response to non-lit. material	1½				
B				100	(folder) (4)	12	At least 4 pieces based on reading, av. length 400 words
WJEC	50	Paper 1 (1) Section A 40% Sect. B 40% Sect. C 20%	2½	50	coursework A (2)	8	Coursework assessed on best 5 pieces
	30	Paper 2 (3) Qu. 1 40/60% Imag writing Qu. 2 20/60% Practical and informative	1½	20	coursework B (4)	2	*Either* Paper 1 + Course A *or* Papers 1 & 2 + Course B. See also note (5)
NISEC	20	Paper I Prose lit. composition	1¼	50	(folder) (1)	5	Coursework based on one of four themes: Family, Love, Nature, Conflict
	30	Paper II A(15) Practic. wr. B(15) Comp. non-lit.	1¾				Total length of coursework folder 2000-2500 words
SEB Scottish Certificate of Ed Standard Grade (1)	15	writing (2)	1	15	writing ⎱(3)	4	Different structure from others. Syllabus recognizes 4-fold nature of English: listening, talking, reading, writing (See notes)
	15	reading ⎱(4)	3×40 m.	15	reading ⎰	4	
	20	listening (5)	3×40 m.				
				20	talking (6)	–	

* see p. xii for longer notes on the requirements of the different examining groups indicated by the numbers in brackets.

NOTES ON SYLLABUSES

London and East Anglian Group (LEAG)

(1) The syllabus refers to this coursework folder as 'Paper 1'. It is required to provide evidence of expressive or creative writing ability. Length required is 400-500 words for each of the five pieces. One must be written under classroom supervision.

(2) This is 'Paper 3' in the syllabus. Work submitted must demonstrate the ability to write for a particular purpose in response to a text, which may be a book, an article or an extract. Guidelines as to length and supervision are the same as in note **(1)** above.

Midland Examining Group (MEG)

(1) This is the most complicated arrangement of the six, with two different syllabuses, Syllabus A and B, the first with three 'Schemes', the second with two 'Schemes'. For practical purposes, Syllabus A/Scheme 3 and Syllabus B/Scheme2 are identical. Schemes 1 and 2 of Syllabus A include an externally set *aural* (listening) test, which accounts for 20 per cent of the marks. A pre-recorded cassette is supplied for this, together with a written transcript of it. Candidates respond in writing, and are allowed to make notes during a second hearing of the tape. The time allowed for the written answers is 50 minutes. Dictionaries may be used.

(2) Dictionaries may be used in this examination. Section A (45 minutes) will consist of a passage and may include a diagram or picture, with questions. Possible responses may be a letter, report, summary or set of notes, a speech or argument. Section B (1 hour) will offer a choice of topics, and will require a piece of continuous writing – personal, descriptive or narrative – between 350 and 600 words long.

(3) The four pieces must include two based on reading during the course, one of about 400 words of a personal, descriptive or narrative nature and one argumentative or informative piece.

(4) Requirements are as in **(3)**, with the addition of at least two pieces of comprehension done 'under controlled conditions'. Dictionaries may be used.

(5) Requirements are as for **(4)**, but other work in the folder may include poems, playscripts etc.

(6) This scheme offers the smallest coursework element, accounting for only 30 per cent. This makes it the most traditional option, with two set papers each of two hours.

(7) Only four pieces of work are required, of which one must be in response to reading during the course.

Northern Examination Association (NEA)

(1) Questions will be on 'literary text or texts' set in the examination. This may be a short story, play episode or poetry. Most questions will be 'open-ended' requiring answers 'sometimes longer than one or two sentences'.

(2) This section will demand longer writing but questions will relate to the passage(s) in Section A.

(3) The five pieces must include evidence that one 'whole work of literature' has been read. A supervised piece involving comprehension of 'non-literary material' is also needed.

(4) While a minimum of ten pieces of work is needed, assessment is made on the basis of five pieces selected from the ten by the teacher. These five must include one done under class supervision and one giving evidence of the ability to respond to close reading.

Southern Examining Group (SEG)

(1) The paper will present a 'literary passage or passages'. Section A will consist of six short-answer open-ended questions; Section B will offer a choice of questions, of which one is to be answered at greater length.

(2) In contrast to Paper 1 this will contain non-literary material, e.g. statistics, picture(s). There will be up to five questions, all of which are to be answered.

(3) Total length of the six pieces is specified as approximately 2500 words, which gives an average of around 400 words. 'At least two of the pieces must be written in response to literature read during the course.' The syllabus also requires at least one each of 'descriptive', 'narrative' and 'creative' writing.

(4) The same average length of pieces is specified, i.e. 400 words, 'or its equivalent in concentrated effort – a poem, for example'. Three categories of work are specified, (a) expressive/imaginative; (b) discursive/argumentative, (c) explanatory/instrumental. The folder's 'table of contents' should say which of these each piece of writing belongs to.

Welsh Joint Education Committee (WJEC)

(1) This is a fairly traditional-style English examination, in three parts: A a literary passage (or passages on a single theme) with comprehension and appreciation questions; B questions based on non-literary material, e.g. advertisements, instructions, illustrations; C a choice of essay topics suggested by the theme(s) explored in A and B.

(2) Final assessment will be on the best five out of the eight pieces submitted. These will have two imaginative, two argument/opinion, one informative.

(3) The paper will have two questions, one—earning two-thirds of the marks—an imaginative essay, the other requiring instructions or practical guidance.

(4) This is the smallest proportion of coursework in any syllabus, requiring only two pieces (argument/opinion) and worth only 20 per cent of the total assessment.

(5) (From syllabus) 'NB Whether candidates are entered for Coursework Option A or for Paper 2 and Coursework Option B, the total weighting for skills of written expression (including an element of extended writing in Paper 1) is 60 per cent: imaginative writing (30 per cent); writing employing argument (20 per cent); and writing conveying information (10 per cent). These categories have been devised to ensure that fair comparisons can be made on the basis of a range of writing skills; they should **not** be interpreted in terms of hard and fast divisions between different types of writing.' (WJEC Syllabus for GCSE, p 5)

Northern Ireland Schools Examination Council (NISEC)

(1) The total length of the five pieces shall be between 2 000 and 2 500 words. It should include responses to reading, creative/imaginative writing and functional/transactional writing (e.g. instructions, reports etc.). The syllabus includes a suggested list of literary texts.

Scottish Examinations Board (SEB)

(1) The Standard Grade Certificate will be awarded in three levels, Foundation (grades 6 and 7), General (grades 3-5) and Credit (grades 1 and 2). It is pointed out in the syllabus, however, that these levels are within a single syllabus, and that 'the grades achieved by a candidate will be based on performance alone'. The syllabus is worked out for the four modes of English—Talking, Listening, Reading and Writing. The grade achieved in each will be recorded on the certificate, as also will the 'aggregated' final grade, formed by combining the four grades. For this final grade the weighting in favour of reading and writing over talking and listening will be 6:4. This is reflected in the per cent marks in the table.

(2) The specimen paper suggests that there will be a wide choice of questions, from which one is chosen to write on. In the specimen paper most of the 21 questions are based on pictures. There is no recommended length for the piece of writing required.

(3) The coursework folio (i.e. folder) must contain eight pieces of work. These must be final drafts done under classroom supervision. Four will be on literary texts and form the coursework part of the Reading assessment; the other four will be extended pieces of writing for the Writing assessment. One piece in each four must be 'designated' as the best for assessment purposes by the candidate.
The minimum length of any piece for grade 6 or above is 100+ words.

(4) The Reading and Listening external tests will each consist of three tests 40 minutes long run consecutively, with 20 minutes between tests; these are at Foundation, General and Credit levels (see Note (1)). Candidates can choose how many they will take.

(5) The Listening test will consist of a pre-recorded tape (no transcript). The piece(s) can be heard twice, and for some, notes can be made before finally answering written questions in an answer book. Teachers provide grade estimates for Listening based on candidates' work during the course, and these will be compared with the standard achieved in the test in arriving at the final grade for Listening.

(6) The grade for Talking will be based on the teacher's assessment, moderated by the Examining Board.

Requirements for Oral Assessment

LEAG

1 This syllabus makes a point of recommending 'reading aloud' as a useful oral exercise for 'some candidates' (not specified).

2 The oral grade will be based on a course assessment and a 'group oral test' (see 3). The coursework mark has to be submitted by 1 May.

3 *Group oral test* This is unique to this syllabus. Groups are normally of five candidates (exceptionally four or six) and the test is carried out by two teachers, one of them the class teacher. Tests last 45 minutes per group, and consist of a three- or four-minute speech by each candidate, followed by a five-minute discussion.

MEG

The grade will be based entirely on the course assessment, which is made on the basis of 'five speech activities'. These are not specified, but a list of twelve examples are given, which we summarize as follows:

group work
1 small group discussion (four to six candidates) on topic from group or teacher
2 small group discussion on one candidate's topic
3 group discussion from given stimulus, e.g. drama, poetry

group or individual
4 formal debate
5 role-play
6 reading aloud/play reading

individual
7 talk on prepared topic
8 conversation with teacher
9 giving instructions
10 reporting back
11 describing, or relaying information
12 giving an account of something learnt

NEA

The oral grade is determined solely by the course assessment. Three 'guidelines' are listed for this:

situation and audience – covering candidates' grasp of appropriate vocabulary, tone etc.

what is expressed – see our heading CONTENT in 'key criteria' (p. 129).

responding – covering candidates' skill in responding to others, listening to them and evaluating what they say.

SEG

The oral assessment will be made by the course teacher. The syllabus stipulates three 'required contexts' for oral work:

1 – pair (both participants collaborating)
2 – group (open-ended discussion)
3 – individual (to audience of one or more)

WJEC

The oral grade is determined from two separate marks, one out of 20 for the course as a whole, the other out of 10 for a specific assignment 'towards the end of the course'. It is suggested that the second is likely to be more 'formal', i.e. set talk, speech etc.

NISEC

The syllabus identifies five 'categories of talk', as follows:

1 description – including personal feelings
2 relaying information – from seeing, hearing or reading
3 persuasive argument
4 collaboration – in conversations and discussion
5 speculation – 'what might be', including role-playing.

It stipulates that 'six tasks' (not specified) should be included in the assessment, which should be completed by the end of the fifth term of the course.

The criteria match ours as given on p. 129, but include one called 'Organization'. This concerns the candidate's ability to 'select key points', direct a discussion, state problems, etc.

SEB

Oral requirements in Scotland are different from those of other examining groups, in that equal weight is given to Talking and Listening in the course (see notes 1, 5 and 6 to SEB syllabus summary, p. xiii).

Examination Boards: Addresses

Northern Examination Association

JMB
: Joint Matriculation Board
Devas Street, Manchester M15 6EU

ALSEB
: Associated Lancashire Schools Examining Board
12 Harter Street, Manchester M1 6HL

NREB
: North Regional Examinations Board
Wheatfield Road, Westerhope, Newcastle upon Tyne NE5 5JZ

NWREB
: North-West Regional Examinations Board
Orbit House, Albert Street, Eccles, Manchester M30 0WL

YHREB
: Yorkshire and Humberside Regional Examinations Board
Harrogate Office – 31-33 Springfield Avenue, Harrogate HG1 2HW
Sheffield Office – Scarsdale House, 136 Derbyshire Lane, Sheffield S8 8SE

Midlands Examining Group

Cambridge
: University of Cambridge Local Examinations Syndicate
Syndicate Buildings, 1 Hills Road, Cambridge CB1 2EU

O & C
: Oxford and Cambridge Schools Examinations Board
10 Trumpington Street, Cambridge CB2 1QB, and Elsfield Way, Oxford OX2 8EP

SUJB
: Southern Universities' Joint Board for School Examinations
Cotham Road, Bristol BS6 6DD

WMEB
: West Midlands Examinations Board
Norfolk House, Smallbrook Queensway, Birmingham B5 4NJ

EMREB
: East Midlands Regional Examinations Board
Robins Wood House, Robins Wood Road, Aspley, Nottingham NG8 3NH

London and East Anglian Group

London
: University of London Schools Examinations Board
Stewart House, 32 Russell Square, London WC1B 5DN

LREB
: London Regional Examinations Board
Lyon House, 104 Wandsworth High Street, London SW18 4LF

EAEB
: East Anglian Examinations Board
The Lindens, Lexden Road, Colchester, Essex CO3 3RL

Southern Examining Group

AEB
: The Associated Examining Board
Stag Hill House, Guildford, Surrey GU2 5XJ

Oxford
: Oxford Delegacy of Local Examinations
Ewert Place, Summertown, Oxford OX2 7BZ

SREB
: Southern Regional Examinations Board
Avondale House, 33 Carlton Crescent, Southampton, SO9 4YL

SEREB
: South-East Regional Examinations Board
Beloe House, 2-10 Mount Ephraim Road, Tonbridge TN1 1EU

SWEB
: South-Western Examinations Board
23-29 Marsh Street, Bristol BS1 4BP

Wales

WJEC
: Welsh Joint Education Committee
245 Western Avenue, Cardiff CF5 2YX

Northern Ireland

NISEC
: Northern Ireland Schools Examinations Council
Beechill House, 42 Beechill Road, Belfast BT8 4RS

Scotland

SEB
: Scottish Examinations Board
Ironmills Road, Dalkeith, Midlothian EH22 1BR

W1 WRITING AND READING

Introduction

The written word is and will remain one of the most versatile means of communication. As explained in the Introduction, your grasp of the three interlinked activities of reading, understanding and practising writing in English will determine to a great extent how well educated you are.

The ability to write good clear English still holds a central place in the subject of ENGLISH and all GCSE and SCE examinations will aim to test this ability in various ways. As we have explained in the Introduction to this book, certain kinds of writing are better tested by means of coursework rather than through one or more written examinations as in the old GCE O-level and CSE papers, and work done during the 18 months or so of your GCSE course may account for anything from 30 per cent to 100 per cent of your final grade. This means that the kinds of writing we describe here (and help you to practise and improve) may be tested either way – by written examination or units of coursework. Sometimes writing will be linked with understanding other written material, or 'directed' in some other way; sometimes it may involve your personal feelings or ideas, or require you to argue and convince. You have only to look around you or to visit a library to see the immense variety of written English.

> When starting to write [you will find] . . . newspapers, signs, notices, advertisements, labels, instructions, guarantees . . . useful as models (SCE)

In this and the following four units we have identified the main points of good writing and show you how to set about improving your control of them and how to revise what you already know. Units W1-W4 deal with four main types of continuous writing, while in unit W5 we gather together some practical help in such matters as grammar, spelling, syntax and general accuracy and correctness of expression.

In this unit we concentrate on *three* kinds of continuous writing: first, setting down and transmitting facts and information; secondly, expressing ideas and opinions; thirdly, more personal writing about your experiences and feelings, or based on your own imagination.

1.1 Information, Factual Writing

Writers of facts and information hope to make their readers understand easily and precisely what they have written. To achieve this the writers must:
- know just what they mean themselves
- find the words which will convey that meaning to their readers.

This is easier to say than to do, as every reader of official documents knows. Writing clearly and comprehensibly takes time and energy but it is effort well spent and a contribution, in the opinion of the authors, to personal, domestic, social, national and even world peace!

This is the language not only of essential official information but also of accounts of activities, scientific expeditions, projects of all kinds and of factual description. The *order* of words and items is as important as the words themselves. In your coursework you will notice how often you need to change the order of points as you rewrite and improve the piece; this is one of the advantages of being able to submit coursework for your assessment. In a written examination we advise you to make a rough plan so that you can see that the order leads to clarity rather than muddle.

To help you with this kind of writing, we first offer five topics, with their respective plans and comments. Then we print six examples, all of good informative writing, although quite different from one another in style, and add to these further comments. The topics all have four things in common:
- they all need to include *facts* as a main ingredient
- they will involve close observation and attention to detail

- they do not require a story line
- they need little or no dialogue

1 Write about the skill you have learned and the pleasure you have found in one of the following: astronomy, archaeology, photography, cooking, making your own clothes, taking part in a play or a concert, skiing, mountaineering.

2 'The familiar sounds of home.' Describe some of the sounds which are typical of your home and the people in it; show how they express its special atmosphere and reveal the activities and characters of those who live there.

3 Describe the process of some craft in such a way as to give a clear impression of what the craftsman is doing and what he might be feeling.

4 The young children's group which you help to run has been on an outing. Part of your responsibility is to write a detailed account of the trip for the records and for reference when another outing is planned. Consider numbers, transport, timing, distance, destination, food, facilities etc. Your last paragraph should deal with any improvements that could be made next time.

5 If you see someone knocked down by a car, your feelings of fear and distress surge up. But as a witness for the police you have to forget feelings and keep to the facts. Write a statement (a factual report) for the police on one of the following:
- a street accident in which someone is killed
- a burglary in a house where you were present
- a Bank Holiday rampage in which your motor bike is damaged.

PLANS

1 Making Your Own Clothes

Introduction (100 words)

Set out briefly the points you will be dealing with in the essay. They might include:
- need for special teaching
- own designs compared to shop-bought patterns
- boys learning sewing
- handling a sewing machine
- personal qualities needed
- advantages as a hobby

Main part (300-350 words)

Deal in some detail with all the points listed. Here is an example: 'My young brother's class were given four choices of craft in their second year at school: metalwork, woodwork, cookery or needlework. Quite a number of the boys chose needlework. My brother soon became proficient in the use of our sewing machine. He loved making things, turning up his new jeans and patching his old ones – with some startling choices of material – even mending towels and pillowcases for my mother. He made a really professional-looking shirt at school: I was quite envious . . .' (80 words). (Four or five such points will be plenty for this part.)

Conclusion (150 words)

An anecdote about a garment you have made recently; your success with it; your family's and friends' reactions to it.

2 The Familiar Sounds of Home

'My older brother plays the trumpet. What we should do if his room were not at the far end of our old house, with 18 inches of solid stone wall between him and the nearest room, I do not know. Fortunately, too, that room is the bathroom. My mother once had a bath after midnight. She told us next day how, as she lay relaxing, ghostly echoes of Haydn's *Trumpet Concerto* came floating upon the night air as if from outer space.'

Introduction

Here are some topics you might deal with:
- the members of your family
- ordinary, routine sounds. (Sit in your bedroom and list the sounds as you hear them.)

– sounds 'special' (peculiar) to your family, perhaps unusual effect of your house's layout on sounds
– effect on visitors
– your own feelings about the sounds

Main part

Cover more closely some or all of the points in your introduction.

Conclusion

A comment on whether your house would really be 'home' for you if the sounds were not there.

3 The Craftsman and his Craft

Introduction

How, when, where and why you came to know this craftsman.

Main part

Comment on all aspects of the work: the workshop, the craftsman's tools and how he keeps them, materials and how they are stored. Describe what he has told you of his apprenticeship or training and any details about the history of the craft. Use your powers of *observation* to describe his processes, his hands and how he uses them, his working position – standing, sitting, squatting cross-legged (e.g. a tailor). Move from the man to his product – how long it takes to complete, where it will go, how much it will cost; and whether its maker gets satisfaction from that, or from making it well.

Here is an example: 'Today I watched him sharpening the blade of the plane he uses for shaping fingerboards. They are made of ebony and need a good sharp tool. He took a flat piece of smooth stone from his right-hand drawer and wetted it by dipping his fingers into a jar of water that had been at the back of his bench for a week. Then he unscrewed the blade and circled it flat upon the stone. The firm pressure bent his broad fingers concave and their tips curved outwards. The steel made wet black rings on the stone. When he had finished he reached for a piece of cotton-wool and wiped the stone clean before putting it away. After wiping the blade well, he stropped it on a strip of hard black leather from his left-hand

drawer – up and down, long strokes, twice each way. Finally he tested it for sharpness by shaving some hairs off the back of his hand.
   "That'll do," he said.'
(A violin-maker)

Conclusion

Imagine yourself in his place. Think, and describe what must be satisfying or tiring or frustrating about this particular job – perhaps comparing it to other crafts.

4 Trip to Paradise Hall

If you have first-hand experience of some group outing you might well choose this topic. Be careful to make it relevant to the various parts of the question and keep your account factually accurate, based on first-hand experience or discussion with others who went.

Introduction

Summarize work done to prepare for outing: 'expert' to talk to group; study of history and site of Paradise Hall; final briefing of group and leaders.

Main part

Give the date and place of the outing and then record the activities, for example: 'The group, thirty children and five adults, met at the Blue Peter Garage at 9.30 a.m. The coach, hired from Wheelers, came promptly at 9.40 and we arrived at Paradise Hall at 10.30 a.m. We could leave bags on the coach while we went through the maze in the garden, watched the fountain make all its different patterns and tried to count the fish in the pool. In the "wild" garden the children had time to try to find five different kinds of wild flowers and to learn their names.
   It was fine and warm at lunchtime, so we collected our things from the coach at 12.15 as arranged and had our picnic. We sat on the grass under a huge tree in the car park. At 1.30 after everyone had been to the toilet . . .' (Continue with afternoon activities.) . . . 'There was time for ice cream and toilets before leaving at 3.30. Children who were not able to make their own way home were met by parents at 4.30 at the Garage.'

Conclusion

The question asks for suggestions for improvements, for example: 'The children got tired on the tour of the Hall in the afternoon; it would be better to do the tour in the morning and leave the garden till the afternoon.'

5 Statement for the Police

Introduction

Give exact time and place of incident, for example: Burglary at 32 Newcombe Street, Oldtown between 10.45 p.m. and 12.30 a.m. Friday/Saturday 20/21 March 1987.

Main part

Statement by Eva Brick, aged 16.
'I was watching the late night film with my boyfriend, Wayne Wake, from number 26 in our street. We made a drink about 10.30 p.m. in the kitchen and took it into the sitting-room to be ready for the film which started at 11 p.m. My parents were out and I did not expect them back until after midnight.
   The first I knew was my mum coming in saying, "Why is the window in the downstairs toilet open?" She made me go with her to look and by this time my dad was shouting from upstairs. I ran up and saw drawers pulled out and shirts and clothes on the floor in their room. I ran into my room, straight to the dressing table for my silver charm bracelet, but it had gone. And the two china dogs which sat either side of the mirror had gone too. I looked for my little alarm clock by the bed; it was still there and it said twenty-five past twelve . . .'
Eva can probably provide more evidence of missing items.

Conclusion

Eva and Wayne try hard to remember if they *did* hear anything after they left the kitchen – a click or a creak – but all Eva can say in her statement is that she heard nothing loud enough to distract her attention from the film.

COMMENTS

Making Your Own Clothes will be more successful the keener you are on the subject. You will be able to show that you know specialized terms and equipment, practical dangers and difficulties, short cuts. Your expertise will convey a professional attitude to the subject. Which of these writers do you think is the better dressmaker?

(a) I would advise any inexperienced dressmaker to use a bought pattern – *Style* or *Simplicity* are the easiest – because the step-by-step instructions are straightforward. The cutting layout saves wasting material; they remind you to notice the grain of the stuff and to check that the pattern is the right way up. They show you where to make alterations to fit your own figure – and all this nowadays in French, German and Spanish as well as English! It's almost like having someone beside you giving you the benefit of her professional know-how.

(b) I love dressmaking; it is nice to be able to tell somebody you have made the dress you are wearing. Even if the clothes have a homemade look, at least nobody else will have one the same. I am not too bothered if my efforts do not turn out very professional-looking; I like casual clothes, loose or tunic styles, gathered skirts. I don't like pleated or tailored skirts.

The Familiar Sounds of Home will be more successful if your home gives you plenty of scope for describing varied sounds. A small, fully carpeted house with only two or three careful occupants may not be the best material for this subject.

The Craftsman and his Craft could be the most successful essay of the five – but only if you know a craftsman and enjoy watching him at work. Your special relationship with the craftsman and your enjoyment in watching his skill will make it easy for you to transmit your interest to a reader. It would be hard to write entirely from the imagination on this topic.

Trip to Paradise Hall could end in disaster if you get carried away into writing a personal account instead of a factual record! Keep in mind what would be useful to next year's planners. An interesting experiment would be to write a second account in which your personal views and feelings are given free rein (see W1.3 p. 40 for advice on this), then compare the two to see what makes the difference. If your friends prefer the second one, you have probably done very well but explain the purpose of the first one clearly so that you get full credit.

Statement to the Police – whichever of the three statements you choose, the method is the same: think out carefully the sequence of significant events, leaving out all inessentials, however interesting. Why did Eva include making a drink?

TRANSMITTING FACTS AND INFORMATION

The examples that follow are from non-fiction; all except one contain personal opinions. These writers want to pass on information and also to interest their readers, since, presumably, they want to sell their books! Information about prehistoric men, life in the Fens, how to keep dry etc. is of course written in very different styles but all the authors are aware of their readers directly or indirectly. The questions that go with these passages are designed to help you to demonstrate your skill. Work like this could well form part of your coursework folder. Read the extracts with a critical eye and ear; they are good models for your own writing.

> . . . order and present factual information such as . . . a piece of research   (NEA)

The Tollund Man

The dead man who lay there was 2 000 years old. A few hours earlier he had been brought out from sheltering peat by two men who, their spring sowing completed, had now to think of the cold winter to come, and were occupied in cutting peat for the tile stove and kitchen range.

As they worked, they suddenly saw in the peat-layer a face so fresh that they could only suppose they had stumbled on a recent murder. They notified the police at Silkeborg, who came at once to the site. The police, however, also invited representatives of the local museum to accompany them, for well-preserved remains of Iron-Age men were not unknown in central Jutland. At the site the true context of the discovery was soon evident. A telephone call was put through straight away to Aarhus University where at that moment I was lecturing to a group of students on archaeological problems. Some hours later–that same evening–I stood with my students, bent over the startling discovery, face to face with an Iron-Age man who, two millennia before, had been deposited in the bog as a sacrifice to the powers that ruled men's destinies.

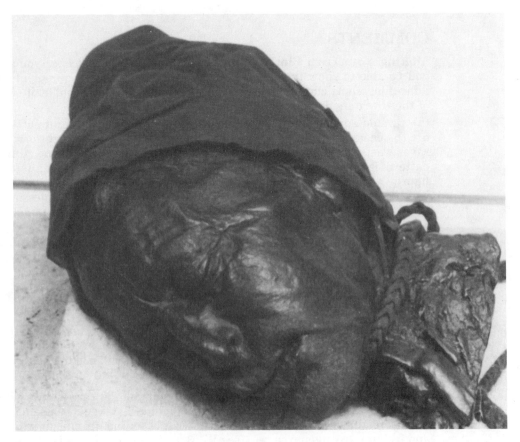

Tollund Man

The man lay on his right side in a natural attitude of sleep. The head was to the west with the face turned to the south; legs were to the east. He lay 50 yards out from firm ground, not far above the clean sand floor of the bog, and had been covered by eight or nine feet of peat, now dug away.

On his head he wore a pointed skin cap fastened under the chin by a hide thong. Round his waist there was a smooth hide belt. Otherwise he was naked. His hair was cropped so short as to be almost entirely hidden by his cap. He was clean-shaven, but there was very short stubble on the chin and upper lip.

The air of general tranquillity about the man was shattered when a small lump of peat was removed from beside his head. This disclosed a rope, made of two leather thongs twisted together, which encircled the neck in a noose drawn tight into the throat and then coiled like a snake over the shoulder and down across the back. After this discovery the wrinkled forehead and set mouth seemed to take on a look of affliction.

Proper study of such an interesting find, and the need to preserve it for the future, called for its immediate removal to the National Museum in far away Copenhagen. Preparations were quickly begun – a local saw-mill was asked to supply planks for a box to be built in the bog round the dead man and his bed of peat, so that everything could be despatched for investigation. The dead man and the surrounding peat were first tightly walled in between the sides of the box. Next, boards were pushed in underneath the whole. When the box had been filled right up to the top with peat blocks so that there was no possibility of its contents shifting during the journey, a lid was nailed on.

The heavy plank box weighed almost a ton when filled. It had to be raised nearly ten feet vertically from the bottom of the bog and on to a horse-drawn cart, then to the nearest railway station. The soft surface of the bog made it impossible to bring a crane up to the spot, and everything had to be done by hand. This was not accomplished without loss. One of the helpers overstrained himself and collapsed with a heart attack. The bog claimed a life for a life; or, as some may prefer to think, the old gods took a modern man in place of a man from the past.

(From *The Bog People* by P.V. Glob, translated by R. Bruce-Mitford, Faber & Faber/Paladin, London.)

1 The author of this extract is a Professor of Archaeology, a scientist, but in this passage he finds room for a few of his own opinions. Can you give an example of one of them?

2 Imagine that you were one of the Professor's students (see paragraph 2) when this find was made. Write a completely factual account for your scientific records of what you saw when all the peat had been removed. The account you have read was of course written by your Professor so change the wording where possible and perhaps the order in which the information is given, but don't add anything.

3 Using information from the last two paragraphs, write a sensational account of the find for the local paper, with an arresting headline. (150-200 words.) (You may prefer your version to ours on p. 167 but finish yours before you look.)

Further comments

This piece has demonstrated to you that informative writing need not be dull and boring. Keep your antennae alert to what makes it good writing. A number of startling revelations are made. Notice how the author moves from ordinary to extraordinary:

– from cutting peat for the winter to finding a body;

– from lecturing to students to looking at an astonishing discovery;

– from the practical details of making a box to philosophical speculation about life and death.

The use of contrast in this way for emphasis and effect is only one aspect of good writing, but while you are alert to it look for it in other factual writing you have been reading or studying. You should not find it difficult to track down other examples.

Our next piece is very different. Instead of an academic professor, a poor country woman; instead of a written account, a *verbatim* (word for word) transcript of some of her spoken reminiscences.

Mary Coe

[Mary Coe is a widow of eighty-six. She lives by herself in a tiny cottage built into the side of the Pits. Most of her children, grandchildren and great-grandchildren still live in the village. Her husband used to be a farm labourer.]

'I've always lived here – I was brought up in the house opposite and I've lived in this cottage for fifty-four years. And the houses – there was nearly fifty houses down this place, the Pits as they're called. There's about fourteen houses now, I think. They didn't have doorsteps, some of them. Just hang the washing on the hedges up the road to dry. And we always used to have to get the water out of the well. And the earth toilets! My old father, he only earned ten shillings a week, and he had to go and feed the animals twice on Sunday. He was just a landworker, with the Coatesworths. They were big farmers. Later, he earned twelve shillings a week.

He'd give my Mum the half sovereign, which he got then, and my Mum used to give him a shilling back. That was his pocket money. And she had nine shillings to keep the house and the family. He'd be able to go and get a pint of beer for tuppence. And perhaps he could do a little job on the side and get a little piece of tobacco, and if not, well he didn't have any. There was Mum and Dad and us four girls. We used to have a penny's worth of sweets a week and have them divided round. We didn't do like they do today – have them every day. And I used to play hopscotch and we used to have one of these wooden hoops and run, and skipping ropes. And for Christmas, if we got a sixpenny toy and an orange or an apple, we thought it was ever so grand. But that's all we got. People say they can't make out how we lived that life. But I say, remember, we'd never had anything else. Our parents before had had the same life. You see, when you've never had anything, you never miss it.

They used to brew the harvest beer where I lived, for the Horkeys. We'd got a big brewing copper in the kitchen – I don't know how much it hold. There used to be two men brewing night and day, a month before the harvest. All the farmers in the village used to come up here and fetch this here beer. We used to live in the house that belonged to Mr Coatesworth, the farmer, and it was his beer and stuff they were doing, but it were in our big old kitchen. And they used to be, night and day, brewing this beer. They used to come up and fetch it, bring these big barrels, and take it away in a horse and cart. I used to think that fun, because there was always someone in the house. Sort of company for us.

Then the men used to come and shear the sheep in the big old barn. I used to love that week, when they come and sheared the sheep. They used to say "Go down the street and fetch us some beer". So I used to go down the pub and fetch these men beer and take it to the big old barn where they was shearing. Oh, it was marvellous. They used to go round them that quick. But it was all the things we got pleasure out of, you see. Those things gave us pleasure. They want everything else ready made today, don't they?

And I remember we used to have Hospital Sunday, Hospital Parade. We used to love them. They'd go round with a big wagon, and one used to sit there dressed as a nurse, and I think there was another one in a cot, and they'd have a collection for the hospital. Once a year they used to have the Forester's Club parade round the village, and us children would have a half holiday from school. They used to have a supper, or something, and go round with the band, and them in the club went round with their green sashes tied with a red bow and they'd march right round the village. And a man was dressed as a clown and he'd have a money box and he'd go round the houses that they knew got money, then he'd come back and buy sweets. They used to get huge tins, not bottles, tins and us children used to stand all along by the Church and all the other side right by the vicarage, and right up past where

Sheep shearers

the butcher's shop was, both sides, and the men used to come round. But they didn't give them to us. They used to toss them up and we'd have to pick them up. You'd get your fingers stamped on then! They'd throw them, no paper, no nothing. Where was the hygiene then? It didn't kill us. We had lovely concerts, the village got up. We got a lovely brass band then. Beautiful band. We used to think that was wonderful. But that went. Wireless, television, done away with that.'

(From *Fenwomen: A Portrait of Women in an English Village,* edited by Mary Chamberlain, Routledge & Kegan Paul/Quartet Books, London.)

Our questions on this passage give us a chance both to respond intelligently in writing to Mary Coe's account and to recognize what makes it a good one.

1 Choose either (a) or (b), and write about 250 words.

(a) Imagine that you were a young child at the Forester's Club parade round the village (see paragraph 5). You decide to write your own account of it for your school or class newspaper. Say where you stood, and what you saw; include the man 'dressed as a clown' and whether you were lucky with the sweets. You can make up more details than are given.

(b) Write your own account of watching a carnival procession, parade, marathon or special outdoor festivity, as if for a local radio broadcast.

2 Mary Coe *spoke* her memories, she did not write them. You have read a *transcript* of what she said. Many writing tasks involve setting down on paper what you hear. Read carefully again paragraphs 1 and 2, or 2 and 3, or 3 and 4 and provide a written version of the two paragraphs you choose, suitable for including in a history essay. (Advice, p. 167).

For our third example we stay in rural surroundings. This passage comes from a book whose purpose is to explain some of the features of country life that are almost taken for granted by the country people themselves.

How to Keep Dry

There are two kinds of thatch – I call them flat thatch and deep thatch – and they are quite different. Flat thatch is used in Africa for most dwelling huts, in the west of Ireland, and for thatching stacks or ricks. Flat thatch is laid almost parallel with the slope of the roof – one layer, perhaps only two or three inches thick – simply overlapping the one below it so as to shed the water. It only lasts two or three years and the cabins in the west of Ireland have to be rethatched this often. As it only takes a day to thatch a cabin this does not matter.

Deep thatch is quite different. The straw or reed is laid almost horizontally, with just a slight slope downhill as it comes outwards. Thus the roof has to be nearly as thick as the straw or reed is long. Invariably with deep thatch the ears of the reed are laid inwards. This thatch is much longer-lasting but is fearfully expensive in labour to put on, and expensive also in material: it takes an enormous stack of it to thatch a house.

In good husbandry nothing is wasted, however. When thatch is finished and pulled off to be replaced, it is thrown into the bullock yard or the pig sties to be used as bedding, trodden into manure, and carted out to fertilize the land, perhaps seventy years after it, itself, grew out of the land. Other roofing material is earthenware tiles – either small and flat or the kind of big curling pantiles you get in Suffolk and which originally came from Holland. Tiles are comely, long-lasting, trouble-free, but need plenty of good seasoned sawn timber to support them. You see them, as you would expect, in the stoneless areas of the country. Caernarvon slate, in Victorian times, spread far and wide, being light, cheap, and easily put on, and bid fair at one time to supplant all other materials.

In our century, though, corrugated iron, which inevitably rusts, looks horrible, and lets the water in, has come to replace much roofing of farm buildings if not of farmhouses. Somehow the true Briton jibs at *living* under a corrugated iron roof – whatever the South Africans, South Americans or Aussies may do. (In those countries they roof *cathedrals* with corrugated iron.) Corrugated asbestos is one better (whatever horrible diseases the workers who mine it may die of) in that it lasts longer and does not rust. It does gradually decay though. There are new lightweight flexible plastic roofing materials now which don't rust at least, but nobody knows how long they will stand up to direct sunlight and other factors.

(From *The Countryside Explained* by John Seymour, Faber & Faber, London.)

1 This passage shows you how everyday things – things you take for granted – can be made interesting when facts about them are skilfully presented. Choose a similar 'taken-for-granted' feature of your own surroundings, find out some facts about it and write three or four paragraphs that could interest people of your age from a different area – or even country. Possible topics might be flooring, methods of heating (or cooling!), front doors, back doors, boundaries – fences, hedges, walls etc. If you have a newspaper round, you could write with authority on front gates and letter boxes!

2 The author of the book this piece is taken from goes on to describe different kinds of farmhouse. Write about 400 words on advantages and disadvantages of different types of housing that you know, e.g. bungalow, semi-detached, detached, terraced, flats, high-rise flats, old, new etc. Choose at least six different types; include other ideas of your own if you like. (Hints on answering, p. 168.)

Thirty years ago the milk preparation 'yoghurt' was almost unknown in Britain; now it is almost as familiar as milk itself. The next piece is an example of the kind of writing anyone living at home might encounter and demonstrates how to convey information clearly and without fuss.

Yoghurt

Yoghurt is made by adding a 'culture' or bacteria to milk, which then breeds in the milk and produces a creamy substance with a distinctive soured flavour. There are a number of cultures available on the market, the most easily available being *Lactobacillus Bulgaris*, a culture supposedly originating from Bulgaria. There are also innumerable yoghurt culture kits, yoghurt-making machines and yoghurt thermos activators etc. available, but they are all totally unnecessary and a gross waste of money. If you can just get hold of a few lumps of the culture, that is all that is needed, for it breeds in milk reasonably quickly so that after a few weeks, large quantities of yoghurt will be produced and the culture will then have to be split and one half given away to a friend. A culture I was given about two years ago has been split in this way about two dozen times and the culture sent all over the country.

Having obtained the culture all one needs is a glass bowl (don't use steel or plastic). Pour in a pint of milk and add the culture. The culture looks rather weird – white lumps rather like pieces of polystyrene. Part cover the bowl with a plate and put it in a warm place. The quantity of resulting yoghurt will vary according to the proportion of culture to milk and the temperature at which they are left. For instance, a little culture in a lot of milk in a cool place will create yoghurt very slowly. As a general guide, half a cupful of the culture to 1 pint of milk in a warm place will take about 24-30 hours to make a solid bowl of yoghurt. To separate the culture from the yoghurt a metal strainer or sieve is needed. Simply pour the contents of the bowl into the strainer and work the yoghurt through gently with a wooden spoon. All that will be left in the strainer will be the lumps of culture, which are then placed back in the bowl and covered with another pint of milk. A sort of greyish mould will appear on top of the milk when the culture is working but don't worry about this as it is all good stuff and disappears on straining. One important point is to try and get a strainer with a medium-sized mesh: too fine a mesh will tend to liquify the yoghurt.

The strained yoghurt can then be eaten immediately, or left for another day which tends to thicken its consistency. There are other methods for yoghurt making, but all of them involve special temperatures and other complications; anyway, no yoghurt tastes as good as that which is obtained from a culture.

From *Country Bazaar* by A. Pittaway and B. Scofield, The Architectural Press, London.

Good sense and good advice make this writing more than a mere recipe for making yoghurt, but it also has the virtues of a recipe; i.e. clear instructions which you can follow. Think of something that you have often made or done (e.g. baked bread, cleaned a bicycle) so that you know the best method to achieve the desired results and what to avoid. Write a helpful account for a friend who wants to learn. (Hints on answering p. 168).

> . . . accounts or explanations of how problems might be solved or tasks performed
>
> (LEAG)

It is not always activities that prompt the kind of writing we are considering in this section. For our fifth example we turn to a different source of ideas – a picture. Just as we were concerned in *Mary Coe* with transcribing what was *heard*, so here we concentrate on putting into writing what has been *seen*.

Heath Robinson's Balancing Acts

Before you read the paragraph on p. 28, look at the picture below. You are going to write a description of what you see, so look carefully and work out an order of events that will make 'sense' of what is happening in the picture. Of course, the picture is 'non-sense', it comes from a book called *Absurdities*, so point out in your description some of the most impossible ideas.

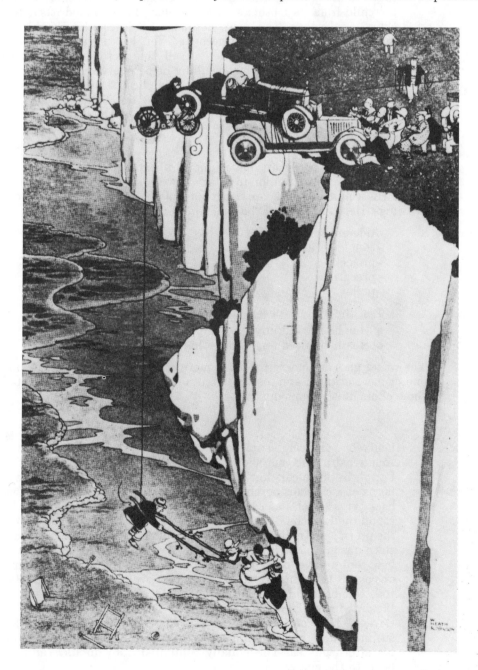

Heath Robinson, 'Plucky attempt to rescue a family overtaken by the tide,'
from *Absurdities* (Duckworth, London)

Give yourself at least five minutes to study the picture; 20-30 minutes to write the description.

Now read the description given below and do the observation test.

The design, the draughtsmanship and the content of these humorous drawings are worth some consideration. For instance, 'Plucky Attempt to Rescue a Family Overtaken by the Tide': the drawing shows the unhappy father standing on a tide-encircled rock at the bottom of a high cliff, holding his fat wife in his arms with their two children sitting on her back. The rescue apparatus consists of a motor cycle tied to the back of a motor car which is strapped on the back of yet another motor car. This conglomeration projects over the top of the cliff and is held in precarious position by eleven stout helpers and a twelfth beneath, who is supporting it with his umbrella. A back wheel of the motor cycle is being used for a pulley and the line from this supports a little man who dangles near the marooned family. He is holding two forked branches to act as tweezers and is in the process of lifting the first child off its parent's back. It could work, except that the three vehicles could never have remained balanced in this precarious manner, and anyhow, how did they get on top of one another? The little man with the sticks could never have lifted the child from its mother's back, let alone have landed it safely on the top of the cliff . . . and so on. The more detailed the description of the drawing, the more improbable the whole thing becomes. Yet, looking at the drawing, because of its precise and careful delineation of all the factors, including the chopped-down telegraph pole from which the willing helpers have collected their rescue lines, one is convinced that this is a viable but complicated method of rescue. The precarious balance, the literal cliff-hanger, provides the tension and at least part of the humour.

In this description the writer has managed to explain just what makes the pictures funny. He has done so by exact attention to detail, as well as by describing how they might (or might not) work. His common sense approach and plain language match the crazy precision of the drawings. Here are some of the exact words:

- tide-encircled
- conglomeration
- projects
- precarious
- pulley

Test the writer's observation (and your own!)
● Has he left out anything important in describing the 'cliff-hanger'?
● Has he noticed any details that you would have missed?

The writer goes on to describe three more of Heath Robinson's drawings. Try to find a copy of one or more of them and test the accuracy of the description. Most public libraries will have some of his illustrations in stock.

Unlikely balancing feats seem to feature in Heath Robinson's comic drawings. Another drawing (not shown here) is called 'Narrow Squeak of an Alpine Touring Party'. In this a car that had plunged vertically over a precipice is balanced on the horns of a chamois perched on a pinnacle of rock. The car is steadied by one of its back tyres which has conveniently stretched out like a rubber band and is looped round the branch of a miserable bush that had a precarious foothold on the edge of the precipice. Another cartoon of the Ark balancing on a pointed rock on which her stern has grounded is a masterpiece of mechanics. All the heavy animals and a few light ones have been crowded into the stern to provide an equilibrium. The onlooker's belief in the balancing act is never in doubt. Heath Robinson was to use the same balancing joke for various of his 'Flat Life' absurdities and particularly in the drawing of 'How the Tenant of the Top Flat can Enjoy the Amenities of a Back Garden'. Here on the most precariously cantilevered framework, a contented gent sits in his armchair smoking a pipe, while his wife does a tight-rope act bringing out his afternoon tea. The equally contented baby in its cradle is suspended from beneath the chair.

(From *Heath Robinson, Artist and Comic Genius* by John Lewis, Constable, London.)

1.2 Opinions and Argument

We have been dealing so far with the straightforward use of writing in English to record or convey facts and information. Now we need to look at more personal and in some ways more varied modes of writing. This time we are concerned with setting down ideas and personal opinions, often in order to pursue an argument or discussion or to persuade the reader in some way. We shall see how similar skills are needed in spoken English in unit 06 Listening and Talking (p. 129). Here are two pieces of writing, one light-hearted in tone, the other more serious, as befits their themes. *Tone* becomes an important part of the total message in this personal kind of writing. The expression, as you may have guessed, is taken over from our primary mode of communication, speech. We all know how much the *tone of voice* in which something is said affects its meaning: a phrase like 'a blue dress' can be made to indicate approval, dislike, amusement and probably many other feelings, by altering the tone in which it is said. Try it with a friend. A good writer will adopt a *tone* that suits her or his subject, as these two have done.

Examples by other writers

The first extract, on the subject of mothers and daughters, comes from America.

'Care and Feeding of Mothers'

This is my code of ethics about mothers. After a daughter is grown and if her mother is in good health, I think the daughter deserves a life of her own and a house or apartment of her own if she wants it, even though the daughter is unmarried. No mentally and physically healthy person would fasten herself on another and say 'Here I am. I am going to be your companion, room-mate, adviser and millstone the rest of your life and how could you even think of refusing? I am your mother.'

During those years of independence, however, I think ideally a daughter stays close to her mother by mail, telephone and personal visits. Hopefully both mother and daughter continue to grow in grace and wisdom.

While I believe that a mother should give her daughter independence and a shove out of the nest after the daughter is grown, I also fervently believe that a daughter should help support her mother if the mother requires this and should physically take care of her when the time comes that the mother can't manage alone, even if it means taking her back home to live.

A friend of mine has just brought her eighty-six-year-old mother, an independent old lady who ran a boarding house for fifty-five years, back to her own home. It was the right thing to do, but now it seems to me the daughter is undoing all the good by treating her mother like an invalid. (I have *nothing* if not strong opinions as to how people should run their lives.) When I was over there the other day, Marian, the daughter, was talking about driving up to see her own daughter and grandchildren. (That makes Marian's mother a great-grandmother.) The old lady wanted to go along. 'Mother, it's a nine-hour drive,' said her daughter. 'You'll just get too tired.'

'No I won't,' snapped her mother. 'If I get too tired, we'll just stop and rest a bit.'

'I wouldn't want to be responsible for you getting ill,' said her 'solicitous' daughter. 'I'll have Mrs Weiss look in on you while I'm away and you can just have a nice rest here.'

'I don't want a nice rest,' said the mother. 'I want to see my great-grandchildren.'

'Remember you got sick the day we drove out to the national park,' the daughter reminded her.

'But I ate blueberry waffles with jam that day,' said her mother. 'I won't do that this time.'

How could there by any question about her mother going along, I wondered. She wasn't asking to be included on a man–woman date but only to see her own kinfolk. I was so moved by the old lady's determination I wanted to shake her silly daughter.

Day after day I see *young* women alone who don't participate – won't try for the better job, won't call up the bachelor whose phone number they have from a friend back home, won't give the party or take the piano lesson. When I see an eighty-six-year-old woman who has get up and go, I want to hand her the *croix de guerre* and also hand her a more understanding daughter.

(From *Outrageous Opinions* by Helen Gurley Brown, NEL, Sevenoaks.)

Although the subject is quite a serious one, Helen Gurley Brown has decided that she can best get her message across – you will have noticed she is quite deliberately arguing her case to her readers – by adopting a light-hearted tone, instead of being pompous about it. We get the message early on with the word 'millstone' (in paragraph 1). See if you can find out other light-hearted touches. Is she self-critical, for instance?

Practice

Write a similar length piece (ours has about 530 words) as a speech to be given at a fifth-form parents' evening, (a) giving your opinion of how working mothers should care for their young children, or (b) expressing your views on whether parents should pay their teenage children for jobs they ask them to do around the house or garden. Write so as to persuade your reader that you are right.

> . . . presentation of opinions or conclusions, persuasion from differing points of view
> (LEAG)

(We have not provided an 'answer' to this exercise, but you will find some further hints on it on p. 168. The best way you can test whether your essay is effective is to ask a friend to read it, then ask whether he or she agrees with you.)

Exam hint

In written English examinations you are often asked to write a piece of about the same length as the one we have just been studying.

Next a rather longer piece, a complete essay on a controversial subject in the world of sport.

George Orwell is well-known for his hard-hitting journalism and his defence of the English language, as well as for his two bestsellers, *Animal Farm* and *1984*. He wrote the essay below more than 30 years ago. Whether or not you like football you should find the argument, and Orwell's way of presenting it, interesting.

Be warned! It is not easy reading; forceful, well-supported argument that is closely reasoned rarely is. But it is worth the effort of reading it carefully.

The Sporting Spirit

Now that the brief visit of the Dynamo football team* has come to an end, it is possible to say publicly what many thinking people were saying privately before the Dynamos ever arrived. That is, that sport is an unfailing cause of ill-will, and that if such a visit as this had any effect at all on Anglo-Soviet relations, it could only be to make them slightly worse than before. 5

Even the newspapers have been unable to conceal the fact that at least two of the four matches played led to much bad feeling. At the Arsenal match, I am told by

*The Moscow Dynamos, a Russian football team, toured Britain in the autumn of 1945 playing against leading British clubs.

Violence at a soccer match

someone who was there, a British and a Russian player came to blows and the crowd booed the referee. The Glasgow match, someone else informs me, was simply a free-for-all from the start. And then there was the controversy, typical of our nationalistic age, about the composition of the Arsenal team. Was it really an all-England team, as claimed by the Russians, or merely a league team, as claimed by the British? And did the Dynamos end their tour abruptly in order to avoid playing an all-England team? As usual, everyone answers these questions according to his political predilections. Not quite everyone, however. I noted with interest, as an instance of the vicious passions that football provokes, that the sporting correspondent of the russophile *News Chronicle* took the Anti-Russian line and maintained that Arsenal was *not* an all-England team. No doubt the controversy will continue to echo for years in the footnotes of history books. Meanwhile the result of the Dynamos' tour, in so far as it has had any result, will have been to create fresh animosity on both sides.

And how could it be otherwise? I am always amazed when I hear people saying that sport creates goodwill between the nations, and that if only the common peoples of the world could meet one another at football or cricket, they would have no inclination to meet on the battlefield. Even if one didn't know from concrete examples (the 1936 Olympic Games, for instance) that international sporting contests lead to orgies of hatred, one could deduce it from general principles.

Nearly all the sports practised nowadays are competitive. You play to win, and the game has little meaning unless you do your utmost to win. On the village green, where you pick up sides and no feeling of local patriotism is involved, it is possible to play simply for the fun and exercise: but as soon as the question of prestige arises, as soon as you feel that you and some larger unit will be disgraced if you lose, the most savage combative instincts are aroused. Anyone who has played even in a school football match knows this. At the international level sport is frankly mimic warfare. But the significant thing is not the behaviour of the players but the attitude of the spectators: and, behind the spectators, of the nations who work themselves into furies over these absurd contests, and seriously believe – at any rate for short periods – that running, jumping and kicking a ball are tests of national virtue.

Even a leisurely game like cricket, demanding grace rather than strength, can cause much ill-will, as we saw in the controversy over body-line bowling and over the rough tactics of the Australian team that visited England in 1921. Football, a game in which everyone gets hurt and every nation has its own style of play which seems unfair to foreigners, is far worse. Worst of all is boxing. One of the most horrible sights in the world is a fight between white and coloured boxers before a mixed audience. But a boxing audience is always disgusting, and the behaviour of the women, in particular, is such that the army, I believe, does not allow them to attend its contests. At any rate, two or three years ago, when Home Guards and regular troops were holding a boxing tournament, I was placed on guard at the door of the hall, with orders to keep the women out.

In England, the obsession with sport is bad enough, but even fiercer passions are aroused in young countries where games playing and nationalism are both recent developments. In countries like India and Burma, it is necessary at football matches to have strong cordons of police to keep the crowd from invading the field. In Burma, I have seen the supporters of one side break through the police and disable the goalkeeper of the opposing side at a critical moment. The first big football match that was played in Spain about fifteen years ago led to an uncontrollable riot. As soon as strong feelings of rivalry are aroused, the notion of playing the game according to the rules always vanishes. People want to see one side on top and the other side humiliated, and they forget that victory gained through cheating or through the intervention of the crowd is meaningless. Even when the spectators don't intervene physically they try to influence the game by cheering their own side and 'rattling' opposing players with boos and insults. Serious sport has nothing to do with fair play. It is bound up with hatred, jealousy, boastfulness, disregard of all rules and sadistic pleasure in witnessing violence: in other words it is war minus the shooting.

Instead of blah-blahing about the clean, healthy rivalry of the football field and the great part played by the Olympic Games in bringing the nations together, it is more useful to inquire how and why this modern cult of sport arose. Most of the games we now play are of ancient origin, but sport does not seem to have been taken very seriously between Roman times and the nineteenth century. Even in the English public schools the games cult did not start till the later part of the last century. Dr Arnold, generally regarded as the founder of the modern public school, looked on games as simply a waste of time. Then, chiefly in England and the United States, games were built up into a heavily-financed activity, capable of attracting vast crowds and rousing savage passions, and the infection spread from country to country. It is the most violently combative sports, football and boxing, that have spread the widest. There cannot be much doubt that the whole thing is bound up with the rise of nationalism – that is, with the lunatic modern habit of identifying oneself with large power units and seeing everything in terms of competitive prestige. Also, organized games are more likely to flourish in urban communities where the average human being lives a sedentary or at least a confined life, and does not get much opportunity for creative labour. In a rustic community a boy or young man works off a good deal of his surplus energy walking, swimming, snowballing, climbing trees, riding horses, and by various sports involving cruelty to animals, such as fishing, cock-fighting and ferreting for rats. In a big town one must indulge in group activities if one wants an outlet for one's physical strength or for one's sadistic impulses. Games are taken seriously in London and New York, and they were taken seriously in Rome and Byzantium: in the Middle Ages they were played, and probably played with much physical brutality, but they were not mixed up with politics nor a cause of group hatreds.

If you wanted to add to the vast fund of ill-will existing in the world at this moment, you could hardly do it better than by a series of football matches between Jews and Arabs, Germans and Czechs, Indians and British, Russians and Poles, and Italians and Jugoslavs, each match to be watched by a mixed audience of 100 000 spectators. I do not, of course, suggest that sport is one of the main causes of international rivalry; big-scale sport is itself, I think, merely another effect of the causes that have produced nationalism. Still, you do make things worse by sending forth a team of eleven men, labelled as national champions, to do battle against some rival team, and allowing it to be felt on all sides that whichever nation is defeated will 'lose face'.

I hope, therefore, that we shan't follow up the visit of the Dynamos by sending a British team to the U.S.S.R. If we must do so, then let us send a second-rate team which is sure to be beaten and cannot be claimed to represent Britain as a whole. There are quite enough real causes of trouble already, and we need not add to them by encouraging young men to kick each other on the shins amid the roars of infuriated spectators.

(From *Collected Essays, Journalism and Letters,* by George Orwell, Martin Secker & Warburg, London.)

George Orwell's piece is a little more than twice the length of the first essay, i.e. a good length to aim at for a piece of writing to include in your coursework folder, but too long for a normal written examination. It illustrates well *two* worthwhile features of this kind of writing:

Strong personal views: Orwell shows us that he has strong views on the subject of international sport. He makes deliberately argumentative statements:
'these absurd contests'
'a boxing audience is always disgusting'
'serious sport has nothing to do with fair play'.

It is easy to hold extreme views or opinions; not so easy to convince your reader that you have a right to hold them. For this you have to show that you are well-informed, and not speaking out of ignorance or blind prejudice.

> ...recognizing statements of opinion and attitude...showing some awareness of underlying assumptions and points of view   (SEG)

Background knowledge: There is plenty of evidence here that Orwell has thought about his subject and that he knows the facts that will support his views:
'e.g. the 1936 Olympic Games'
'the visit in 1921 of the Australian cricket team'
'first-hand evidence of violence in football in Burma'
'a knowledge of the history of sport'.

Structure

This kind of essay gains greatly from careful planning. Let's see how Orwell does it. He uses nine paragraphs for his 1450 or so words – about three times the length you may be expected to write in an examination. The essay is planned in two main parts:

Part A (about 1000 words)
Paragraphs 1 to 6 (lines 1-66), stating the facts, and the writer's views on them.

Part B (about 500 words)
Paragraphs 7 to 9 (lines 67-107), explaining the history of the subject, and making recommendations based on the writer's views.

   Notice the linking sentence between part A and part B:
Instead of blah-blahing about the clean, healthy rivalry of the football field and the great part played by the Olympic Games in bringing the nations together, it is more useful to inquire how and why this modern cult of sport arose.' (lines 67-69.)

We can see the structure clearly if we examine it paragraph by paragraph.

Part A

1 *Introduction* (short)
(a) The news-item on which the essay is based.
(b) Orwell's view on it.

'Even the newspapers . . .'
2 *Facts* to support view given in 1 – carefully selected details.

'And how could it be otherwise?'
3 & 4 *General principles*
The argument developed; his view derived from general principles.

'Even a leisurely game . . .'
5 *Further illustrations*
Extending the argument to other sports.

'In England . . . bad enough, but . . . in young countries . . .'
6 *Context enlarged*
Effects of competitive sport in other countries; opportunity for personal reminiscence.

Part B
'Instead of blah-blahing . . . it is more useful . . .'
7 *Historical background*
Tracing development of phenomenon.

'I hope, therefore, that we shan't . . .'
8 & 9 *Conclusion*
Case fully made; suggestions for remedy.

Notice how Orwell holds the essay firmly together by means of these linking words and ideas – a useful tip for your own discussion essays.

Practice

Using some of the ideas in Orwell's essay, together with your own knowledge and observation to support your view, write an essay on this topic: 'International sporting events promote goodwill between nations'.

. . . and a reminder about the words you or any writer uses:

whenever you write you take it for granted that your intended reader will understand you. Orwell assumed that readers of *Tribune* (a socialist weekly, in which the essay appeared) would understand such words as:

predilections (line 15)

russophile (line 17)

animosity (line 21)

The last of these is a key word. Unless you understand it, a central point in Orwell's argument is obscured.

Dictionary Practice

(see also *Using a Dictionary,* p. 125) Establish the meanings of the three words just discussed and of these four from later in the essay:

obsession (line 51)

sadistic (line 65)

cult (line 72)

sedentary (line 82)

Notice how a full understanding of their meaning helps you to follow Orwell's argument and to understand his feelings more clearly. (When you have found the dictionary meaning of each word, check that it makes sense in the passage.)

You will have realized by now that in this kind of writing you need first to convince your reader that you know what you are talking about. Helen Gurley Brown used an example from her own experience to back up her strongly held views – and they *are* strong, though she avoids sounding too bullying by poking fun at herself ('I have nothing if not *strong* opinions . . . '). Orwell, as we have seen, shows he has the necessary background information.

The writer of this third piece, which appeared in a serious newspaper, bases her whole argument on presenting a lot of detailed facts and statistics. Notice how she first states her case in a sentence 'there is now *concern* . . . taken the *wrong* course' – then proceeds to back it up with the facts. She does not present these uncritically, but uses them to reinforce the view that methods of agriculture need to change.

The Use of Chemicals in Agriculture

In many countries there is now concern that mainstream agriculture has taken the wrong course. Researches at the end of the last century led to the belief that the soil can be virtually by-passed, except as a supporting medium, and the plants fed directly with soluble, often synthetic, chemicals. From this sprang the development of further artificial products – insecticides, herbicides and fungicides. Modern agriculture has become a capitalized industry, supported by feed, machinery, packaging, chemical and pharmaceutical firms and research institutions – a giant network concerned more with production of money than with food. Farms have become factories where plants and animals are injected with every sort of industrial product in order to achieve maximum yields – and maximum return on capital.

The excessive use of chemical fertilizers not only pollutes rivers and lakes, but it also destroys the fertility of the soil itself, and may lock up essential minerals necessary for the health of plants and livestock. One example is that potash will go into insoluble compound with magnesium, thereby denying magnesium to the plant and to the animal which eats the plant; this is one of the causes of hypo-magnesaemia in cattle. The farmer is compelled to resort to an arsenal of poisons against pests and diseases which are not fully effective as controls, and the long-term results of which are unseen.

Also unseen is the waste of energy. To produce one ton of nitrogen fertilizer, between three and five tons of fossil fuels are needed – 50 per cent of which is absorbed by the plant, the rest being lost in run-off or seepage, during which it can turn to poisonous nitrate. A number of recent publications have analysed various aspects of energy use, particularly in United States agriculture. Approximately five times as much energy goes into the production of food as is actually contained in the food itself. Furthermore, as far as scientific research has gone in the past, all work has been directed to improving *quantity* of yield, not quality, and value is assessed by bulk, not nutritive content.

Health, quality and rejection of dangerous practices are the priorities of the alternative movement in organic or biological agriculture, which is supported by

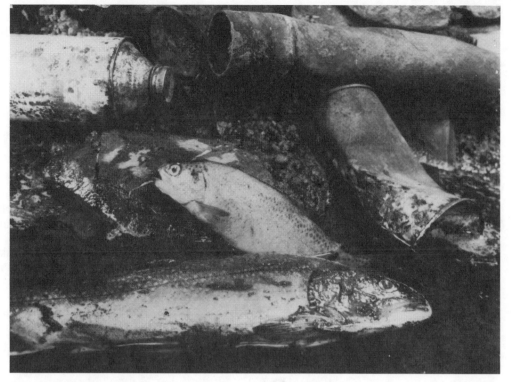

The effects of river pollution

several organizations. (The Soil Association, The Henry Doubleday Research Association and The Organic Farmers and Growers are just three.) These practical people have little time for woolly romanticism, hippies, food faddists and cranks. They have evolved a positive scientific system of agriculture based on a more complete biological view – growing food from the land, rather than transmuting imported chemicals and proteins into eatables using the land as a factory floor.

The central idea is to build up soil fertility (and the population of micro-organisms which create humus and produce natural plant foods to maintain all plants' health and resistance to disease) by returning all organic waste to the land in a cycle of renewal. Feed the soil to feed the plant to feed the animal/human. Animal residues are vital for the health and nutrition of plants – if all animal and human excreta were harnessed, chemical fertilizers could become virtually redundant.

Recent surveys in France and the United States corn belt, together with a preliminary report from the Agriculture Economics Unit at Cambridge University (currently working on British organic farm costings) show that organic farmers can obtain yields as high as those of industrial farming with sometimes greater profits. Moreover these results are achieved without the aid that some conventional agriculturalists receive from chemical and governmental advisory services into which millions of pounds are poured – the British spend £50m on research and development in agriculture, 80 per cent in research. What might these farmers achieve with the backing of scientific research? It is not a question of regression, but of how to go forward.

(From 'Are we feeding ourselves to death?' by Philippa Pullar, *The Times*.)

It is good practice to spend a little time studying a passage like this to see how the argument is built up. You can also use it as an exercise in note-making (see units W2 and W4).

Practice

1 Make a summary or a set of notes
(a) of the evidence given by Philippa Pullar that 'mainstream agriculture has taken the wrong course' (about 80 words)
(b) setting out what alternative she proposes to present methods (about 40 words). (Answer on p. 168).

2 Choose a topic in which you are convinced or can make out a case that present practices are wrong (e.g. methods of adoption or fostering, schemes for roadmending or widening, policing of demonstrations, social security payments, refuse disposal, truancy control) and write a piece presenting the facts so as to support your views. Imagine it is to be published in a local paper,

magazine or youth/peace group newsletter. (The piece on agriculture is about 700 words. You may manage with 400-500 words.)

Next, let us sample a more gentle style of argument. Once again the writer is suggesting alternatives to currently accepted ideas and once again he is able to demonstrate that he knows what he is talking about. But this time a more quietly persuasive, friendly tone is in order, suiting the subject of herbs and their medical uses.

Herbal Remedies

Suffering from a cold? Well, take a handful of peppermint leaves, crush them and infuse them in boiling water. This peppermint tea will give symptomatic relief from a headache and runny nose. If you are troubled by a cough, rub garlic on your chest. It will not only 'loosen' your chest; it will also keep your friends and family away so that they do not catch your bug! 5

Herbal remedies for everyday ailments are part of our folklore. They are associated with old crones stealing out to the crossroads under the full moon to find ingredients for their magic potions and with a multitude of other whimsical superstitions. As a result, not many people with a modern scientific turn of mind feel inclined to take the subject of herbalism too seriously. It is regarded as a quaint 10 reminder of our simple and ignorant past, when we knew little of chemistry and pharmacology. Nevertheless, herbal medicine still flourishes in this country, and in many Third World countries it is the basis of available medical care. Moreover, although the historical roots of herbalism are interwoven with astrology and magic, a great deal of the herbal medicine practised today is based on scientific principles 15 and practical experience.

DIGITALIS PURPUREA

FOXGLOVE
It has a gentle, cleansing quality, and withal very friendly to nature.
A tall plant with reddish-purple flowers, with some black on white spots within them, the Foxglove has many long and broad leaves, dented upon the edges. The leaves have a hot and bitter taste.

Where to find it: It grows on dry sandy ground and under hedge-sides and is also cultivated in gardens.

Flowering time: It seldom flowers before midsummer.

Astrology: Under the dominion of Venus.

Medicinal virtues: It is used by the Italians to heal fresh wounds, the leaves being bound thereon. The juice is used to cleanse, dry and heal old sores. The decoction with some sugar or honey cleanses and purges the body both upwards and downwards and opens obstructions of the liver and spleen.

Modern uses: For the past 200 years Digitalis has been the leading cardiac drug for heart failure. The dried leaf is listed as an official drug in the British Pharmacopoeia. Pharmaceutical companies make synthetic versions of it for use by the orthodox medical profession. Recent evidence, however, suggests that the synthetic versions are more toxic than the dried leaf. Herbalists do not use Foxglove because of its reputed toxic effects. They have several other remedies to choose from, including Hawthorn and Lily of the Valley.

The cardiotonic properties were reported to the medical profession by Dr William Withering in 1775. He learned of its use from a medical herbalist of that time who cured a patient of heart failure when the college physicians had failed. Whereas modern physicians use Digitalis as a specific heart tonic, the herbal method would be to include it in a prescription aimed at treating the whole person. Used in this traditional way, the dosage would be such that toxicity is unlikely. This is not to say that Digitalis is recommended for domestic use. It is not. The drug is available only on a doctor's prescription.

An infusion of one teaspoonful of the dried leaves to 1 pt (568 ml) boiling water should not be taken in more than teaspoonful doses. The toxicity tends to be cumulative.

An extract from *Culpeper's Colour Herbal* (Foulsham, Slough)

Herbalism did, of course, begin as a practical art. Leaves or moss would be used to protect wounds and sores and our forebears would notice that some of these plants appeared to make the wound heal faster. They would also have realized that some plants had an effect on the digestive system, soothing the gut in some cases and 20 causing constipation or diarrhoea in others.

The magical, religious or astrological qualities attributed to these plants came later. Once it was realized that they had some healing power, the plants were respected and revered. As their power could not be explained in the kind of chemical terms we use today, it was assumed to be a gift from the gods or due to the presence 25 of a spirit. In the Middle Ages, astrologers drew great significance from correlations between the time at which a plant came into flower and the position of the heavenly bodies. Alchemists, the mystical predecessors of modern research chemists, believed that dew was one of the purest substances in the universe, and therefore put great value on plants which held dew. They mistook the sticky syrup which the sundew 　30 plant secretes to attract insects as a kind of everlasting dew, and therefore came to the idea that the plant was a recipe for eternal youth. Other plants were held in awe because of their shape: much of the mystique which surrounds ginseng and mandragora, for instance, is due to the rather humanoid shape into which their roots often grow. 　35

These associations are very poetic, but they tended to turn herbalism into more of an art than a science. Although some herbalists today see beauty and significance in the myths and legends about their raw materials, most want to establish herbalism on a more contemporary scientific footing.

One of the first and most famous attempts to separate fact from legend in herbal 　40 medicine was Dr William Withering's study of the foxglove. In 1775, this English physician was shown a herbal brew which a 'wise woman' in Shropshire was selling as a cure for dropsy. Dropsy is the oedema, or swelling, which results from the body retaining water, and it occurs most often in heart disease, when the heart is not strong enough to flush fluid from the tissues. The wise woman's brew was very 　45 effective in curing the dropsy, but it was a concoction of several herbs, any of which could have been the effective ingredient. By means of trial and elimination Dr Withering ascertained that the important ingredient in the brew was root of foxglove. He subsequently made his own foxglove preparations, using various parts of the plant and trying them on his patients. He finally discovered that the most 　50 useful part of the plant was in fact the leaf, and that it was at its most potent when the flower was in bloom. The leaf of the foxglove (or *Digitalis*, to give it its botanical Latin name) is still used by doctors today. We now know that it acts on the heart muscle, encouraging it to beat more strongly.

(From *A Guide to Alternative Medicine* by Robert Eagle, BBC Publications, London.)

(*Reminder:* It is always worth making sure you understand what a writer is saying by checking unfamiliar words with a dictionary or a friend with a bigger vocabulary than yours – or even your teacher! As a check, what do these words mean from the passage above?

　infuse (line 2), *revered* (24), *correlations* (26), *secretes* (31), *elimination* (47))

Here the writer is *defending* herbal remedies against those who pooh-pooh them as unscientific ('it is regarded as . . . pharmacology' 10-12). To do this you need to state the case *against* your point of view in order to defend that view.

Practice

1 List the different points that Robert Eagle makes belittling or ridiculing herbal remedies, then against each one set down what he says in defence of herbalism.

2 Using the information here, write – as though in a letter to a friend whose father has a heart condition – recommending foxglove leaves as treatment. Present your argument in such a way that you are taken seriously. (Answer and comment, p. 169).

The author's own views could be easily recognized in the last passage. In our next one, on a far less comfortable topic, the writer's opinions, although strong, are not so easy to identify. Notice, however, how quickly he moves from the general – 'the subject of all this talk . . .', 'you are in a city . . .' – to his own personal viewpoint: 'the only ancient city I have ever seen . . .' etc. After this, when he says 'you', we know he is describing his own responses, his own recognition of the contrast between 'civilized', ordinary life, and the violence that accompanies it in Israel today.

An American Jew in Jerusalem

[The writer, an American Jew, is visiting Jerusalem. He describes meal-time conversations.]

The subject of all this talk is, ultimately, survival – the survival of the decent society created in Israel within a few decades. At first this is hard to grasp because the setting is so civilized. You are in a city like many others – well, not quite, for Jerusalem is the only ancient city I've ever seen whose antiquities are not on display as relics but are in daily use. Still, the city is a modern city with modern utilities. You shop in supermarkets, you say good morning to friends on the telephone, you hear symphony orchestras on the radio. But suddenly the music stops and a terrorist bomb is reported. A new explosion outside a coffee shop on the Jaffa Road: six young people killed and thirty-eight more wounded. Pained, you put down your civilized drink. Uneasy, you go out to your civilized dinner. Bombs are exploding everywhere. Dynamite has just been thrown in London; the difference is that when a bomb goes off in a West End restaurant the fundamental right of England to exist is not in dispute.

Yet here you sit at dinner with charming people in a dining room like any other. You know that your hostess has lost a son; that her sister lost children in the 1973 war; that in this Jerusalem street, coolly sweet with night flowers and dark green under the lamps, many other families have lost children. And on the Jaffa Road, because of another bomb, six adolescents—two on a break from night school— stopping at a coffee shop to eat buns, have just died. But in the domestic ceremony of passed dishes and filled glasses thoughts of a destructive enemy are hard to grasp. What you do know is that there is one fact of Jewish life unchanged by the creation of a Jewish state: you cannot take your right to live for granted. Others can; you cannot. This is not to say that everyone else is living pleasantly and well under a decent regime. No, it means only that Jews, because they are Jews, have never been able to take the right to live as a natural right.

(From *To Jerusalem and Back* by Saul Bellow, Martin Secker & Warburg, London.)

Question:

In order to illustrate his final statement, the Jewish writer Saul Bellow points out in this passage the contrast between ordinary life and violent death. In about 300 words describe another situation that brings out this contrast, as though for a local newspaper. Try to make your personal view come through in your description.
(We cannot provide an answer to this question. Ask a friend to read your answer.)

Finally, a passage from a rather different travel book. In it the writer Geoffrey Moorhouse gives a very vivid personal impression of a journey by camel across the Sahara desert. Notice he includes his feelings and ideas about his companions, whose response to their surroundings is so different from his own.

Sahara Journey

The morning of my forty-first birthday, we had been marching for half an hour or so in the early cool of a low sun when young Mohamed, immediately ahead of me, suddenly swivelled to his left, hauling the camels after fast to get them away from a clump of dried grass, pointing with excitement as he did so. A snake, a horned viper,

was coiled there beautifully camouflaged, its skin matching exactly the colour of the sand and the grass. I never would have noticed it. The young man hit out with his long riding stick and the reptile writhed horribly. Then Mohamed came up and stoned it to bits with large rocks, in a savage reflex of elemental fear. He had already, a day or two before, killed a scorpion he found crawling a couple of feet from my head as I lay asleep after a midday meal. I had found another, between my sleeping bag and ground blanket, when I awoke and shook my things out one morning. It, too, was beautiful, a delicate shade of jade green, almost translucent. But as I bent down to look, its sting arched over with menace; and when I touched its back lightly with my stick, it struck, struck, struck wickedly at the wood.

I was too obsessed with the physical struggle of the march to pay proper attention to the most exciting discovery of all. We were crossing a hollow of sand strewn with rocks when Mohamed pointed to an object a yard or so from our tracks. It was a block of red sandstone rounded across its base, its flat top hollowed ovally towards a beak, the whole shaped crudely like an avocado cut in half and stoned. How very curious, I thought, as I gazed at it blankly. My eye registered its details: about two and a half feet long, perhaps eighteen inches wide, maybe fifty-two pounds in weight. Then I trudged on to catch up with the others. It wasn't until that night, when I was writing in my notebook, that the implications of what I had seen dawned on me. It was a quern, in which food could be pounded and then poured out, and it may have been very old indeed. Any museum in Europe would have grabbed at this piece of bric-a-brac belonging to primitive man, and I almost could not have cared less about it in that great wilderness of sand.

Next morning young Mohamed stopped to pick something from the ground and turned to hand me a perfectly formed arrowhead of flint, its point slim and sharp, its base notched into a V, its sides finely serrated by meticulous knapping. I marvelled at the eyesight that could spot something so minute in a confusion of rubble. The older man, Mohamed, was perpetually searching the ground for flints suitable for tinder with which to light his long, straight Mauritanian pipe.

(From *The Fearful Void* by Geoffrey Moorhouse, Hodder & Stoughton, Sevenoaks.)

Questions:

1 Explain Moorhouse's mixed feelings about the snake and the scorpion.

2 How was it that neither he nor his guides paid proper attention to the archaeological discoveries?

3 Comment on the differences between Moorhouse and his Arab guides.

4 Describe a journey in which you either made or missed an interesting discovery.
(Answers p. 169)

1.3 Personal Experience, Imagination, Emotions

This kind of writing includes much of the world's best literature, so you are in good company in practising it. Writing about first-hand personal experience always involves your feelings, and usually means some exercise of your imagination. When we move over to the infinite possibilities of fiction, feelings and imagination are central. No one can write a good story without using his or her imagination and much of the appeal of fiction depends on the reader believing in the people in the story and how they feel. That depends in its turn on the writer's ability to convey her or his feelings through the behaviour of the characters.

> . . . relating experience and expressing what is felt and what is imagined (NISEC)

We shall look at five examples of such writing as models for your own attempts, two of them fictional, three written from personal experience. First a complete short story such as you might plan to include in your coursework folder. It runs to between 4000 and 5000 words. One great advantage of the GCSE emphasis on coursework is that you have the opportunity to include complete, finished work of this kind.

River Afternoon

'Are you ever coming?' asked the boy.

'Soon,' she said. She knew he would not go fishing without her. He had bought bait, made sandwiches, filled a bottle with lemonade, sorted his tackle – everything was put ready by the open door. He was waiting outside the door in the sunlight.

'Come on, it's late.'

'It's not.'

'What are you doing?'

She was at the mirror by the sink fixing her hair into a pony tail with a new tortoiseshell clip. Trying to.

'I'll go alone.'

She just knew he wouldn't; it was for her to watch him bait up, watch him cast; to wait patiently, clamping her lips together not to make a noise, to defer to his patience, knowledge and skill, to fix her eyes upon the striving line. He wanted someone to wail his disappointment if he lost a fish, to leap and shout his satisfaction if one swung clear of the water and fell twitching silver upon the green at his feet. And he preferred that she should be the one to relate to his father in the evening, sipping his mother's sweet cocoa by the fire – 'I watched Peter catch two trout.'

Or three – or four – or five – once I caught a fish alive – she sang the rhyme as they walked along. She'd had to leave her hair loose, it was like a black mane, too thick and wiry for the new clip; she was used to it round her shoulders but it made her hotter. Today it was sweating hot and there were a lot of flies – the high strong sun, no wind, no clouds –

'Peter, let's stop here.'

'We're going to the loop,' said Peter. His father's farm had water meadows, but Peter had planned that they should cross by the road bridge and fish away from home on the opposite bank on Ron Evans' land. The fishing was better; in fact Ron had let it to a Birmingham doctor – 'you'll be all right, he only comes down weekends,' Ron had said. A public footpath ran along his bank, skirting two meadows before the river curled back on itself in a wide, deep loop. Ron's Herefords were grazing in the second meadow.

'Lysander's out,' she said. Lying on the grass with the cows, lazy in the heat, the old bull was obviously not going to stir; old and slow and docile, Lysander frightened nobody except visitors.

They reached the place where Ron's meadow bordered the inner curl of the loop. The high bank here jutted out almost like an island; to the right and left of it black alder trees stuck their angular branches out over the shining mirror beneath them. This jutting grassy knoll commanded a fine curving stretch of water, deep under this bank and in mid-stream, levelling out to stony shallows by the farther bank, where yellow willows drooped in suspense above the still water. These shallow pools under the willows were great places for resting trout, likewise the deep water under the overhang on which they were standing. The almost imperceptible current, unfortified by any breath of wind, hung merely a transparent veil between the rocks and roots of the river bed proper and the shafts of sunlight which cleaved clear to the bottom. In this clarity the children's sharp eyes missed nothing.

'By Christ there's a big 'un!' She also had seen a large fish lying along the current in mid-stream. Quickly and excitedly Peter dumped the gear. He began to fix up his rod.

'Get us a worm out.'

She found a piece of flat slate from a place where the bank fell away, and went for the bait tin. She so hated the warm feel of the tin and the stirring of the white grubs within; and worse, as she prized the lid up, the familiar nauseating smell which made her stomach heave. She shut her eyes and held her nose with her free hand, offering him the tin at arm's length.

'Yuk!' she said, 'ugh, horrible!'

Peter knew but he didn't care. He picked out a worm, fixed it to the hook, reeled out sufficient line.

'Keep still.'

'I'm putting the tin back.'

'He can see us easy. It's too bright.'

He cast quite skilfully up-river from the resting trout; they watched the white blob of worm wriggling its way down the current. Peter reeled in gently, bringing the bait within striking distance. The fish ignored it as it floated past.

'Try again,' said Peter. He tried a dozen times. She sat on the dry grass, relaxed, quietly absorbing the rhythm of his movements; today she felt treacherously withdrawn and careless of his success or failure. She was thinking, 'I'm never going to open the bait tin again.' And she was thinking, 'That fish lives there, it's his home' – when suddenly the fish was there no longer.

Peter looked up. 'Bloody cows,' he said. Upstream from them the Herefords were ambling into the water at a shallow muddy place. Some stooped to drink, others stood aimless – cooling their heels, staring –

'Stupid bloody animals. Go and chase them off,' Peter said.

'You go,' she said. She held his rod while he ran along the bank shouting and waving at the cows. While he was gone she saw a small fish jump. Also she saw the incredible lightning-blue flash of a kingfisher; he skimmed the water's surface in front of her, travelling the surprising curve of the loop with brilliant precision. She thought, he must know all the winding shapes of the river; before he got to the loop he must have remembered the shape of it, to go so fast.

Peter came back, hot.

'I saw a kingfisher,' she said.

'I wish Ron didn't turn his cows into that meadow.' He took the rod from her. They both saw a fish jump, near the other bank.

'Only a little one. There's not enough wind, the big 'uns are all lying close. There'll be a few lying under this bank.' He dropped the worm straight down in front of where they both crouched. Quite soon, a smallish fish ventured out from beneath their feet; Peter swayed the rod tip, the worm danced obediently to his baton, weaving a tiny pattern in the water.

'Come on, come on!' He moved the rod a little more, the worm responded and the fish darted away.

'You ought to hold it still.'

'I know what I'm doing. They're used to things moving. They're all fed already, they've had plenty.'

'There's not many mayfly.'

'That's why they're not jumping.'

'They don't jump for mayfly, they wait till they get waterlogged.'

'What do they jump for then?'

'They jump for joy.'

'Oh don't talk daft!'

'They do. I read it.'

'They jump for bloody mayfly. Everyone knows that.'

She pointed. A sizeable trout had leaped some distance downstream; the rings lapped gently wider.

'I'll try there.' She made no move to follow him.

'I'm going to have a drink.' The lemonade Peter had mixed was weak and tepid, but she was thirsty. And hungry. She opened the sandwiches. Brown bread with honey in. She counted them; he had made four double slices and cut them in half.

'Four halves each,' she called to him.

'It's not tea time.'

'I'm hungry.'

'Shut up shouting.'

She lay on her stomach on the warm grass munching sandwiches and staring into the water. The big trout they had first seen was back again. She tried to imagine herself looking out, from his angle, at the sun, the alders, the willows, at her own

self looking down. She reckoned he was big enough to defend the place that was his home against all other fish; and at night it would be a safe place, no poachers along the bank could reach him there. Fish were wily and wary, but fishermen were crafty and skilful – she hoped that the big trout could feel the altered flow of the current at his back when a strong nylon fishing line sliced the water in two, that he could also see the line like a thin crack in his watery window as he stared through it up at the sunlight. She hoped he knew the danger of it.

Peter was making his way back – he looked tall, striding along. His jeans were tucked into his wellingtons, and his check shirt was tucked into his jeans at the front – it was out at the back. Before he reached her she picked up a stone and threw it into the water.

'What you doing? What you chucking stones for?' He sounded peevish. She glanced at where the big fish had been.

'You should know not to chuck stones.'

'Have a sandwich,' – she held the packet out. He took one and ate it absent-mindedly, staring into the water.

'They're just not interested. Not a single bite. It's no good today.'

She knew his mood – blaming the sunshine, the lack of wind, blaming the scarcity of mayfly, blaming her for speaking, for moving –

'D'you want to go home?' she asked.

'We only just got here.'

'If you didn't want to fish we could bathe. It's hot.'

'It's too bloody bright; we need a bit of wind. If you hadn't have shouted at me up there – I nearly had a bite –'

'It's no fun if you can't talk.'

'You better bloody go home then.'

A bathe, she thought. A lovely cool bathe.

'Hey, look,' said Peter, 'there's that big 'un again.'

'He's too wily; you'll never catch him.'

'Want to bet?'

She clenched her fists and stared at the line where it entered the water, willing the fish to sense danger. She did not watch the bait as it drew nearer to the fish; she watched the motionless fish himself, willing him to stay still, to ignore it – not to feel hungry, not to feel tempted – no, no, no – Peter kept drawing the worm across his field of vision – 'he doesn't want to know' – ten times, and each time she had counted, she had breathed 'no' under her breath. Peter had tried ten times, ten skilful, careful attempts, and each time no –

'You've tried ten times. He doesn't want to know.'

Peter cast again. Get past thirteen, let him get past thirteen. She picked up a small stone. Tense and nervous, she held it. She held her breath –

'Fourteen,' she said, fingering the stone.

'Quit counting. You've got to have patience, you've got to spend hours. Quit that stupid counting.'

But still she counted. Twenty casts. Then the hook caught itself in a piece of weed and the worm came off.

'Get the bait tin.'

'You get it,' she said. She jumped up and walked away a little.

'You're no help. What d'you come out for I wonder?' Peter was cross. He put his rod down and went for the tin. While his back was turned she quickly threw the little stone. Peter heard the splash, turned and saw the rings in the water, and saw that the fish was gone.

'He's gone! You threw another stone!'

'No I didn't!'

'You bloody did. I heard it.'

'Something fell into the water.'

'Oh yes, bloody likely, out of the skies, right by my fish, scared him off—'

'It must have.'

'You try to fool me—'

I don't like Peter.

'You chuck stones—'

I don't like him.

'—and then tell lies you didn't.'

I hate him.

'I hate you,' she said.

'Well, I hate people who tell lies. You're no fisherman.'

'No I'm not. I hate fishing. I'm glad I scared him off.'

'Well hard luck,' said Peter, 'because he's back. If you're stopping, keep your hands in your bloody pockets.'

Miserable, she now hated the fish. She didn't care what happened to him. He deserved to be caught—good riddance to him; another fish could have his place. All she had done for him, and there he was, stupid, back in the same place, mesmerized by the stupid horrible worm. Persistently, Peter repeated the same routine. She lost count—hundreds of times—for ever—

'Oh so boring!' she said loudly. 'I think fishing is stupid!'

But she failed to goad him because just then the fish moved slightly. Peter was holding the worm steady about four inches from his nose and he altered his position fractionally.

'Come on, come on,' muttered Peter, 'come on, come on—'

'He won't,' she said, again loudly.

'Shut up!' Peter's voice was muted and savage. The fish moved again, but still maintaining the same distance between him and the bait.

'He will. Come on.' Peter moved the worm a half inch closer. Nothing.

Suddenly a much smaller fish darted from some distance away and took the worm in its swift forward path; the line travelled and tightened. Peter easily controlled his puny catch and landed it on the bank. She laughed unkindly at it.

'Better than nothing,' said Peter.

'It's not. You'll have to throw it back.'

'It's big enough, just about.'

'Oh, nowhere near, it's tiny. You know it's too little.'

Peter extricated the hook, and gripped the fish in his hands. It flipped strongly.

'You're no fisherman if you keep that.'

'I caught it didn't I—'

'Whatever d'you want it for?'

Peter had no answer. The fish arched itself frantically.

'You just want it to prove something, to prove you can catch something. It's so young it doesn't know anything; you don't prove anything unless you'd caught the big one—'

'You didn't want me to.'

'No. But if you had you'd be a good fisherman—I'd respect you even if I do hate fishing. I'd tell them at home, I'd even tell I tried to scare him off. Anybody can catch little ones; they're for kids.'

'I landed it.'

'It just took the bait; you weren't trying for it.'

'When you're fishing you're trying to catch a fish, stupid.'

'You just had to land it to get the hook free; it got itself caught. You've held it; now put it back. You know you don't want it.'

Obstinately he still held it tight. The poor thing opened its bleeding mouth pitifully.

'It'll die in a minute. I shan't say at home you caught a fish. I shan't say anything. You can show it to your father.'

The fish was almost at its last gasp.

'You won't want to show him. He'll be angry and Ron Evans will—Ron thought you were a proper fisherman. And I did; I'll never come with you again.'

'Big deal!'

Her eyes were hot and sharp with tears. The little fish lay limp in Peter's hand.
'What a baby, crying for a fish!'

'I'm not. I'm crying for – because –'

She couldn't say why. But something she knew suddenly found its only expression in loud childish sobbing. Peter went to the water's edge and flung the fish as far as he could. It disappeared with a small splash.

Gradually, as the hard lump in her chest eased and melted, her tears ceased. She heaved a big sigh. Peter sat down without speaking and unwrapped what was left of the sandwiches; presently she sat down beside him and together they finished them, and the lemonade.

'D'you want to have a go for him?' asked Peter, 'You see Mister Big 'Un's back again. D'you want to try for him?'

She nodded. He got to his feet and baited the hook for her; in a short while she became as absorbed as Peter had been. She asked his advice but he didn't give her much. 'He's a crafty bugger, I reckon we won't catch him in a hurry', he said.

The kingfisher flew down the river again, and almost immediately flew back past them both – they both saw it. Presently she gave the rod back to Peter. They sat side by side on the bank; Peter just dangled the worm out of sight under the bank. A slight breeze sprang up, ruffling the river's surface at the farther side; the willows moved trailing their sun-yellow fingers in the water.

'A bit of wind. Let's have some action,' said Peter. He bounced his rod up and down in an amateurish manner, flicking the worm in and out of the water. He made her laugh; he was funny, fooling about. In one movement he looped the worm into the air and flipped it carelessly over at the big fish. She thought it landed right on him.

With an incredible outraged turbulence of the water in which he had lain so still for so long he flashed up, showering spray from his galvanized body. Peter couldn't believe it. He leaped up too, nearly dropping the rod. Both the children were desperately excited – she screamed in surprise, clapping her hands, jumping up and down, and Peter's hands shook as he began to reel in; it was a bigger fish than he had ever caught before.

'What if he gets away! Oh, don't let him!' She chewed her fingers, she was sweating. So far, the trout was still hooked –

'What if he breaks the line?' Peter was sweating too.

The tip of the rod bent to the water; the woodpecker rattle of his reel clocked up a timeless period of suspense. Peter drew his catch relentlessly closer, and closer – till he judged the time was right and swung the big fish up in a triumphant arc on to the bank.

'Oh Peter, if you could see your face!'

'And yours –' he grinned at her. They were both crouching by his panting catch. A huge confidence born of success out of failure wrapped them both in unutterable content.

'He's swallowed the hook right down.'

'Can you get it out?'

'Sure.' While she waited for Peter to unhook the fish the wind swayed in the willows again; the river seemed to be coming alive. Many fish were growing active; several random sets of rings appeared on the surface. She imagined the urgent upward fling of solid bodies made light in the water by a strange compulsion. Peter came and stood by her.

'He's heavy. I reckon he weighs a pound and a half, maybe.'

'Look at them jump! They must feel so light and cheerful to jump like that.' They could clearly see many fish darting and gliding the length of the loop.

'Something gets to them,' said Peter.

'The rings only show where they've been, not where they are now.'

'They're all over the bloody place.'

'I wonder what it is that gets to them –'

They didn't feel like going home. Peter took a fresh worm. He had some luck; he had several strikes and landed two more fish. She watched him, watched the fish swimming, watched the willows and the river. She went a little way along the bank, took her sandals off and played about in the water. She crouched on the rocky floor of a small pool fringed with weed, where boatmen skated and a school of tiny minnows flickered.

The sun beat down upon her head and upon her back – the breeze blew more strongly – she was conscious of no time but now, no place but here – the stream flowing cold round her bare feet might well have had neither source nor destination – this day might well have had no dawning – nor be approaching any nightfall . . .

(Hilary Tunnicliffe, printed by permission of the author.)

If you have enjoyed this story, it is partly because:
- there is enough *description* included to enable the reader to imagine the pleasant country setting;
- the writer has made sure that the *narrative* tells us how the boy and girl feel as well as what they do;
- the *dialogue* is natural (some might think it *too* natural in places!) and helps to bring the characters to life.

These are general reasons; any careful reader could have found them. There may also be personal reasons, unique to each reader:
- a reader who has ever been fishing can share the feelings of the boy or the girl.
- Those who have never gone fishing can take part, through their imagination, in what is happening.

Perhaps there is a particular point of contact for you:
- a detail that awakens a vivid memory
- a feeling that is echoed in your own experience
- words or expressions that mean something special to you.

Think about such contact points between yourself and the writer of this story or for that matter any writer whose work you have enjoyed reading. If you choose to write a fictional piece you yourself need to *make contact* with your reader. In your case the examiner may be the most important one!

> Imaginative literature ... offers complete contexts for reflection on human values and behaviour and at the same time provides activities for the exercise of talk, listening, reading and writing
>
> (SCE)

WRITING FICTION

When *planning* your story:

1 Try to be original. Given the title 'A Close Finish', consider possibilities other than the last five minutes of a football game. That idea will occur to so many people that the examiner will welcome a less obvious story.

2 Positively avoid treating the subject as you may have seen it treated on television, or written about in a magazine. For instance, if you are writing about family life, rid your mind of *Coronation Street*; if your story concerns crime and the law, forget about *Miami Vice*. Such programmes are based on a ready-made pattern, so to copy them will do nothing for your story except make it ordinary.

A story usually contains description, narrative and dialogue.

Description

Be direct, clear, vivid and above all lively in setting a scene or capturing a character. One or two memorable descriptive words are far more effective than a number of commonplace ones.

Which of these descriptions brings the scene to life more?

(a) He shrugged himself into his coat, flicked his fingers at his Labrador dog and marched past the men seated round the big, scrubbed table, a tell-tale of angry colour on each cheek.

(b) He got up angrily and put his coat on. Impatiently he snapped his fingers at his Labrador dog to tell him he was ready to go. He walked quickly past the men who were sitting round the table and his face was flushed with the anger that he felt.

Narrative

The pace or speed of your narrative will be determined by what you are relating. If you vary the pace your story will be much more effective:

If what you are relating is leisurely, use leisurely words ...

The village lay sleepy and quiet in the noon sunlight. The river, spanned by the old stone bridge, flowed peacefully over the pebbles in its wide, shallow bed. Thus it had flowed for centuries from the Welsh hills of its source down through the valleys to the broad Severn, and thence to the open sea.

But then ... suddenly the peace was shattered. A shot rang out in the High Street, two men dashed from the post office and flung themselves into their waiting car. Doors slammed, engine leaped, and they were away. The car reached 50 in 15 seconds; the panic whine of their high gear tailed them down the road ...

Dialogue

From what people say, we learn what they are like. By studying the way they say it we learn even more about them. When you want to practise this, see unit W5 (p. 113) for the special techniques of writing speech.

Getting started

The more closely a writer is involved in what he is writing the more convincing the story is likely to be . . . so . . . *use your five senses.* They are tools and can be made to work for you.

Sample question

'Concentrating on atmosphere, write a story entitled *A Door into the Dark.*' (From specimen paper, Oxford and Cambridge Schools Examination Board.)

> Although I was clutching Karl's arm, feeling his comforting warmth through the rough sleeve of his sweater, holding tightly to the reassurance of his daytime self, I could still feel my heart pounding in near panic at the slow creaking of the door as it opened. (I think I had been praying that it would not.) Stone steps – we could see six or seven steps, uneven from use, curving away, leading downwards into total, terrifying blackness. 'Oh no, Karl, no!' I tried to pull him back. 'We must go on now,' he said.

The writer here placed himself or herself in the centre of the action at a dramatic moment, concentrating on the sense of *touch*.

Touch emphasizes Karl's 'comforting', 'reassuring' presence and, by contrast, makes the 'heart pounding', 'near panic' more real.

Having started the story at the centre of the action, the writer can see clearly what the outline would have to be:

1 how the two people embarked upon their adventure;

2 where the stone steps led to, and what they found;

3 how the episode ended.

The story started with 2, which is not yet complete. Next the writer could fill in 1 before continuing with 2.

But beware

A title like this may tempt you to use unoriginal ideas and obvious words and phrases, like this:

> Suddenly the tunnel widened out into a space where we could stand upright. Karl shone his torch and revealed a cobwebby, dusty room. In one corner we could see an old oak chest with brass hinges. I held my breath as he inched forward, and gingerly lifted the lid. What would he find?

What *could* he find? Treasure, charts, a skeleton? The tone of the writing, through the choice of words – not wrong but ordinary – makes us fairly certain that this won't be different from a hundred such stories examiners have had to read.

You lose marks by being dull.

Practice

Use the opening just given for *A Door into the Dark*, and continue the essay; concentrate on conveying atmosphere, both around you and within you, as you go down the steps. Use your *senses* to connect you with what is happening.

Sample question

'*The Day of the Party.*' Describe such a day from your own experience. You may choose a recent party or a children's party you remember well.'

> I put on my new dress, and stood admiring myself in the long mirror. Plain brown cord, with an Empire waist and long sleeves, frilled with cream lace at the neck and wrists. I turned this way and that, studying the effect.
>
> 'With your blonde hair and fair skin,' my mother said, 'it's just right for you.'
>
> I liked myself in it. As I walked round to Sarah's house for her party I felt good; I was looking forward to the evening . . . until Sarah opened the door to me. She is also blonde and fair-skinned and – you guessed it – we stared at each other's brown cord dresses in disbelief.
>
> 'We look like twins!' Sarah laughed. She did not seem to mind too much. But I was mortified . . .

By using the sense of *sight* the writer has started to portray a girl who cares about colour and design, who likes plain things, and who is insecure in a situation which she sees as

embarrassing. She will describe the people at the party *subjectively*, as they affect her. This essay subject is more 'open-ended' than the first example, and so less predictable. You would have a better chance of writing a story that will be new to the examiner.

Details drawn from your own experience can be used effectively; a single incident, insignificant in itself, can colour one's whole feeling towards people at a party:

> I heard Sarah's younger sister – she's in the fourth form at our school – saying to Graham: 'She'll have bought it on purpose to copy Sarah'.
>
> She did not know I heard her. After that Graham seemed to keep away from me. I *hated* my wretched brown dress. Everybody seemed to be absorbed, laughing, playing records. 'I'm not enjoying this party one little bit,' I said to myself miserably.

Practice

If the suggested opening appeals to you, use it and finish the story. Your rough plan could be:

1 what you expect of the party;
2 a description of meeting people there;
3 how your enjoyment of the party was affected by meeting them.

Our second piece comes from a travel book, a personal account of a train journey from Lima, the capital of Peru situated almost at sea level, to Huancayo almost 4 000 metres up in the Andes, where the atmosphere is thin. Most people have experienced the effects of small changes of air pressure; the massive changes in such a journey are less easy to bear.

The Old Patagonian Express

It begins as dizziness and a slight headache. I had been standing by the door inhaling the cool air . . . Feeling wobbly, I sat down, and if the train had not been full I would have lain across the seat. After an hour I was perspiring and, although I had not stirred from my seat, I was short of breath. The evaporation of this sweat in the dry air gave me a sickening chill. The other passengers were limp, their heads bobbed, no one spoke, no one ate. I dug some aspirin out of my suitcase and chewed them, but only felt queasier; and my headache did not abate. The worst thing about feeling so ill in transit is that you know that if something goes wrong with the train – a derailment or a crash – you will be too weak to save yourself. I had a more horrible thought: we were perhaps a third of the way to Huancayo, but Huancayo was higher than this. I dreaded to think what I would feel like at that altitude.

I considered getting off the train at Matucana but there was nothing at Matucana – a few goats and some Indians and tin-roofed shacks on the stony ground.

None of the stops contained anything that looked like relief or refuge . . . And now my teeth hurt, one molar in particular began to ache as if the nerve had caught fire. I did not know then how a cavity in a bad tooth becomes sore at a high altitude. The air in this blocked hole expands and creates pressure on the nerve, and it is agony. The dentist who told me this had been in the air force. Once, in a sharply descending plane, the cockpit became depressurized and an airman, the navigator, screamed in pain and then one of his teeth exploded.

Some train passengers had begun to vomit. They did it in the pitifully unembarrassed way that people do when they are helplessly ill. They puked on the floor, and they puked out of the windows and they made my own nausea greater. Some, I noticed, were staggering through the cars. I thought they were looking for a place to puke, but they returned with balloons. *Balloons*? Then they sat and held their noses and breathed the air from the balloon nozzle. I stood unsteadily and

made for the rear of the train, where I found a Peruvian in a smock filling balloons from a tank of oxygen. He handed these out to distressed-looking passengers who gratefully gulped from them. I took my place in the queue and discovered that a few whiffs of oxygen made my head clear and helped my breathing.

(From *The Old Patagonian Express,* by Paul Theroux, Hamish Hamilton/Penguin, London.)

In our first example an important part of the story's vividness was conveyed by the actual conversations between the boy and girl. In this journey there was not so much conversation, because all the passengers were feeling the effects of depressurization. Theroux, who is suffering with the others, makes us share his discomfort; 'And now my teeth hurt . . .' – bad enough without the appalling example he uses to bring it home to us! Look for other vivid details as the travellers' pain and distress increase. Yet there must have been some talk, perhaps about the oxygen seller. Paul Theroux has not given us any of the talk – perhaps because it might have been difficult for him to catch the flavour of it in an English translation. If you feel as we do that he has helped his readers share his experience and sensations you may like to exercise your own imagination by supplying some conversation.

Practice

1 Write the conversation Theroux might have had (a) with a fellow-passenger, (b) with the oxygen seller. (For this exercise imagine they all speak English. See p. 121 for help in setting out direct speech.)

2 Think of a situation you have been in when you felt pain or physical discomfort. Describe it as vividly as you can in a letter to a friend, including your surroundings, other people present and any treatment you had and its effects on you.

(Answers and hints, p. 170)

Next, an extract from a famous novel by an American poet, Sylvia Plath. The novel is autobiographical, and demonstrates well how close the connection is between real life and fictional writing of this kind. Sylvia Plath had herself won a writing contest of the kind she describes here and drew heavily on her own recollections of the experience – a method you could easily make use of in writing a fictional piece in an examination or for a coursework folder.

In the Amazon Hotel

There were twelve of us at the hotel.

We had all won a fashion magazine contest, by writing essays and stories and poems and fashion blurbs and as prizes they gave us jobs in New York for a month, expenses paid, and piles and piles of free bonuses, like ballet tickets and passes to fashion shows and hair stylings at a famous expensive salon and chances to meet

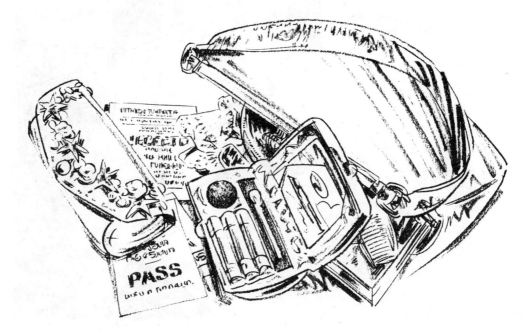

successful people in the field of our desire and advice about what to do with our particular complexions.

I still have the make-up kit they gave me, fitted out for a person with brown eyes and brown hair: an oblong of brown mascara with a tiny brush, and a round basin of blue eyeshadow just big enough to dab the tip of your finger in, and three lipsticks ranging from red to pink, all cased in the same little gilt box with a mirror on one side. I also have a white plastic sun-glasses case with coloured shells and sequins and a green plastic starfish sewed on to it.

I realized we kept piling up these presents because it was as good as free advertising for the firms involved, but I couldn't be cynical. I got such a kick out of all those free gifts showering on to us. For a long time afterwards I hid them away, but later, when I was all right again, I brought them out, and I still have them around the house. I use the lipstick now and then and last week I cut the plastic starfish off the sun-glasses case for the baby to play with.

So there were twelve of us at the hotel, in the same wing on the same floor in single rooms, one after the other, and it reminded me of my dormitory at college. It wasn't a proper hotel – I mean a hotel where there are both men and women mixed about here and there on the same floor.

This hotel – the Amazon – was for women only, and they were mostly girls my age with wealthy parents who wanted to be sure their daughters would be living where men couldn't get at them and deceive them; and they were all going to posh secretarial schools like Katy Gibbs, where they had to wear hats and stockings and gloves to class or they had just graduated from places like Katy Gibbs and were secretaries to executives and junior executives and simply hanging around in New York waiting to get married to some career man or other.

These girls looked awfully bored to me. I saw them on the sun-roof, yawning and painting their nails and trying to keep up their Bermuda tans and they seemed

bored as hell. I talked with one of them, and she was bored with yachts and bored with flying around in aeroplanes and bored with skiing in Switzerland at Christmas and bored with the men in Brazil.

Girls like that make me sick. I'm so jealous I can't speak. Nineteen years, and I hadn't been out of New England except for this trip to New York. It was my first big chance, but here I was, sitting back and letting it run through my fingers like so much water.

I guess one of my troubles was Doreen.

I'd never known a girl like Doreen before. Doreen came from a society girls' college down South and had bright white hair standing out in a cotton candy fluff round her head and blue eyes like transparent agate marbles, hard and polished and just about indestructible and a mouth set in a sort of perpetual sneer. I don't mean a nasty sneer, but an amused, mysterious sneer, as if all the people around her were pretty silly and she could tell some good jokes on them if she wanted to.

Doreen singled me out right away. She made me feel I was that much sharper than the others and she really was wonderfully funny. She used to sit next to me at the conference table, and when the visiting celebrities were talking she'd whisper witty sarcastic remarks to me under her breath.

Her college was so fashion-conscious, she said, that all the girls had pocket-book covers made out of the same materials as their dresses, so each time they changed their clothes they had a matching pocket-book. This kind of detail impressed me. It suggested a whole life of marvellous, elaborate decadence that attracted me like a magnet.

The only thing Doreen ever bawled me out about was bothering to get my assignments in by a deadline.

'What are you sweating over that for?' Doreen lounged on my bed in a peach silk dressing-gown, filing her long, nicotine-yellow nails with an emery board, while I typed up the draft of an interview with a best-selling novelist.

That was another thing—the rest of us had starched cotton summer nighties and quilted housecoats, or maybe terry-towel robes that doubled as beachcoats, but Doreen wore these full-length nylon and lace jobs you could half see through and dressing-gowns the colour of skin, that stuck to her by some kind of electricity. She had an interesting, slightly sweaty smell that reminded me of those scallopy leaves of sweet fern you break off and crush between your fingers for the musk of them.

(From *The Bell Jar,* by Sylvia Plath, Faber & Faber, London.)

Note: Americanisms in this extract include 'bawled me out', 'Bermuda tans', 'talked with'—and many of the ideas, e.g. 'hats and stockings and gloves to class'.)

Comment

Good writing, like good building or good joinery, stands firm or gains its strength from the care and skill that has gone into its construction. Even in so short a piece, taken from a 250-page novel, we can see some methods of *construction*. Three sentences are given paragraphs to themselves—three plain facts, like firm planks to build on. Ideas stem from each one, which can be coloured in the speaker's own personal, American, way.

'There were twelve of us at the hotel.'

'I guess one of my troubles was Doreen.'

'The only thing Doreen ever bawled me out about was bothering to get my assignments in by a deadline.'

You will have noticed from all three examples of this kind of writing so far that accurate and vivid *description* forms an important element. Hilary Tunnicliffe makes sure we can visualize the river setting. Look again at the paragraph beginning 'They reached the place . . .' (p. 40). Paul Theroux, in a few well-chosen phrases, brings to life the sordid scene in the train compartment. And Sylvia Plath draws our attention to many details, insignificant separately but building up an authentic setting for the characters.

Sylvia Plath's novel is about a girl of 19 (the narrator) who is (by the American standards of the time) very unsophisticated for her age. Description is used here to help us to share the girl's new experiences, so the writer appeals to our *senses* by, for example,

- the look and the feel of things in the make-up kit;
- the appearance and the voices of the other girls;
- the appearance, the voice and even the smell of Doreen;
- the feel of her cotton nightdress contrasted with Doreen's nylon and lace négligé.

If the story is to come to life we, the readers, must be helped to see what an unsophisticated 19-year-old would see. Good descriptive writing depends on careful selection of details: here everything selected is important to a young person. For example:

- all the free bonuses, ballet tickets, hair styling, etc.;
- the make-up box in all its details;
- the admission that she 'got a kick out of' all the free gifts;
- the comparison of the hotel with her college dormitory;
- her envious attitude to the richer girls;
- her pride at being singled out by Doreen and her fascination with Doreen's behaviour, wit, clothes;
- her anxiety to do well in her work.

The writer does not need to state background information outright; instead we are allowed to discover it *obliquely,* (that is, indirectly).

How do we know . . .

1 the colour of her hair and eyes?
2 that she is a writer?
3 that all the twelve in the group were girls?
4 that she had had some illness after this award?
5 that she now has a baby?

(Answers on p. 170)

Now that we have studied these examples of good writing and how it is achieved, here is a chance for you to practise.

Practice

You have been given the essay title *A Red Woollen Sweater*. Here are four possible openings:

1 Completely plain, bare, straightforward statement of fact.

Example

'As it happened, on that particular day I was wearing a bright red woollen sweater.'

2 Straightforward, but with more descriptive words.

Example

'On that memorable Saturday I decided when I was dressing to put on my new sweater. It was pure wool, bright red and very warm.'

3 Obliquely, connecting the fact to something else.

Example

'By the time the sun reached its height there was no cloud in the sky, no breath of wind. I had stripped off my woollen sweater, and it lay, a splash of brilliant red, on white sand by the rocks.'

4 More obliquely, i.e. stressing the other item so that the original fact seems of casual importance.

Example

'We were startled to hear voices nearby. At first we thought nothing of it, until a woman's voice said: "But I'm known to the police; I'd be recognized". We crept as close as we dared, fascinated. She and her companion were behind some rocks; we could get closer without being seen – or so we thought until the woman said: "There's something red moving". They stood up, a man and a woman, and sauntered casually away, not glancing in our direction. The others glared at my red woolly sweater accusingly.'

Sight is the sense being used here – a good choice because the title of the essay set was *A Red Woollen Sweater.*

Here are four plain bare statements like the first of the four openings just given. Each emphasizes a particular *sense* (given in brackets). Write versions **2, 3** and **4** for each in turn, on the lines of *A Red Woollen Sweater.*

1 The grandfather clock in the corner of the room struck eight o'clock. (Hearing.)
2 I thought I was in an empty house until I heard the sound of someone hammering. (Hearing.)
3 The postman handed me a small but heavy parcel. (Touch or feel.)
4 People who have a weight problem need a calorie-controlled diet. (Taste.)

(Answers, p. 170)

PICTURES AS A STIMULUS FOR WRITING

Quite often English written examinations include essay questions based on pictures. These offer opportunities for the kind of writing we have been discussing here (see also W1.1 p. 17). The question might be: 'Write a story or a description or a number of thoughts suggested by one of the pictures A and B'.

Picture A

Picture B

... Write an exciting adventure story suggested by the picture   (Sample question SCE)

One way to start is to *be* one of the people you see in the picture (or the person taking the photo). Use your senses again.

in A Does the man standing behind look as though he will speak out to back up his mate?
in B Is the protest peaceable?
in A Are the man's eyes afraid or steady?
in B Are most of the sitters occupied while they wait?
both Where might the photographs have been taken? What time of year? Or time of day?
in B What could be the purpose of the protest?
both What might there be nearby, but off the picture?
both Where is the camera situated? Do the people in the picture react to being photographed?

Examples

A 'I stood behind Jack, backing 'im up like. I knew the way he would play it – cool, with his trap tight shut and his eyes wide open. I was fair hugging myself against the moment when the gaffer would run out of steam. Pick your time, Jack, let him have it, straight from the shoulder, I'm right behind you . . .'

B 'On the morning of the demonstration my grandpa got dressed in his best suit. "Got to show them we're not riff-raff," he said. And when we went out, he sat in the middle of the road, at the front . . .'

Description

If there is plenty of detail in the picture (as in picture B) *one way* of starting your description is to describe first the parts furthest away, and work towards those nearest to you. This brings the picture closer:

e.g. the walkers,

the parked van,

the one readable poster,

the spread plastic sheeting,

then the two lads at the back of the group, the man leaving, front right.

Another method is to fasten on to the particular feature or detail that strikes you most, and to let that lead you further into the ideas suggested by the picture . . .

e.g. in picture A it might be the two men's caps.

Thoughts

The third choice in the question gives more freedom for the *imagination*. As long as the thoughts spring directly from something in the picture they need not be confined to what is in the picture. Thus:

● Picture A might lead you to consider other clashes between workers and officialdom.

● Picture B might lead you to write about the way a common cause such as fighting for a new by-pass helps people to forget the generation gap.

Practice

Find an open-air scene in a newspaper or magazine, *or* an old family photograph at home, and write an essay using the question we have quoted. If you choose a photograph, ask one of the people in it to read and comment on your essay.

Our fourth example takes us back 30 years or so to the London of the 1950s, when the post-war generation of teenagers shared in the 'boom', with more money to spend and fewer responsibilities than any other teenage generation before or since. This brought with it, as a less desirable by-product, the beginnings of the teenage drug problem. Colin MacInnes grew up through this period, and draws on his own recollections for both the setting and the style of his account.

Absolute Beginners

[This extract describes part of the London teenage scene in the 1950s.]

If you have a friend who's a junkie, like I have the Dean, you soon discover there's no point whatever discussing his addiction. It's as senseless as discussing love, or religion, or things you only feel if you feel them, because the Dean, and I suppose all his fellow junkies, is convinced that this is 'a mystic way of life' (the Dean's own words), and you and I, who don't jab hot needles in our arms, are just going through life missing absolutely everything worth while in it. The Dean always says, life's just kicks. Well, I agree with him, so it is, but personally, it seems to me the big kick you should try to get is by how you live it sober. But tell that to the Dean!

Why I'd not recently seen him, is that he'd until then been away inside. This has fairly often happened to the Dean, owing to his breaking into chemists' shops, and as he suffers a lot when he's cut off from the world and all it gives in there, he doesn't like you to refer to it when he emerges. At the same time, he *does* like you to say you're glad to see him once again, so it's all a trifle dicey.

'Hail, squire,' I said. 'Long time no see. How is you, are we? Won't you say tell?'

The Dean smiled in his world-weary way.

'Doesn't this place stink?' he said to me.

'Well certainly, Dean Swift, it does, but do you mean its air or just its atmosphere?'

'The both. The only civilized thing about it,' the Dean continued, 'is that they let you *sit* here, when you're skint.'

The Dean gazed round at the teenage products like a concentration camp exterminator. I should explain the Dean, though only just himself an ex-teenager, has sad valleys down his cheeks, and wears a pair of steel-rimmed glasses . . . so that his Dean-look is habitually sour and solemn. (The Swift part of the thing comes from his rapid disappearance at the approach of any cowboys. You're talking to him and then, tick-tock! he's vanished.) I could see that now the Dean, as usual, when skinned and vicious, was going to engage in his favourite theme, i.e. the horror of teenagers.

'Look at the beardless microbes!' he exclaimed, loud enough for everyone to hear. 'Look at the pram products at their plotting and their planning!'

And, as a matter of fact, you could see what he meant, because to see the kids hunched over the tables it *did* look as if some conspiracy was afoot to slay the elder brethren and majorities. And when I'd paid, and we went out in the roads, even here in this Soho, the headquarters of the adult mafia, you could everywhere see the signs of the un-silent teenage revolution. The disc shops with those lively sleeves set in their windows, the most original thing to come out in our lifetime and the kids inside them purchasing guitars, or spending fortunes on the songs of the Top Twenty. The shirt-stores and bra-stores with cine-star photos in the window, selling all the exclusive teenage drag I've been describing. The hair-style saloons where they inflict the blow-wave torture on the kids for hours on end. The cosmetic shops – to make girls of seventeen, fifteen, even thirteen, look like pale rinsed-out sophisticates. Scooters and bubblecars driven madly down the roads by kids who, a few years ago, were pushing toy ones on the pavement. And everywhere you go the narrow coffee-bars and darkened cellars with the kids packed tight, just whispering, like bees inside the hive waiting for a glorious queen bee to appear.

'See what I mean,' the Dean said.

(From *Absolute Beginners* by Colin MacInnes, Allison & Busby, London.)

You will remember that at the beginning of unit 1.2 we referred to the *tone* of a piece of writing, and its importance in shaping the reader's response (p. 29). Tone forms a significant part of MacInnes's piece, which uses the casual, friendly, sloppy language of the teenage world he is describing, with a liberal use of slang (some of it sounding old-fashioned by now)–'junkie', 'kicks', 'dicey'. At the same time, he leaves us in no doubt of his own critical view of the scene; read his final paragraph and the 'Dean's' comment. If you want to experiment with this kind of writing, make sure it is authentic. Listen carefully next time you go to a disco, or a club, or wherever the people you want to describe meet one another.

Practice

Write an impression of a crowded teenage gathering today, including some conversation. Write in the first person, and try to catch the *tone* of the language spoken there. (We cannot provide an answer to this question. Ask a friend to read and comment on your description.)

For our last piece of writing from personal experience and the emotions we travel in space as well as time, to the United States of America. It comes from the justly famous autobiography of a black American woman, Maya Angelou. Her rich and varied life is described in four vividly written volumes; this passage comes from the first.

I Know Why the Caged Bird Sings

[This passage comes from the autobiography of a black American, Maya Angelou. She grew up in Arkansas in the Southern United States in the 1930s. At the age of 15 she ran away from her loose-living parents. This describes her first night alone.]

I spent the day wandering aimlessly through the bright streets. The noisy penny arcades with their gaggle-giggle of sailors and children and the games of chance were tempting, but after walking through one of them it was obvious that I could only win more chances and no money. I went to the library and used a part of my day reading science fiction and in its marble washroom I changed my bandage.

On one flat street I passed a junkyard, littered with the carcasses of old cars. The dead hulks were somehow so uninviting that I decided to inspect them. As I wound my way through the discards a temporary solution sprang to my mind. I would find a clean or cleanish car and spend the night in it. With the optimism of ignorance I thought that the morning was bound to bring a more pleasant solution. A tall-bodied gray car near the fence caught my eye. Its seats were untorn, and although it had no wheels or rims it sat evenly on its fenders. The idea of sleeping in the near open bolstered my sense of freedom. I was a loose kite in a gentle wind floating with only my will for an anchor. After deciding upon the car, I got inside and ate the tuna sandwiches and then searched the floorboards for holes. The fear that rats might scurry in and eat off my nose as I slept (some cases had been recently reported in the papers) was more alarming than the shadowed hulks in the junkyard or the quickly descending night. My gray choice, however, seemed rat-tight, and I abandoned my idea of taking another walk and decided to sit steady and wait for sleep.

My car was an island and the junkyard a sea, and I was all alone and full of warm. The mainland was just a decision away. As evening became definite the street lamps flashed on and the lights of moving cars squared my world in a piercing probing, I counted the headlights and said my prayers and fell asleep.

The morning's brightness drew me awake and I was surrounded with strangeness. I had slid down the seat and slept the night through in an ungainly position. Wrestling with my body to assume an upward arrangement, I saw a collage of Negro, Mexican and white faces outside the window. They were laughing and making the mouth gestures of talkers but their sounds didn't penetrate my refuge. There was so much curiosity evident in their features that I knew they wouldn't go away before they knew who I was, so I opened the door, prepared to give them any story (even the truth) that would buy my peace.

The windows and my grogginess had distorted their features. I had thought they were adults and maybe citizens of Brobdingnag, at least. Standing outside, I found there was only one person taller than I, and that I was only a few years younger than any of them. I was asked my name, where I came from and what led me to the junkyard. They accepted my explanation that I was from San Francisco, that my name was Marguerite but that I was called Maya and I simply had no place to stay. With a generous gesture the tall boy, who said he was Bootsie, welcomed me, and said I could stay as long as I honoured their rule: No two people of opposite sex slept together. In fact, unless it rained, everyone had his own private sleeping accommodations. Since some of the cars leaked, bad weather forced a doubling up. There was no stealing, not for reasons of morality but because a crime would bring the police to the yard; and since everyone was underage, there was the likelihood that they'd be sent off to foster homes or juvenile delinquent courts. Everyone worked at something. Most of the girls collected bottles and worked weekends in greasy spoons*. The boys mowed lawns, swept out pool halls and ran errands for small Negro-owned stores. All money was held by Bootsie and used communally.

(From *I Know Why the Caged Bird Sings* by Maya Angelou, Virago, London.)

Maya Angelou

It is easy to tell, even from this short extract, why the book it comes from has been such a success. Although her life had been tough and was still precarious she wastes no time on self pity. She observed her own behaviour with detachment – 'with the optimism of ignorance I thought . . . solution' (para. 2). Here and there her plain straightforward narrative moves into poetic language – 'I was a loose kite . . .' (para. 2), 'My car was an island . . .' etc. (para. 3).

*'greasy spoons' are cafés.

> This [i.e. coursework] must include response to literary texts (e.g. short stories, novels, autobiography, poetry, plays)   (NISEC)

Writing acquires richness and life from the writer's ability to vary her style, to add such touches. For instance, can you say what is particularly apt about the reference to Brobdingnag (*Gulliver's Travels*) (para. 5)? (Answer p. 171).

Practice

Either

1 A little later in the book Maya Angelou comments on this period of her life: 'Odd that the homeless children, the silt of war frenzy (the period was now 1943-4) could initiate me into the brotherhood of man.' With this as a clue, write a continuation of Maya's story, a piece of about the same length. (You can compare your version with hers if you get the book from the library, but write your version first.)

or

2 Using this as a model, describe an episode in your life that involved you in totally new experiences. (For hints on answering, see p. 171.)

W2 INFORMATION AND FACTS

2.1 Comprehension and Summary

In this unit we turn our attention to what used to be called 'comprehension' or comprehension and summary ('precis') in GCE and CSE courses. The kinds of writing dealt with make even greater demands on concentration and understanding than those we looked at and practised in unit W1. The passages are not simply to be read as stimuli and examples for your own writing; they are source material for all kinds of investigation and analysis.

> . . . demonstrate the ability to select material relevant to a particular task   (LEAG)

Reading has to be for many different purposes: finding information, selecting facts, summarizing, so your understanding has to operate on many different levels. Writing in this section usually follows specific instructions; you are rarely left free to make your own response. The ability to write as instructed is very important not only for examination purposes but in everyday life.

In fact you have practised these skills since you learned to talk and to read! You are using them when you tell someone the story of a book or a film, when you look at a timetable and catch the right bus, and when you do your homework. In the first two examples that follow, you may not be writing but you are using the skills of passing on information and of selecting certain facts.

The same skills are also required for some aural work (see Listening and Talking on p. 139) but in this section the work is based on written material or diagrams.

When you are looking for information in a passage, your mind flashes as fast as a computer through various stages of investigation. Reading the *words*, as you know, is only a small part of reading with full understanding. As you read, your mind is occupied with many different levels and aspects of understanding. We are going to work with the following five possible stages.

OBSERVATION

Your first reading will tell you what the passage is about. You may be asked to set out the *argument*, i.e. the line of thought or reasoning, to show how one point depends on another. Sometimes particular points may be dealt with in separate questions, to see whether you have noticed them.

COMPARISON

Your full understanding of the passage will involve comparing things. The commonest and most useful kind of comparison will concern the actual words used, the writer's *vocabulary*. Words you have used before, or seen used in your reading, provide you with meanings to compare with the ones you are asked about. Even when a word seems quite new to you, you can compare the way it is used with expressions, sentences, contexts familiar to you. Many questions test your word skill, often by asking you to put the words in sentences of your own – an active comparison, so to speak – or to provide synonyms (i.e. words closely similar in meaning).

REFLECTION

This is the heart of understanding. To understand fully what is written, we have to draw inferences. This includes the ability to read between the lines, to catch the tone of voice, the change of mood. Just as when we are talking to someone, we take into account the *way* they say things (and who is saying it), so we may be expected to notice the way something is written, and relate it to the writer. Is he being serious here? Does he mean just what he says? What kind of person is he? What kind of person is he describing?

SELECTION

Many questions test your ability to select the appropriate points. From your close reading and observation of the passage you will be able to select the features that illustrate different aspects of the subject written about, or of the writer's methods.

CONCLUSION

Once the preliminary work has been done you can draw conclusions about the passage as a whole, what it is aiming at, and the way it is written.

These methods and processes of reading all lead to a full understanding of what is written, but this part of the GCSE also tests your ability to write clearly, accurately and especially concisely. Only a few questions leave you free to develop your own ideas; usually a short answer is the best indication that you know exactly what the question requires. Good spelling, punctuation and layout all contribute greatly to the accuracy and adequacy of your answers. Where an indication is given of the number of marks that can be earned for a question, or part of a question, divide your time sensibly so that you give more to a question worth 10 marks than to one worth 2.

A word of warning

It can be dangerous to use direct quotations from the passage as an answer to a question; better to change the original into words of your own. The questions test your understanding, so take all opportunities offered to show that you do understand.

For example, George Orwell writes on p.31 '. . . international sporting contests lead to orgies of hatred'.

Question:
What is the outcome of international sporting contests according to George Orwell?

Answer:
International sporting contests lead to uncontrolled outbursts of ill feeling.

The words 'orgies of hatred' need to be 'translated' so that the examiner knows that you know what they mean. Even if the meaning of some phrases seems blindingly obvious, be helpful to the examiner and find other words! Unimportant words like 'and', 'if', 'the', etc. do not matter, nor do common words like 'space' where there are no satisfactory substitutes. It is a good idea to practise this good practice (it will help your vocabulary) in all work of this kind.

TYPES OF QUESTION

The following questions and directions are grouped under the same headings – observations, comparison etc. – we have just used; they include almost every kind of question that can be asked on this aspect of English. If you can recognize what type of question you are being asked, you are halfway to answering it properly.

Sometimes you need to summarize the argument or main points of a passage and to *draw inferences* from what you read. We have dealt with these techniques of writing in greater detail later in this unit.

Type 1 (Observation)

– Summarize in x words the argument of the second paragraph . . .
– Basing your answer on information given in the passage, state what different occupations A has . . .
– Mention briefly the *four* ways in which . . .
– Explain the meaning of '. . .' on line x . . .
– List three ways in which, according to the author . . .

Questions of this type are all testing your powers of intelligent observation of what you have just read. Keep a clear head, and all the material for your answers is there in front of you.

Type 2 (Comparison)

– Explain why the word '. . .' is used on line x . . .
– Give the meaning of *five* of the following words as used in the passage . . .
– Express in your own words '. . .' (line x).
– Give one word or one short phrase meaning the same as each of the following as used in the passage: . . .

In this type of question you are often reminded that the meaning asked for is the one used in the passage. This is because words take much of their meaning from the context they are used in. You may be allowed a dictionary but will still need your own powers of comparison and selection to catch precisely the meaning required. Small dictionaries may even be a hindrance, misleading you in your answers. Look at the example given in 'A word of warning'. If you had looked up 'orgy' and found 'drunken or licentious revel', George Orwell's meaning would have been distorted.

Type 3 (Reflection)

– Describe the tone in which *A* speaks.
– Say why *B* thinks it would be better if he did grumble?
– Describe the relationship of *C* and *D* as demonstrated by the passage.
– What does the expression '. . .' (line *x*) tell us about the general public's attitude to *B*?
– What do you infer from *A*'s sudden departure?
– (This question is a combination of Types 1 and 3.) Explain the meaning, and comment on the effectiveness of . . .

Questions of this type are often set on extracts from stories or novels.

Type 4 (Selection)

– Select two statements in the passage which indicate . . .
– Quote three sentences or phrases which mean the same as . . .
– What details suggest that *E* has been carefully prepared and might be dangerous?

Type 5 (Conclusion)

– Summarize *A*'s and *B*'s attitudes to writing novels. (On a passage portraying two contrasting approaches to writing)
– Say whether you think the author is right.
– Is . . . necessarily true? Explain why or why not.

With a little practice, you will quickly be able to recognize what type of question you are being asked and then your answer is more likely to be on target.

Most passages given for this kind of writing will either be from fiction (novel or story) or set out a discussion or argument, often including a good deal of 'evidence' in the form of factual statement. The first example here comes from argument/discussion writing: three short pieces on advertising. The next two are from fiction. In the answer section we have sorted the questions of the first two pieces into their different categories but left you to work out most of the answers. For the third piece from *Kes* we have worked through the answers in a more detailed way.

PRACTICE

1 *Read the following extracts carefully. Answer the questions that follow.*

(a) Advertising has done much to raise the standards of physical well-being. The catalogue of its benefits, real and claimed, is a long one. It has speeded the introduction of useful inventions to a wide as distinct from a select circle. It has brought prosperity to communities which did not know how to sell their rotting crops. By widening markets it has enabled costs of raw materials to be cut, accelerated turnover, lowered selling prices. It has spread seasonal trade and kept people in employment. It has given a guarantee of dependability – for who (as that advertisement used to ask) would buy a nameless motor-car put together in a back-street workshop? Its defenders claim that advertising has abolished heavy underwear, made people clean their teeth (which was more than their dentists could persuade them to do), and made them Nice to be Near. These gratifying results have been achieved not only by informative, but by persuasive and indeed intimidating advertisements. The prime object of the exercise was not, of course, to benefit humanity, but to sell more fabrics, more toothpaste, more disinfectant.

(From The Shocking History of Advertising *by E.S. Turner, Michael Joseph, London.)*

(*b*) Sir,

What is responsible for the decline in values in Britain today? Seldom is one of the chief culprits mentioned – I refer to advertising.

The way people are persuaded to live beyond their means, spending on frivolous things that fulfil no real need, is nothing short of scandalous. To sell these fringe products advertisers resort to tricks. The English language is misused to deceive us. Our fears, hopes and weaknesses are exploited. Exaggerated and misleading claims are employed to make us buy things, including those that do us harm, such as drugs and tobacco.

Contrary to all we once believed we have learnt to accept the philosophy of advertisement – that happiness can be measured by what we possess. At all costs we must keep up with the Joneses.

Much space is devoted to 'brand' advertising which is an expensive waste of time. All this does is to push up prices. Does it really matter which soap, toothpaste or petrol we use? There's not a hap'orth of difference.

It's about time large-scale advertising was banned. Then we'd all *really* be better off.

Robert Blunt

(*c*) 1 *Everyone* is changing into Levi's.
2 Slimfit fashions for *the fuller figure*.
3 Cinzano Bianco – the *bright lights* taste.
4 Try Walls's *Country-Style* Pork Sausages.
5 *Invest* in Littlewood's Pools.

Answer *all* the questions that follow. Brief answers *only* are required to the questions on extracts (*a*), (*b*) and (*c*).

Extract (a)
1 What does the writer mean by referring to some benefits as 'claimed'?
2 The writer has used a short phrase to say that advertising has increased sales. Give the phrase.
3 Why does the writer believe advertised goods are more dependable?
4 What is meant by making people 'Nice to be Near'?
5 Give the three words which Turner uses to describe the three types of advertising.
6 Which type of advertising is likely to cause most concern, and why?

Extract (b)
1 The writer starts by speaking of the 'decline in values'. Later in his letter he gives an example of what he considers to be such a decline. What is it?
2 The expression 'fringe products' is explained in a short phrase. Give the phrase.
3 Give two 'tricks' of the advertisers' trade of which the writer complains.
4 What is meant by 'keeping up with the Joneses'?
5 Why is 'brand' advertising said to be a waste of time and money?
6 In his last sentence, Blunt refers to a point made early in his letter. What is it?

Extract (c)
The writer in extract (*b*) complains of the language in advertising being used to deceive us. Study the five slogans. Comment *briefly* on the words italicized in each, explaining in each case how they seek to persuade the reader.

General Questions
The writers of extracts (*a*) and (*b*) appear to hold very different opinions. Write a paragraph (not more than 100 words) to support ONE of the writers. Do not copy his words. Try to introduce one or two ideas of your own.

(Answers on p. 171.)

2 The following passage describes the first visit of a young British actor to America. He is to play the part of the composer Liszt in a film. Read the passage carefully, and then answer the questions that follow.

Playing Liszt

My room was disturbingly dark and smelled of conditioned air. Ominous glitters of light slitted through the shutters. I groped my way across the room, hit a table, and pushed open the windows. Hot smoggy air came up from the studio yard. Six men pushing half a snow-capped mountain trundled up the yard. A woman came
5   running down, a bundle of sequined dresses over her arm, a paper cup of coffee in

her hand. To my far left, by the carpenter's shop, plants and sawdust and gilded doors were leaning against the concrete walls. To my right, high up, were the misty smog-smudged ridge of the hills and the great wooden sign striding the skyline, one letter missing, long since fallen: 'Hol-ywood'.

10   I had arrived at last. I was there where it all started: the most chaotic city on earth west of Calcutta. My heart fell with despair: six months to go.

I examined the room. It was pine-panelled – fake plaster pine-panelled. The tweed carpet looked like old porridge and the chairs and settees were covered in violent tartan. There were hunting prints on the walls, a sword, a galleon in full sail, two
15   refrigerators disguised as oak chests, lamp-shades with maps of the world on them, a small table with a flat bowl of plastic sweet peas and dahlias. The bathroom, entered between the 'oak chests', was plain, clinically white, very masculine. A note told me to report to Room 2456 for a 'Music Conference'.

When I arrived, Victor Aller, small, benign, with glittering rimless glasses and
20   beautiful hands, was sitting at the Broadwood piano playing something sad. I didn't interrupt him but sat quietly in the chair beside him. He switched music and went into something extremely fast, short and vaguely familiar. He placed his hands on his knees and smiled at me.

'That's Chopsticks.'
25   'Oh.'
'You know it?'
'I think so . . . somewhere.'
'*Everyone* knows it. It's a child's exercise. Play it.'
'I have never played a piano in my life. I couldn't.'
30   A pause like a century.
'You gotta be Liszt.'
'I know that.'
'Liszt played piano.'
'Yes.'
35   'You don't dispute that?'
'No.'
'He played piano like no one else played piano.'
'I believe. . . .'
'And you don't?'
40   'No. Never.'
'Well, we gotta start then. That's what I'm here for. To teach you to play the piano and fast. And like Liszt.'
'Thank you.'
'Don't thank me till I have.' He played some scales rapidly. Dull with fear, I
45   watched his hands. 'These are just scales . . . we'll have to do a lot of this, just to exercise your fingers . . . show me your span.'
'What's that?'
'Hell! Put your hands out in front of you and spread your fingers . . . that's a span.'
I did as he asked. My hands looked supplicating. They were.
50   'Nice span you got. You play tennis?'
'No.'
'Football?'
'No.'
'Ping pong . . . table tennis?'
55   'No, neither.'
Another long stupefied pause. The air-conditioner hissed and throbbed.
'You play that game you have in England . . . with a bat and a ball . . . like rounders?'
'Cricket?'
60   'That's it. Cricket. You play that?'
'No.'
'Hell.' He played another set of scales. 'And you gotta be Liszt?'
'They tell me so.'
'In five weeks we start shooting in Vienna. You going to be ready?'
65   'What do *you* think?'
'Not in a million years, let alone five weeks. You got 85 minutes of flaming music in this production. Eight-five minutes, not including the conducting.'
'Well, I'd better start. I mean, perhaps you could show me, very slowly, a bit of something to play . . . not Chopsticks. It's too fast.'
70   'So is the First flaming Concerto. . . .' He started, very gently and softly, to play. It was good. He played with deep feeling and tenderness. I listened and watched, horrified. How could I ever remember where the fingers went, which keys to use, the black or the white?

Questions

1 In what way do the things seen by the author from his window (in the first paragraph) confirm the fact that he is in the centre of the American film industry?

2 The author clearly dislikes his room. From lines 1 to 18, write down *six* of the phrases which show his dislike of the room's appearance or furnishings and in each case state briefly the reason for his dislike.

3 What can be learned from the passage about the abilities, attitudes and personality of Victor Aller?
Justify each point you make by a brief reference to the passage.

4 What does the encounter with Victor Aller (line 19 to the end of the passage) tell us about the author?

5 (a) Suggest a reason for the author's writing: 'My heart fell with despair' (line 11).
(b) Explain carefully:
the reasons for the pause mentioned in line 30;
and the reason for the pause mentioned in line 56.
(c) Victor Aller is an American. Quote *one* of the sentences he speaks (not including the expression 'gotta') which shows his American style of speech, and after it write what a British musician would have said (in standard English).

6 Explain *briefly* the meaning of each of the following words as used in the passage:
(a) trundled (line 4); (b) chaotic (line 10); (c) supplicating (line 49).

(Answers on p. 171.)

3 The Football Game

[This extract is from *Kes*. Billy Casper is the boy who keeps and trains a kestrel. He enjoys little of his school life and certainly not football, for which he has none of the right kit and no sympathy from the teacher.]

Mr Sugden used the lengths of bandage to secure his stockings just below the knees, then he folded his tracksuit neatly on the ground, looked down at himself, and walked on to the pitch carrying the ball like a plum pudding on the tray of his hand. Tibbut, standing on the centre circle, with his hands down his shorts, winked at his left winger and waited for Mr Sugden to approach.

Sugden (teacher): 'Who are we playing, Tibbut?'
'Er . . . we'll be Liverpool, Sir.'
'You can't be Liverpool.'
'Why not, Sir?'
'I've told you once, they're too close to Manchester United's colours, aren't they?'

Tibbut massaged his brow with his fingertips, and under this guise of thinking, glanced round at his team.
'We'll be Spurs then, Sir. There'll be no clash of colours then.'
'. . . And it's Manchester United v. Spurs in this vital fifth-round cup-tie.'

Mr Sugden (referee) sucked his whistle and stared at his watch, waiting for the second finger to twitch back up to twelve. 5 4 3 2. He dropped his wrist and blew. Anderson received the ball from him, sidestepped a tackle from Tibbut then cut it diagonally between two opponents into a space to his left. Sugden (player) running into this space, raised his left foot to trap it, but the ball rolled under his studs. He veered left, caught it, and started to cudgel it upfield in a travesty of a dribble, sending it too far ahead each time he touched it, so that by the time he had progressed twenty yards, he had crash-tackled it back from three Spurs defenders. His left winger, unmarked and lonely out on the touchline, called for the ball. Sugden heard him, looked at him, then kicked the ball hard along the ground towards him. But even though the wingman started to spring as soon as he read its line, it still shot out of play a good ten yards in front of him. He slithered to a stop and whipped round.

'Hey up, Sir! What do you think I am?'
'You should have been moving, lad. You'd have caught it then.'
'What do you think I wa' doin', standing still?'
'It was a perfectly good ball!'
'Ar, for a whippet perhaps!'
'Don't argue with me lad! And get that ball fetched!'

Back in goal, Billy . . . touched the ball for the first time. Tibbut, dribbling in fast, pushed the ball between Mr Sugden's legs, ran round him and delivered the ball out to his right winger, who took it in his stride, beat his full back and centred for Tibbut, who had continued his run, to outjump Mr Sugden and head the ball firmly into the top right hand corner of the goal. Billy watched it fly in, way up on his left, then turned round and picked it up from under the netting.

'Come on Caspar! Make an effort, lad!'
'I couldn't save that, Sir.'
'You could have tried.'
'What for, Sir, when I knew I couldn't save it?'
'We're playing this game to win you know, lad.'
'I know, Sir.'
'Well, try then!'

He held his hands out to receive the ball. Billy obliged, but as it left his hand the wet leather skidded off his skin and it dropped short in the mud, between them. He ran out to retrieve it, but Sugden had already started towards it, and when Billy saw the stare of his eyes and the set of his jaw as he ran at the ball, he stopped and dropped down, and the ball missed him and went over him, back into the net. He knelt up, his left arm, left side and left leg striped with mud.
'What wa' that for, Sir?'
'Slack work, lad. Slack work.'

He retrieved the ball himself, and carried it quickly back to the centre for the restart. Billy stood up, a mud pack stuck to each knee. He pulled his shirt sleeve round and started to furrow the mud with his finger nails.
'Look at this lot. I've to keep this shirt on an' all after.'

The right back was drawn by this lament, but was immediately distracted by a chorus of warning shouts, and when he turned round he saw the ball running loose in his direction. He ran at it head down, and toed it far up field, showing no interest in its flight or destination, but turning to commiserate with Billy almost as soon as it had left his boot. It soared over the halfway line and Sugden started to chase. It bounced, once, twice, then rolled out towards the touchline. He must catch it, and the rest of his forward line moved up in anticipation of the centre. But the ball, decelerating rapidly as though intended to be caught, still crossed the line before he could reach it. His disappointed forwards muttered among themselves as they trooped back out of the penalty area.
'He should have caught that, easy.'
'He's like a chuffing carthorse.'
'Look at him, he's knackered.'
'Hopeless tha means.'

Tibbut picked the ball up for the throw in.
'Hard luck, Sir.'

Sugden, hands on hips, chest heaving, had his right back in focus a good thirty seconds before he had sufficient control over his respiration to remonstrate with him.
'Come on, lad! Find a man with this ball! Don't just kick it anywhere!'

The right back, his back turned, continued his conversation with Billy.
'SPARROW'
'What, Sir?'
'I'm talking to you, lad!'
'Yes, Sir.'
'Well pay attention then and get a grip of your game. We're losing lad.'
'Yes, Sir.'

Manchester United equalized soon after when the referee awarded them a penalty. Sugden scored.

(From *A Kestrel for a Knave* by Barry Hines, Michael Joseph, London.)

When you have read the extract carefully, look at it again to find answers to these questions.
1 What parts does Mr Sugden play and how good do you think he is at each of them?
2 How do the boys respond to Mr Sugden?
Answer both these questions from information in the extract.
3 In paragraph 9, the boy playing 'right back' turns to talk to Billy, 'to commiserate' with him. Write a few lines of what they might have said to each other. Set out the conversation as in the passage.

Your own imagination is needed for this answer but it must depend on your understanding of what has happened in the passage.

(Answers and advice, p. 172)

HOW TO SUMMARIZE

One of the most useful of all skills in the handling of English is the ability to select from a piece of writing just those facts, ideas or opinions – and no others – that we need for a particular purpose. We do this all the time in our listening to spoken English – or, if we are lazy or uninterested, we let others (reporters, newscasters, TV personalities, even our parents or friends) do it for us. Here is an example:

A boy's father has agreed to take him for his first camping holiday. They have planned to drive to the Brecon Beacons in Wales, then garage the car and hike for a few days, carrying their gear in rucksacks. The evening before the day they had planned to set off the weather seems uncertain. They turn on the radio, and the father says to his son: 'Let me know what they have to say about the weather over the weekend. We don't want to be drowned.'

The son has to listen very closely, first isolating from nationwide reports and forecasts only the items that might apply to the Brecon area; then deciding which particular forecasts are likely to affect camping conditions. When his father says: 'What did they say?' he must be ready with his *summary*. In his own interest he is probably alert and careful; a missed item may mean a soaking, or at least a very uncomfortable night.

> . . . demonstrate the ability to select material relevant to a particular task   (LEAG)

Let's compare this boy's experience with an English examination candidate's, faced with a 'summary' question. A radio or television weatherman may speak between 100 and 150 words a minute, and his weather report may last five minutes – the equivalent of a written passage from 500 to 700 words long. You will be faced with a similar task to the boy's, with regard to length and content. Like him, too, you may be asked to select for a particular purpose, or to pick out information on one particular aspect of the topic. Alternatively, you may be asked to summarize the whole passage, either in a set number of your own words, or in about one third or a quarter of the length of the original.

If someone said to you: 'What's in the paper today?' or 'Did you watch the news? What's been happening?' they would again be asking you to summarize. Your replies are not likely to be very carefully planned; after all, no marks are awarded for *accuracy* and *completeness* in our daily life. Both are expected of the good GCSE answer.

Here is an example of a question, followed by an explanation of how you can set about summarizing the passage that follows it.

Question

As a contribution to a debate that 'animals are superior to humans', summarize the ways in which wolves resemble human beings, as described in the passage below. A good clear summary need not be more than 100 words.

Most of the great carnivores of Africa and Asia form family groups, but it is the pack hunters whose social system bears the closest similarity to that of man. It may come as a surprise to those who are acquainted with the promiscuous behaviour of our domesticated canines to learn that in their natural state wolves form permanent male-female pair relationships, and that wolf packs are in fact extended families.

Wolf packs have now been recognized as family or kinship units that hunt co-operatively. They grow up around a pair of adult wolves and their offspring. Adult males pair off with adult females, establishing a permanent or semi-permanent pair-bond, each pair possessing their own 'den' in which, as a nuclear family, they raise their own litter. Since the females have to care for offspring during the 'denning' season, hunting becomes the responsibility of the male at this time, and food sharing develops on a family basis because of a basic dichotomy of role – a basic division of labour – between the paired male and female. At times when the female is unable to join the chase, the male, on his return from a successful hunt, will regurgitate sufficient food for her sustenance. On occasion, adults leave the parental pack to set up their own pack. Having a permanent family-type society, wolves take a great interest in their offspring, extending much care not only to the nourishment and protection but also to the socialization and education of their young. Wolf fathers share their consorts' interest in the litter and appear to educate the cubs in the techniques of hunting.

(From *Introduction to Anthropology,* by Roger Pearson, Holt, Rinehart and Winston, New York.)

Method

Read through fairly fast. Don't stop at difficult words or points not understood.
Re-read more slowly, ticking or underlining points that seem important.
Jot down the points in note form. This makes it easy to spot repetitions and irrelevant material.
Write your summary. It will probably need a rough copy then a re-write.

This is how the method worked with us. First the jotted points:

Male and female wolves stick together.
Wolf packs are big families – they hunt cooperatively and they are formed round an adult pair, with a den.
When female has to stay at home in breeding season the pair divide up the necessary work; the male hunts for food while the female looks after the young.
Sometimes adults leave to start up a pack on their own.
As well as nourishing and protecting their young, wolves take an interest in educating them.
The father teaches the cubs the technique of hunting.

When it came to writing our continuous prose, we made a false start. It was much too long-winded:

> Male and female wolves pair off, often permanently; and round them is formed a large family group, which also forms the pack for hunting purposes.

So we scrapped it and began afresh. Finally we produced this:

> Male and female wolves pair off, like human beings, and start a big family, which hunts as a pack. The pair has a den; and the female shares with the father the responsibility and work of looking after the cubs – he hunts and fetches food home while she looks after the family. (Sometimes members of the family leave and start packs of their own.) Again like human parents, wolves not only feed and protect their young, but also educate them, with the father helping the mother and teaching the cubs how to hunt.

Notes

1 In line 1 of our version we've put in 'like human beings' because the question set asks for this.
2 We have hardly used paragraph 1 at all; two relevant points, about pairing, and about the pack being a big family, are repeated in the main paragraph.
3 We've left out technical language like 'pair-bond', 'nuclear', 'basic dichotomy', 'socialization'.
4 Also omitted are the details about providing sustenance.
5 We've left in the piece about wolves setting up on their own because, though it's not in the main stream of argument, it is something which human beings do (see question again).
6 Near the end we have inserted 'Again like human parents' to show that all the time we have kept in mind the resemblances of wolf to man.

The following passage is taken from an article on the packing of goods.
Using it as a source, write two short paragraphs on:
(*a*) the advantages of modern packaging; *and*
(*b*) the problems caused by modern packaging.
Select from the passage only the material you need for your two paragraphs, and write in clear, concise English using your own words as far as possible. Obviously, some words and expressions must be kept.

Packaging

Almost everything bought nowadays has to be broken out of its box, packet, tube, carton or tin before it can be used. Non-returnable wrappings impose serious strains on local authorities, whose responsibility it is to collect and dispose of our rubbish. Ratepayers have to find the 50 million pounds annually required to deal with the
5   processing of 14 million tons of refuse. The destruction of waste is also difficult, as much of the packing we use consists of materials which stubbornly refuse to be broken down naturally by decomposition. Expensive incinerators have to be installed and the smoke they produce causes some pollution of the atmosphere. Packaging, too, in the form of litter spoils the environment we all share, whether it
10   is in the town, in the countryside, or on the beach.
    Industry and selling agencies, however, continue to introduce more and more packaging every week. One large agency argues its views without the trace of an apology: cigarettes, wrapped in tinfoil and placed in a box, which is then wrapped in cellophane, retain their flavour better and have a longer shelf-life than products less
15   carefully packaged; products sold in jars are protected from the contamination which would be bound to occur if they were handled continually by shop assistants or, in self-service stores, by intending purchasers. The higher cost of wrapping goods carefully is reflected in their higher prices, but money spent on ensuring greater freshness and the higher standard of hygiene achieved by good wrapping is money
20   well spent.
    The housewife, surrounded by clamouring young children, needs to be able to make her purchases both quickly and economically. Packing goods in such a way that their price and weight are seen at a glance will help her to make her choice. Some unscrupulous manufacturers may try to deceive her by increasing the size of a
25   carton whilst reducing the quantity of its contents, or by changing the shape of a bottle in order to conceal the fact that it contains fewer fluid ounces or cubic centimetres; but recent attempts to standardize packet-sizes by introducing 'Eurosizes' help to make the housewife's task easier. Uniformity in the size of packets also leads to quicker transportation and more efficient display and storage
30   of goods. If marketing costs are held down, some of the savings can be passed on to

the consumer in the form of stabilized prices. Not everyone approves of standardization, however. Colourful wrappings do make goods look attractive and provide variety; they can stimulate a healthy demand, which leads to increased competition between manufacturers and the maintenance of employment for the workers in the
35 companies.

Those who watch over the interests of the consumer sometimes argue that wrappings are unnecessarily complicated and merely serve to confuse the shopper; it is difficult to compare accurately in the bustle of a supermarket the value of a pear-shaped bottle of shampoo containing 1300 ccs. and sold for 35p with that of a
40 round-shaped bottle containing 1650 ccs. and sold for 42p. To make the necessary comparisons a housewife needs a pocket calculator and an escape from her clamouring children. In the end the article will sell on the strength of its attractive packaging. Only when she reaches the check-out will she realize just how bulky the cartons, bottles, and tins have made her shopping; two journeys to the shops will be
45 necessary instead of the one she made in the days when packaging was less elaborate.

Nevertheless, anything which helps to brighten our lives is worthwhile. The merest suggestion on a packet that we shall be fitter, more loved, richer, or happier if we buy the product will lure us to spend more than we can afford and ignore the
50 blatant waste of the earth's resources in the making of unnecessary boxes, packets, tubes, cartons and tins.

(Answers on p.173.)

Litter

The next passage is an imaginative commentary on the tools and cave paintings of Early Man by a well-known scientist. This makes it harder to use as a source of ideas than the ones we have been looking at so far in this unit. However, there is plenty if material here for the exercise that follows.

The Art of the Cave-dwellers

The culture of man that we recognize best began to form in the most recent Ice Age, within the last hundred or even fifty thousand years. That is when we find the elaborate tools that point to sophisticated forms of hunting: the spear-thrower, for example, and the baton that may be a straightening tool; the fully barbed harpoon; and, of course, the flint master tools that were needed to make the hunting tools. . . .

[The author goes on to describe how man survived the Ice Age by means of 'the master invention of all – fire'.]

Fire is the symbol of the hearth, and from the time *Homo sapiens* began to leave the mark of his hand thirty thousand years ago, the hearth was the cave. For at least a million years man, in some recognizable form, lived as a forager and a hunter. We have almost no monuments of that immense period of prehistory, so much longer than any history that we record. Only at the end of that time, on the edge of the European ice-sheet, we find in caves like Altamira (and elsewhere in Spain and southern France) the record of what dominated the mind of man the hunter. There we see what made his world and preoccupied him. The cave paintings, which are about twenty thousand years old, fix for ever the universal base of his culture then, the hunter's knowledge of the animal that he lived by and stalked.

One begins by thinking it odd that an art as vivid as the cave paintings should be, comparatively, so young and so rare. Why are there not more monuments to man's visual imagination, as there are to his invention? And yet when we reflect, what is remarkable is not that there are so few monuments, but that there are any at all. Man is a puny, slow, awkward, unarmed animal – he had to invent a pebble, a flint, a knife, a spear. But why to these scientific inventions, which were essential to his survival, did he from an early time add those arts that now astonish us: decorations with animal shapes? Why, above all, did he come to caves like this, live in them, and then make paintings of animals not where he lived but in places that were dark, secret, remote, hidden, inaccessible?

The obvious thing to say is that in these places the animal was magical. No doubt that is right; but magic is only a word, not an answer. In itself, magic is a word which explains nothing. It says that man believed he had power, but what power? We still want to know what the power was that the hunters believed they got from the paintings.

Here I can only give you my personal view. I think that the power that we see expressed here for the first time is the power of anticipation: the forward-looking imagination. In these paintings the hunter was made familiar with dangers which he knew he had to face but to which he had not yet come. When the hunter was brought here into the secret dark and the light was suddenly flashed on the pictures, he saw the bison as he would have to face him, he saw the running deer, he saw the turning boar. And he felt alone with them as he would in the hunt. The moment of fear was made present to him; his spear-arm flexed with an experience which he would have and which he needed not to be afraid of. The painter had frozen the moment of fear, and the hunter entered it through the painting as if through an air-lock.

For us, the cave paintings re-create the hunter's way of life as a glimpse of history; we look through them into the past. But for the hunter, I suggest, they were a peep-hole into the future; he looked ahead. In either direction, the cave paintings act as a kind of telescope tube of the imagination: they direct the mind from what is seen to what can be inferred or conjectured. Indeed, this is so in the very action of painting; for all its superb observation, the flat picture only means something to the eye because the mind fills it out with roundness and movement, a reality by inference, which is not actually seen but is imagined.

Art and science are both uniquely human actions, outside the range of anything that an animal can do. And here we see that they derive from the same human faculty: the ability to visualize the future, to foresee what may happen and plan to anticipate it, and to represent it to ourselves in images that we project and move about inside our head, or in a square of light on the dark wall of a cave or a television screen.

We also look here through the telescope of the imagination; the imagination is a telescope in time, we are looking back at the experience of the past. The men who made these paintings, the men who were present, looked through that telescope forward. They looked along the ascent of man because what we call cultural evolution is essentially a constant growing and widening of the human imagination.

The men who made the weapons and the men who made the paintings were doing the same thing – anticipating a future as only man can do, inferring what is to come from what is here. There are many gifts that are unique in man; but at the centre of them all, the root from which all knowledge grows, lies the ability to draw conclusions from what we see to what we do not see, to move our minds through space and time, and to recognize ourselves in the past on the steps to the present. All over these caves the print of the hand says: 'This is my mark. This is man.'

(From *The Ascent of Man,* by Jacob Bronowski, BBC Publications, London.)

Question

'Art and science . . . derive from the same human faculty: the ability to visualize the future, to foresee what may happen and plan to anticipate it . . .'/'. . . the imagination is a telescope in time . . .'
You have undertaken to represent Jacob Bronowski's views to a Young Scientists' club. Take over his phrase 'a telescope in time' as the title of a short article for their newsletter, based on the passage.

(Answers on p.173.)

2.2 Drawing Inferences

First, let us establish clearly what the words mean:

infer (verb), **inference** (noun)

A Was it a good dance?

B Yes, terrific! I met this really nice boy who works at _____. He's taking me out again tonight.

C I think it was dead boring. The group played all old stuff – not a single number that's in the charts.

From this conversation we get certain *information*: B and C both went to a dance which A did not go to; B made a new friend. We can also *deduce* (i.e. arrive at a logical conclusion) that C is interested in pop music. But if we are alert to the tone of the remarks we might also *infer* that B is an extrovert, fond of good company, whereas C is a bit of a 'loner'. The inference about B, being based on slightly fuller evidence, is more likely to be accurate; further talk with C may establish other reasons for her boredom. But the conclusions about both girls are *inferences* drawn from the tone of their replies as much as from what is said.

(**Warning** Don't confuse **infer** with the similar sounding and often misused word **imply** (noun: **implication**). To imply something is to suggest or hint at it without stating it outright, e.g. 'Are you implying that I'm a liar?')

> . . . demonstrate the ability to . . . recognize implicit meaning and attitudes (LEAG)

Some questions ask for the meanings of individual words and phrases; others give you an opportunity to show how much more you understand by asking what you can infer from the passage. This is one reason why you are always advised to read the passage first and then answer the questions. It is impossible to draw valid inferences from a piece of writing until you have read the whole thing; something at the end may change the way you look at it.

Now for practice consider a question on the short story *River Afternoon* on pp. 40-4.

Question

What can you gather from the story as a whole about both children's attitude to fishing and about the girl's attitude to Peter?

The word 'gather' here tells you to draw inferences. To gather is more than to observe; you have to look, select, weigh up evidence, think about it and arrive at conclusions. This shows why you need to read the whole story before you can begin to *infer* the children's attitude to fishing or the girl's feelings about Peter. If you read only as far as the point where the girl bursts into tears, you might infer that she hated fishing and thought it cruel. Read on and it becomes clear that she can be as enthusiastic and as engrossed as Peter, as they try for the big trout.

The girl's attitude to fishing is a mixture of like and dislike; what about her attitude to Peter? The author does not need to give an answer to this question in an explanatory paragraph, because the reader can find it in what she does and says. But we are given special insight into the girl's thoughts and feelings. How? From whose point of view is the story told? Not exclusively from the girl's, but we are taken inside her head more than Peter's.

The girl knows Peter well; he depends on her support so she can afford to make him wait. But she does what he says:

'Peter, let's stop here.'

'We're going to the loop,' said Peter.

She brings him the bait but makes him go and chase the cows. They are close as they argue about mayfly, apart as he goes to find a better place to fish and she begins to sympathize more with the fish than the fisherman. Their quarrel reaches its climax partly in the girl's mind:

I don't like Peter . . .

I hate him.

'I hate you,' she said.

'. . . I hate fishing . . .'

Miserable, she now hated the fish . . .

Her mood changes but the quarrel continues until she bursts into tears; he finally throws back the undersized fish; they share the rest of the sandwiches and he offers her the rod, which she accepts. The big fish is caught:

A huge confidence born of success out of failure wrapped them both in unutterable content.

The story ends on a note of complete satisfaction and tranquillity.

After a careful reading, or a fully absorbed reading (letting the story have its full effect on you), many of these points will be filed away in the mind and the memory; a quick re-read will recover enough material for a good answer to this question.

EXAMPLES FROM NON-FICTION:
Interpreting Statistics, Persuasive Writing and Filling in Forms

Interpreting Statistics

At first this looks very different from what we have dealt with so far in this unit. Instead of a passage to read you are faced with facts, expressed in the form of charts or diagrams, like those on the page opposite.

This is merely a different, and often a more vivid, way of presenting factual information. Once you have understood its layout your work usually consists in first identifying and *selecting* the relevant facts from those that the diagram presents. To remind you of our five stages: this kind of exercise in interpretation tends to concentrate on **observation** (1) and **selection** (4). Sometimes you may also need to draw **conclusions** (5) from what you have discovered.

Paper 2 . . . may include information in statistical form	(SEG)

As a test of your powers of observation see if you can answer this from the diagram:

On the evidence of the 1982 General Household Survey, how much bigger or smaller is the percentage of men to women who drink only occasionally or not at all? What conclusion can you draw from this?

The question concerns the top right diagram, and refers to the two top portions of each figure, i.e. 35 per cent for women, 16 per cent for men. We can conclude that more than a third of all women drink either occasionally or not at all, but one is only half as likely to find men in this category. This suggests that men's lifestyles offer more opportunities, perhaps convivial ones, for drinking.

It is good practice to make inferences like this on the basis of the facts you have discovered. Now try it for yourself. Our answers to the five questions are on page 173.

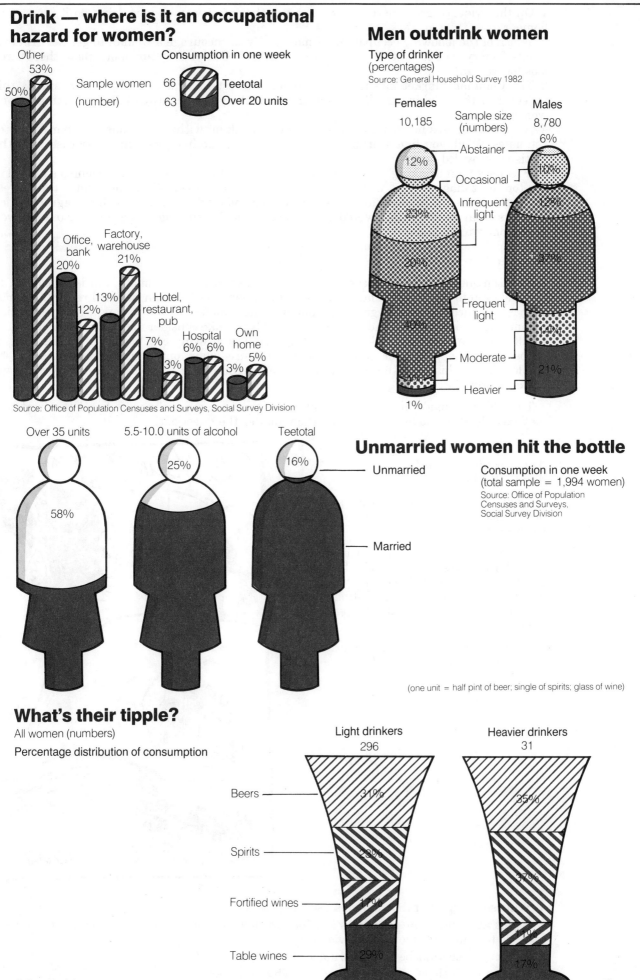

Drink — where is it an occupational hazard for women?

Other
53%
50%

Consumption in one week

Sample women 66 Teetotal
(number) 63 Over 20 units

Office,
bank
20%
12%

Factory,
warehouse
21%
13%

Hotel,
restaurant,
pub
7%
3%

Hospital
6% 6%
3%

Own
home
5%

Source: Office of Population Censuses and Surveys, Social Survey Division

Men outdrink women

Type of drinker
(percentages)
Source: General Household Survey 1982

Females   Sample size   Males
10,185   (numbers)   8,780
                               6%

Abstainer
12%   10%
Occasional
Infrequent light
Frequent light
Moderate
Heavier
1%   21%

Over 35 units
58%

5.5-10.0 units of alcohol
25%

Teetotal
16%
Unmarried
Married

Unmarried women hit the bottle

Consumption in one week
(total sample = 1,994 women)
Source: Office of Population
Censuses and Surveys,
Social Survey Division

(one unit = half pint of beer; single of spirits; glass of wine)

What's their tipple?

All women (numbers)

Percentage distribution of consumption

Light drinkers
296

Heavier drinkers
31

Beers — 31% 35%
Spirits — 23% 37%
Fortified wines — 17% 11%
Table wines — 29% 17%

Crown copyright

1 On the evidence given here is it true to say that most women who drink do it secretly at home, rather than at work?

2 Which of the following occupations is most likely to encourage a woman to get the drinking habit – factory worker, state-enrolled nurse, barmaid? Can you say any more about these three jobs for women?

3 The Common Market has led to a greater interest in wine-drinking in Britain. Is this reflected in the drinking habits of women? Is it likely to encourage heavy drinking among women?

4 A mother advises her daughter not to go out drinking with her friends, and her daughter retaliates: 'Well, you like a drink too!' How could the mother strengthen her case from the statistics provided here?

5 'Frequent light drinking' describes the drinking habits of almost half the women sampled in the top right diagram, and nearly the same proportion of men. What constitutes the biggest contrast between their drinking habits? Can you find evidence from another diagram which supports what you have discovered here about women's drinking? What conclusions can you draw from your findings?

(Answers on p. 173.)

Persuasive Writing

Advertisements usually have some factual ingredients, but their main aim is, of course, to persuade you to buy a particular product. As the differences between two or three or 20 brands of mass-produced consumer goods get smaller and smaller, so the techniques of persuasion become more sophisticated. Advertising copy-writers make considerable use of psychology and a full understanding of this kind of writing involves drawing conclusions about its real, as opposed to its apparent or stated, intentions. Once again our standard practices can be employed; but this time the emphasis will be on **reflection** (3) and on drawing your own **conclusions** (5).

The following 'made-up' advertisement demonstrates some of the more familiar advertising methods. Read the advertisement and then answer the questions.

Are your *pits the pits?*
Ask for Pit Flit.

Already millions of satisfied users know just how welcome is new *Pit Flit* . . . country-fresh *Pit Flit*.

No other deodorant brings such thrilling over-all freshness to you. *Pit Flit* has all the sparkle of spring to keep you fresh and confident all the day long. Its lasting natural fragrance is as fresh as the flowers of the field, – so refreshing!

For you today – zap anti-social odour. Get *Pit Flit*.

1 Why is it suggested that millions use the product?

2 If this advertisement persuades someone to buy the deodorant, what has he or she been made to think of? Quote your evidence.

3 How can deodorant be said to bring 'confidence'?

4 Find an example of alliteration and say why it is used.

5 What actual information are we given about the deodorant?

Your answers need to be brief and lucid. An answer to the first question could be:

The purpose of the (unverifiable) claim that there are already millions of *satisfied* users is to reassure readers who are unfamiliar with the product name. It deliberately plays on their emotions and on the well-known human traits of wanting to be like others, and fearing to miss out on benefits others are getting.

Try answering the other questions for yourself. There is a set of answers on page 173 (including a shorter answer to 1), but in questions of this sort there can never be a particular answer that is the only right one. You can get more practice by picking up the nearest colour supplement or by reading advertisements next time you are travelling by public transport or walking down the street, giving a more critical look at the way they try to engage your emotions.

Filling in Forms

The English language needs to be used very carefully in official documents and forms. Often they come with explanatory notes, and these may also provide practice in understanding English. As a simple self-test in this important application of English, here are four sections of the standard form to be filled in for a passport. Try completing them, imagining you are a Jamaican-born married woman called Mrs Rose Clarke, now working as a nurse in an English state hospital. You had a passport to enter the UK but it has expired. Fill in all the details possible, inventing any we have not given you. Check your completed form with the one on p. 174.

Please write in CAPITAL LETTERS and in ink

1 TO BE FILLED IN BY ALL APPLICANTS

Tick correct box Mr Mrs Miss Ms or title _____

Your surname _____

Christian names or forenames _____

Maiden surname (if applicable) _____

Tick correct box Married Single Widowed Divorced Separated

Age last birthday _____ Country of birth _____

Present address _____

_____ Postcode _____

Daytime telephone no. _____
(We may need to get in touch with you urgently)

Job/occupation _____

Town of birth _____

Date of birth _____

Country of residence _____

Height (in metres) _____ ✳ See note 1 for a conversion chart

Visible distinguishing marks _____

Have you changed your name other than by marriage or adoption? Yes No

What was your previous name? _____

Go to section 2a

6a TO BE FILLED IN BY ALL APPLICANTS ✳ Read note 6

Have you had any sort of passport before or applied for any passport? Yes No

Is your last passport attached? Yes No

Previous passport number _____

Please complete **section 11**

Is your husband/wife to be included on your passport? Yes No

Have they had any sort of passport before? Yes No

Is their previous passport attached? Yes No

Previous passport number _____

Please complete **section 11**

CAUTION
You are warned that the making of an untrue statement for the purpose of procuring a passport is a criminal offence. Passport Office procedures include a check on the authenticity of countersignatories. The application should not be countersigned until the form has been completed, signed and dated by the applicant.

Please write in CAPITAL LETTERS and in ink

➜ 6b Declaration To be signed by all applicants

And by husband/wife if they are to be included on your passport
I the undersigned, declare that
1 I have made no other application for a passport, other than that stated above.
2 (delete if not appropriate) If the passport mentioned in section 11 comes again into my possession, I will return it immediately to a British Passport issuing authority.
3 No one included on this application owes money to Her Majesty's Government for repatriation or similar relief.
4 I am a British citizen *or*
    British Dependent Territories citizen *or*
    British Overseas citizen *or*
    British subject *or*
    British protected person.
  And I have not lost or renounced this status.
5 I (and any children shown in section 3) am/are today in the United Kingdom.
6 The information given in this application is correct to the best of my knowledge and belief.

Sign _____ Date _____

Your husband's/wife's signature (if he/she is to be included in your passport)

10 TO BE COMPLETED BY ALL APPLICANTS ✳ Read note 10

Countries to be visited _____

Purpose of journey _____

Please give the names of two relatives or friends who can be contacted if you meet with an accident. This information will only be used in an emergency.

Name _____

Address _____

Telephone number _____ Relationship (if any) _____

Name _____

Address _____

Telephone number _____ Relationship (if any) _____

Space below is for Passport Office use only
MISC 314

Note 6

If you or anyone on this application has held or been included on a British Passport, a British Visitor's Passport, a Commonwealth Passport, a foreign passport or other travel document of any description you should tick YES, state the passport number(s) and enclose it (them).

If you have not held a passport or travel document of any kind you should tick NO.

If you were included in your husband's/wife's British Passport, you should enclose it with this application so that your particulars may be deleted from it.

If you were born abroad, and you have not previously held a passport of your own, please give details in section 13 of the passport on which you travelled to this country.

If you are unable to write, you should impress a left thumb print as signature. The impression should be witnessed by the person who completes section 8 of the form. If you are unable to write because of a physical or mental disability a declaration by the person responsible for your welfare (e.g. parent or doctor) may be accepted. In these circumstances the signatory should explain in Section 13 that the applicant is disabled and that he/she has signed on the applicant's behalf.

Note 10

Your passport will be made valid for all countries in the world. But it is to your advantage to state the countries you wish to visit and the purpose of your journey. This will enable us to advise you about passport problems which may arise in certain countries.

A SELF-TEST METHOD

Finally here is a way of practising all the five stages of observation, comparison, reflection etc. which we set out on p. 60-1. With the help of a friend you can easily find more practice passages.

Choose a paragraph in a newspaper or magazine (not less than 100 words) and black out every tenth word – except for the first and last sentences. The test is to fill in the gaps with words that make sense. Count full marks for more or less exact synonyms. Only single words are blacked out, but it is better to insert a group of words that make sense than a single one that doesn't. Work out a method of scoring to take this into account. A score of 50 per cent or more is creditable. If you want to make it more difficult, black out words more often, e.g. every ninth, eighth etc.

Follow the often repeated advice: 'Read the whole passage first'. Even if it is difficult to make any sense of it, you may find clues or be able to draw inferences from repeated words or ideas in the passage.

We have prepared three short passages in this way for you on pp. 146-7 and 154. Here are some clues to help you with one of them.

In Test 21 on page 154 the first word omitted must be in the same group of things as factories and houses because it is sandwiched between them in a list; and it must be something you see in a city. How about 'tenements' or 'blocks of flats'? Not bad, but they are similar to 'houses' which comes straight after. Is there something more distinctive? The best word is 'offices'.

There is only one possible word for the next gap. Which word in the sentence must it be linked with? – 'eating'. Therefore it can only be 'into'. ('In' doesn't make sense; it is possible to 'eat *up*', but not to 'eat further and further up . . .'.)

Look at the twelfth gap. Can you tell that it must be some sort of opposite to 'ease'? The blank after this, in the same sentence, follows a 'but', so there an opposite to an opposite to 'ease' is needed! To put this more simply, the thirteenth gap requires a word expressing something more than 'ease'.

That should give you a lead into this kind of quiz. Do the rest for yourself. All the answers are on pp. 185 and 187, but don't cheat!

Most English examinations include assignments or questions about books you have read. Sometimes the syllabus will suggest recommended reading – even if there is a separate syllabus and examination for English Literature. There is a good reason for this: no one can write fluently or acquire a wide vocabulary without making a habit of reading. Some of your written work about books will certainly be included in your coursework folder for the examination, but you will also need to be prepared to answer questions on your recent reading in the written examination.

It is a good plan to read one really interesting book just before your examination – say, within six weeks of exam day. If it has really gripped your attention you will have no difficulty in remembering details, though after six months they will have faded in your memory. Choosing the right book is half the battle. It needs to be worthwhile in its own right – a librarian, or an older friend keen on reading, or one of your teachers, will help you on this if you're not sure. Don't choose too long a book – 150 to 200 pages should be plenty for you so soon before the examination. If the book is in paperback get your own copy. But don't choose one that everybody is reading; the examiner will hear plenty about that one without your help! If you possibly can, choose a book that you know you will enjoy. Maybe you have read others by the same author, or in the same series. Maybe it is about a place, or a sport, or a job, or a hobby that you are very interested in or know a lot about.

> Two out of four [coursework] pieces must show response to the candidate's reading during the course
> (MEG)

The following are places to look for ideas about what to read:

Book-lists in your English classbook, or given to you by your English teacher or school librarian.

'Further Reading' suggestions at the end of a book you have enjoyed, or that is about a subject you are interested in.

Book Clubs These are often formed in school nowadays and usually have a newsletter with information about the club's choices.

Magazines often have a 'Books' section listing new books and saying a bit about them.

Newspapers Some of them have a special review page once or twice a week. (Sunday papers usually have more space for book reviews.)

Once you have chosen your book, do make time to read it. Go to bed earlier – take a drink, some biscuits, make yourself comfortable. Leave the others watching television – you won't miss much!

In this section we have provided samples of some of the best recent literature, partly to tempt you to read the books they come from or others like them, partly to give you practice in *writing about books* and partly to provide you with *models* for your own original writing. In an English examination you may expect to be faced with topics like these:

1 An important incident in the story.
2 Relationships between the characters.
3 The setting of the story.
4 A child character and his relation to adults, or animals, or strangers, or old people.
5 An important conversation.
6 Minor characters in the book.
7 A book's suitability for television or radio serialization.

In some form or another all of these have been set in recent examinations. You will easily recognize them, even if the wording is not quite the same as ours. Try it! Here are four questions on books. Beside each one put the number of topic (1 to 7) you think it is asking about:

(a) Think of two people in the story who are not in the centre of the action but still stick in your mind. Write about their contribution to the story as a whole.

(b) Describe one person in the book who is younger than you and tell of his or her behaviour with a pet or other animal(s).

(c) Many television plays or serials are based on books. Think of *one* book you have read that has been adapted for television or would be suitable for it and explain what came (or would come) over best in the screened version and what came (or would come) over least well or not at all.

(d) Think of a book you have read in which the place or places where the story was set makes an important contribution to the effect. Explain how and why this is so.

As you can tell from these questions, when you are writing about books some of the most interesting topics are about the people portrayed in the books and the way they behave (e.g. nos. 2, 4, 5 and 6 above). The most vivid form of literature about people is drama. Most of your experience of this has probably been from television; but even television plays or 'soap operas' have to be written or scripted. For our first example we have chosen an excerpt from a stage play written in 1982 by the white South African dramatist, Athol Fugard. The play it comes from, *'Master Harold' . . . and the Boys*, is autobiographical, centring on a traumatic moment in Fugard's own childhood when as a teenager he was brought up sharply against – or 'bumped into', to use the play's expression – the race laws of his own country.

The play is set in Harold's (or Hally's) mother's cafe in Port Elizabeth, in 1950. Hally, just back from school, is trying to plan an English essay about a ballroom dancing contest for blacks, with the help of the two black servants he has grown up with, Willie and Sam. Both are keen dancers and Willie has entered for the contest in a fortnight's time. Underlying the friendly, trusting atmosphere is Hally's anxiety that his crippled, racist and drunken father may be returning home from hospital after a blissful (for Hally) reprieve from his presence at home.

HALLY: How are the points scored, Sam?

SAM: Maximum of ten points each for individual style, deportment, rhythm and general appearance.

WILLIE: Must I start?

HALLY: Hold it for a second, Willie. And penalties?

SAM: For what?

HALLY: For doing some things wrong. Say you stumble or bump into somebody . . . do they take off any points?

SAM: (*Aghast*) Hally . . . !

HALLY: When you're dancing. If you and your partner collide into another couple.

(*HALLY can get no further. SAM has collapsed with laughter. He explains to WILLIE*)

SAM: If me and Miriam bump into you and Hilda . . .
(*WILLIE joins him in another good laugh*)
          Hally, Hally . . . !

HALLY: (*Perplexed*) Why? What did I say?

SAM: There's no collisions out there, Hally. Nobody trips or stumbles or bumps into anybody else. That's what that moment is all about. To be one of those finalists on that dance floor is like . . . like being in a dream about a world in which accidents don't happen.

HALLY: (*Genuinely moved by* SAM'S *image*)   Jesus, Sam! That's beautiful!

WILLIE: (*Can endure waiting no longer*)   I'm starting!
(*WILLIE dances while SAM talks*)

SAM: Of course it is. That's what I've been trying to say to you all afternoon. And it's beautiful because that is what we want life to be like. But instead, like you said, Hally, we're bumping into each other all the time. Look at the three of us this afternoon: I've bumped into Willie, the two of us have bumped into you, you've bumped into your mother, she bumping into your Dad. . . . None of us knows the steps and there's no music playing. And it doesn't stop with us. The whole world is doing it all the time. Open a newspaper and what do you read? America has bumped into Russia, England is bumping into India, rich man bumps into poor man. Those are big collisions, Hally. They make for a lot of bruises. People get hurt in all that bumping, and we're sick and tired of it now. It's been going on for too long. Are we never going to get it right? . . . Learn to dance life like champions instead of always being just a bunch of beginners at it?

HALLY: (*Deep and sincere admiration of the man*)   You've got a vision, Sam!

SAM: Not just me. What I'm saying to you is that everybody's got it. That's why there's only standing room left for the Centenary Hall in two weeks' time. For as long as the music lasts, we are going to see six couples get it right, the way we want life to be.

HALLY: But is that the best we can do, Sam . . . watch six finalists dreaming about the way it should be?

SAM: I don't know. But it starts with that. Without the dream we won't know what we're going for. And anyway I reckon there are a few people who have got past just dreaming about it and are trying for something real. Remember that thing we read once in the paper about the Mahatma Gandhi? Going without food to stop those riots in India?

HALLY: You're right. He certainly was trying to teach people to get the steps right.

SAM: And the Pope.

HALLY: Yes, he's another one. Our old General Smuts as well, you know. He's also out there dancing. You know, Sam, when you come to think of it. that's what the United Nations boils down to . . . a dancing school for politicians!

SAM: And let's hope they learn.

HALLY: (*A little surge of hope*)   You're right. We mustn't despair. Maybe there's some hope for mankind after all. Keep it up, Willie. (*Back to his table with determination*)   This is a lot bigger than I thought. So what have we got? Yes, our title: 'A World Without Collisions.'

SAM: That sounds good! 'A World Without Collisions.'

HALLY: Subtitle: 'Global Politics on the Dance Floor.' No. A bit too heavy, hey? What about 'Ballroom Dancing as a Political Vision'?
(*The telephone rings.* SAM *answers it*)

SAM: St George's Park Tea Room . . . Yes, Madam . . . Hally, it's your Mom.

HALLY: (*Back to reality*) Oh, God, yes! I'd forgotten all about that. Shit! Remember my words, Sam? Just when you're enjoying yourself, someone or something will come along and wreck everything.

(From '*Master Harold*' . . . *and the Boys* by Athol Fugard, Oxford University Press.)

Drama is a social art form, like dancing. A dramatist worth his salt cannot insulate his work from the reality around him. In Fugard's case it is a harsh one, involving racist attitudes crystallized in the laws of the land. Think about this as you try to answer these questions – ones that might well be asked in an examination.

PRACTICE

1 (a) Up to this point most of the play has been about the way Hally has over the years been passing on his school learning to Sam, who had no such educational opportunities. In this passage, who is teaching and who is learning?

(b) What is the passage about besides dancing?

2 Imagine an occasion before this when Hally comes home from school and tells (or 'teaches') Sam what he has been learning. Write it in a play form like this, or as a first-person narrative by either Sam or Hally. (Answers/suggestions p. 174.)

> Candidates will be required to respond to questions on a literary text or texts (e.g. a short story, an episode from a play, a poem or poems)   (NEA)

Drama *involves* its audience – or even its readers – closely in the action or human behaviour it is revealing to us. *Poetry* involves its readers or listeners in different ways, through its qualities of rhythm, imagery and verbal patterning. Like drama, it started (and for many people in the world still remains) a spoken and heard art; writing came later. You may want to include poems you have written in your coursework folder. This is such a wide field that it is almost impossible to offer you advice and help on that part of your English assessment here. What we can do is to show you how one or two good poets set to work and the results they achieve and help you to know what to look for in good poetry, and how to write about it. We need to remember that poetry has always been and still remains the language form capable of containing the greatest intensity of feeling, as well as the greatest precision. Some examining bodies recognize this and ask you to read and respond to poems, either in connection with compositions or in other ways. Poetry written in our own time is usually chosen.

Here is a recently written poem that might well form the basis of an examination question.

Cathedral Builders

They climbed on sketchy ladders towards God,
With winch and pulley hoisted hewn rock into heaven,
Inhabited sky with hammers, defied gravity,
Deified stone, took up God's house to meet Him,

And came down to their suppers and small beer;
Every night slept, lay with their smelly wives,
Quarrelled and cuffed the children, lied,
Spat, sang, were happy or unhappy,

And every day took to the ladders again;
Impeded the rights of way of another summer's
Swallows, grew greyer, shakier, became less inclined
To fix a neighbour's roof of a fine evening,

Saw naves sprout arches, clerestories soar,
Cursed the loud fancy glaziers for their luck,
Somehow escaped the plague, got rheumatism,
Decided it was time to give it up,

To leave the spire to others; stood in the crowd
Well back from the vestments at the consecration,
Envied the fat bishop his warm boots,
Cocked up a squint eye and said, 'I bloody did that.'

John Ormond

(From *Requiem and Celebration*, Christopher Davies (Publishers), London.)

We have printed the poem first, before saying anything about it, because a good poem makes its own impact best for itself. Perhaps this one has caught your interest, amused you, made you think. If so it has already started doing its job. Sometimes, however, readers feel baffled or even cheated when they encounter a poem. What is it *for*? Why is it printed like that instead of in the 'normal' way, i.e. like prose? Some even let their prejudices prevent them from enjoying or understanding poetry at all and 'switch off' as soon as they see the way it is set out on the page. We can't help such people until they help themselves. What we can do is to suggest to more open-minded readers a few ways of approaching poetry, whether in an examination, in school, or in reading for their own enjoyment.

Title

If the poem has a title, it usually plays an important part. In *Cathedral Builders* it is like a label or a headline, defining the subject clearly. As we start reading, the first word – 'They' – simply continues the idea, so that we are prepared for what follows.

Subject matter

With most of the things we read we have some idea what to expect, because of the setting or form – newspaper, travel brochure, driving licence application, instruction manual or recipe book, letters ... they all set up particular expectations in the reader and aim to satisfy them. A brochure describing a package holiday in Benidorm is *not* likely to include things like this, for obvious reasons:

There are so many hotel tower blocks that the Mediterranean is invisible to most visitors for much of the time and its waters are often polluted by sewage.

Poems are not so predictable. Instead, they often please by surprising you, by presenting things in a new light, or by using words in new ways. Most of us have seen cathedrals. The older ones in particular may be connected in our minds with feelings of awe or solemn thoughts. It is startling to put our ideas next to the ones in the poem about the men who actually built them; yet as we read of their daily lives – supper, beer, having children, growing old – we are convinced that this is how real labourers would have been, even centuries ago. By the time we reach the last verse we are sympathetic to these anonymous craftsmen and the poet can count on our support when he contrasts them with 'the fat bishop' in his boots (a rare luxury!) The last line, with its irreverent but genuine exclamation 'I bloody did that', brings the man who says it into sharp focus. We may laugh at the comment, but we now have a vivid idea of the true 'cathedral builders'.

Tone
(*See also 1.2 p. 29*)

When we talk, our tone of voice is often as important as what we say. Sometimes it is much more important: small children learn to recognize and respond to it long before they grasp actual meanings of words. Good writers also convey their feelings and attitudes through tone and for poets it can be one of the most valuable ways of getting their full meaning across. We can tell from John Ormond's tone that he feels warmly towards the thousands of humble workmen who made cathedrals possible, who, as they grow older

> . . . greyer, shakier, become less inclined
> To fix a neighbour's roof of a fine evening.

It is our response to this tone of friendly sympathy that makes the last verse so effective.

Shape and language

Poems have one great advantage over prose, which is that their actual shape on the page, their arrangement into stanzas (verses), sometimes with a particular pattern of line length, or rhythm, or rhyming words, can be made to contribute to their total effect. Here the five four-line stanzas, with a basic five stresses to the line

> They climbed on sketchy ladders towards God,

give the poem a progress: first the work routine – 'They climbed . . .', 'And came down . . .', 'And . . . took to the ladders again'; then they watch the cathedral grow without them (notice the dynamic words 'sprout', 'soar' in the fourth stanza); and finally see the finished building.

We said just now that the language of poetry is capable of the greatest precision. This may seem surprising; perhaps you connect precision more with science or engineering than with poetry. This need not be so; you must remember that poetry has a great advantage over other language forms, because the poet, if he knows his job, can include as much of the total meaning of word or expression as he wants. His words are not merely restricted to one sense like scientific terms or public notices. They can set off chain reactions in your mind, can explode in your imagination; and the poet's skill can control the direction in which his words 'take wing'.

Look at the word 'sketchy' in the first stanza. A dictionary tells us this means 'giving only a slight or rough outline of the main features, facts or circumstances without going into details'. One would not normally expect ladders to be described like this. But the very unexpectedness of the adjective makes us alert to other possibilities in the word. A sketch is an outline drawing; thin ladders scaling a vast cathedral structure can be seen in just this way. Even the sound of the words '*sk*etchy la*dd*ers' seems to be describing the precarious climbing of the builders, making it seem more real. If we think more about it we realize that the ladders do 'sketch out' the lines of the great cathedral by enabling the builders to do their work.

Now think about 'defied' and its deliberate half-echo 'deified' (i.e. made a god of), or the word 'inhabited', or the alliterative phrase '*h*oisted *h*ewn rock into *h*eaven' – all in this same first stanza – and you can get some idea of the rich resources of poetic language.

Conclusions

When we have looked at the details like this, it is a good idea to stand back, like the cathedral builders and survey the poem as a whole. We cannot claim that we 'bloody did that', but we can, if we have responded to its tone and language, see something of its shape, and understand more fully the poet's intention. Ormond is not just mocking 'fat bishops', nor is he merely writing social history, though both these contribute to the poem. The freshness and modernity of his vision show us the discomforts, the pettiness and drudgery involved in building a medieval cathedral; but he also conveys the shared sense of achievement in 'taking up God's house to meet Him', and the way in which a cathedral represents in a solid and permanent form the lives and faith of its human creators.

PRACTICE

Here are some questions that might be set in a GCSE or SCE paper on *Cathedral Builders*. If you have followed our comments carefully, you should have no difficulty in answering most of them.

1 (a) How is the routine, humdrum nature of the builders' lives emphasized in the poem?

(b) What details help to make the builders seem real people like ourselves? Quote two of them.

(c) Why does the poet say '. . . into heaven' in the first stanza (verse)?

(d) Explain what is meant by
'Impeded the rights of way of another summer's
Swallows . . .'

2 Imagine you are one of the builders. Describe the scene, and your feelings, on the day the cathedral is consecrated. (Answers on p. 174.)

Cathedral Builders could be described as a comfortable poem. It is written from a safe, prosperous environment and observes with wry humour, amusing and interesting but not disturbing us. Yet most of the world's population, many of them English speakers, do not share such a privileged setting. Poetry is not just a luxury art and it often means more to the poor and deprived than any other form of language. The Malaysian poet Cecil Rajendra believes passionately that poetry has a moral purpose in society. He says in a poem called *My Message*

> . . . i want the cadences
> of my verse to crack
> the carapace of indifference
> prise open torpid eyelids
> thick-coated with silver.

The following poem, *Glass*, is a good example of how Cecil Rajendra sets about his task. Note that Karol Wojtyla was the present Pope's name when he was a Polish priest. He published many poems of his own before being made Pope. UPI/Reuter are press agencies responsible for sending out news messages around the world.

Glass

A visit by the Pope to families in two small shacks of wood and corrugated iron occupied by 10 and 14 people respectively in a squalid, muddy back alley without sewage was cancelled at the last minute for unexplained security reasons.

UPI/Reuter

Nothing else was cancelled

The glittering ceremony
in the Presidential palace
The carefully orchestrated
motorcade across the city

Nothing else was cancelled

The solemn meeting
with the august Cardinal
The Mass for masses
in the majestic cathedral

Nothing else was cancelled

For neither chandelier
nor stained glass
nor pointed mitre
nor rear-view mirror
can cut and reflect
cut and reflect like
the naked and the poor

And their squalid
back alley shacks
their open latrines
their armies of flies
bugs and cockroaches
the sharply pointed
ribs of their children
will ever pose the greater
threat to the security
of thieves who have stolen
their birthright and
rooted themselves in power

The poor have nothing
to lose but their poverty.　*Cecil Rajendra*

That world will come like a thief
and steal all we possess
Poor and naked, we will be transparent as glass
that both cuts and reflects.

Karol Wojtyla

John Ormond's poem is self-contained, i.e. one does not require any special knowledge in order to respond to his theme. By contrast, Rajendra needs the press report and the extract from the Pope's poem (printed just after the press report) as a basis for his own poem. Notice how he takes up the idea of glass 'that cuts and reflects'. This is just the sort of point you might be asked in an examination question, e.g.

1 Comment on the appropriateness of the poem's title (60-70 words)

> . . . understanding of and response to close reading [in coursework folder]   (LEAG)

Another way in which you are often asked to record your response to a poem is by means of a more 'open-ended' question. Try your hand at this one:

2 You are travelling with the Pope on this occasion. Write your view of the cancelled visit as though in a letter to a friend, taking into account Rajendra's comments.

(Answers p. 175)

You may also have to answer questions on fictional writing, including short stories. As we have already given you a complete short story to read, *River Afternoon* (pp. 40-4), we shall choose a passage from there. Such extracts often have a few words of introduction. (See *River Afternoon* p. 43 'Suddenly a much smaller fish . . .' to p. 44 '. . . it was a bigger fish than he had ever caught before.')

This passage comes from a short story about a boy and girl who go fishing in a river near their home. The boy has spotted a big trout.

1 *There are five short sentences at different points, describing the fish in Peter's hand. Quote three of them and say what they add to the story.*
This is a matter for observation and selection, but the second part of the question demands more careful reflection. Here is an adequate answer.

Answer
  (i) It flipped strongly.
 (ii) The fish arched itself frantically.
(iii) The poor thing opened its bleeding mouth pitifully.

The wording of these three helps the story in two ways: first, it describes vividly the gradual exhaustion of the fish; secondly, it shows the fish through the girl's eyes – especially (iii) – and helps to express her feelings.

   Notice that this answer does not quote the other two sentences about the fish – 'The fish was almost at its last gasp' and 'The little fish lay limp in Peter's hand.' They are purely descriptive, and illustrate only the first of the two points given in the answer. A good answer to this question involves selecting the three that you can say most about.

2 *Why does the girl say – 'You're no fisherman if you keep that' and '. . . even if I do hate fishing . . .'?*
Make up your own mind about this question before looking up the answer on page 175, and jot down an answer in rough.

3 *What is the tone of Peter's words 'Big deal!', and what does this tell us about his thoughts?*
'Tone' – the way words convey attitudes and feelings – is always an important part of the meaning in imaginative writing. From it you can often **draw inferences** (see p. 71) about the characters and their feelings, or about the writer's intentions. A satisfactory answer to this question would be:

Answer
Peter responds sarcastically to the girl's threat never to come fishing with him again, because at this moment he is antagonistic to her and wants her to know that, far from feeling threatened, he would be pleased if she never came again. The slang expression 'Big deal!' also carries a note of contempt that suits the boy's mood.

4 *The paragraph starting 'The kingfisher flew down . . .' adds a number of descriptive details – the kingfisher, the breeze, the willows, etc. Why are they given at this point in the story?*
This question demands careful reflection on the placing of this paragraph rather than its actual content. Decide which of the following openings would lead to the better answer (see p. 175) and try completing the answer for yourself.

Answer
   • This paragraph comes immediately after the children have made up their quarrel and are on good terms again . . .
   • The paragraph describes how Peter dangled the worm under the bank, and how the willows dangled in the water too . . .

5 *What words or phrases bring out the change of atmosphere when the big fish is hooked? Comment on their appropriateness.*
Obviously this is first a matter of careful selection. In the following list two are wrongly chosen. Which are they? (Answer on p. 175.)

> incredible outraged turbulence
> lain so still
> flashed
> showering spray
> galvanized
> leaped
> screamed in surprise
> began to reel in

The second part of the question – 'Comment on their appropriateness' – asks you to draw conclusions about the way the paragraph is written. Conclusions are also needed for the final question; this time you are expected to draw on the passage as a whole in your answer:

6 *How old do you think the boy and the girl are? Sum up their relationship as revealed in this passage.*
Try answering this question for yourself. An adequate answer would require between 50 and 70 words. Ours is on page 175 but don't look at it until you have written your own.

River Afternoon showed how even in imaginative writing the writer must draw on her or his experience. Without some idea of what it feels like to grow up in the countryside and to catch a big fish Hilary Tunnicliffe could not have brought the two children and their afternoon excursion so vividly to life in our imaginations. Now we turn to a very different setting, a sugar cane plantation in Trinidad. It is an extract from a short story. As you read it, try to decide how you could answer someone who asked you 'What is it about?'.

> [This passage describes how a Trinidadian boy, Romesh, who has come back to his family after being educated away from home, decides to *leave* home.]

He went into the kitchen to wash his face. He gargled noisily, scraped his tongue with his teeth. Then he remembered his toothbrush and toothpaste in his suitcase. As he cleaned his teeth his sister stood watching him. She never used a toothbrush: they broke a twig and chewed on it to clean their mouths.
  'You going to go away, *bhai?*' she asked him timidly.
  He nodded, with froth in his mouth.
  'If you stay, you could teach we what you know,' the girl said.
  Romesh washed his mouth and said, '*Baihin*, there are many things I have yet to learn'.
  'But what will happen to us?'
  'Don't ask me questions, little sister,' he said crossly.
  After he had eaten he left the hut and sulked about the village, walking slowly with his hands in his pockets. He wasn't quite sure what he was going to do. He kept telling himself that he would go away and never return, but bonds he had refused to think about surrounded him. The smell of burnt cane was strong on the wind. He went to the pond, where he and Hari used to bath the mules. What to do? His mind was in a turmoil.
  Suddenly he turned and went home. He got his cutlass – it was sharp and clean, even though unused for such a long time. Ramlal never allowed any of his tools to get rusty.
  He went out into the fields, swinging the cutlass in the air, as if with each stroke he swept a problem away.
  Hari said: 'Is time you come. Other people start work long time, we have to work extra to catch up with them.'
  There was no friendliness in his voice now.
  Romesh said nothing, but he hacked savagely at the canes, and in half an hour he was bathed in sweat and his skin scratched from contact with the cane.
  Ramlal came up in the mule cart and called out, 'Work faster! We a whole cartload behind!' Then he saw Romesh and he came down from the cart and walked rapidly across. 'So you come! Is a good thing you make up your mind!'
  Romesh wiped his face. 'I am not going to stay, *bap*.' It was funny how the decision came, he hadn't known himself what he was going to do. 'I will help with the crop, you shall get the bonus if I have to work alone in the night. But I am not going to get married. I am going away after the crop.'

'You are mad, you will do as I say.' Ramlal spoke loudly, and other workers in the field stopped to listen.

The decision was so clear in Romesh's mind that he did not say anything more. He swung the cutlass tirelessly at the cane and knew that when the crop was finished, it would be time to leave his family and the village. His mind got that far, and he didn't worry about after that . . .

(From 'Cane is Bitter' in *Ways of Sunlight* by Sam Selvon, Longman, Harlow.)

We asked you to decide what this passage – or the story it came from – is about. Let us put this in the form of questions of the kind you might be faced with in an examination:

1 Which, in your opinion, is more important in this story, the setting or the characters? Explain your choice by referring to particular passages or phrases.

2 Point out any differences between Romesh and the rest of his family.

3 On the basis of your answers to 1 and 2, explain in three or four sentences of your own why Romesh behaved as he did.

4 The title of the story this extract comes from is 'Cane is Bitter'. Suggest an alternative title, giving a reason.

5 Write the story as you imagine it might have been up to the point where this extract begins. (For hints on answering see p. 175.)

Coursework assignment

Write a short story (1000-1500 words) involving a clash of opinion between two generations in a family.

It is sometimes a good idea to give an 'overview' of a whole book, rather than picking out extracts for close attention. Consequently English examinations or coursework assignments may ask for a more general account of a book you have read. Let's look at one book and see what might be expected of us. We have chosen a fast-moving adventure story of events taking place about a hundred and fifty years ago – *A High Wind in Jamaica*, by Richard Hughes. We hope to convince you that it is a good choice: it has, in fact, often been set for close study in English Literature examinations – but don't let this put you off!

Summary

The opening chapter gives a wonderful description of an old house on a ruined sugar plantation in the West Indies – its slave quarters, sugar grinding and boiling houses. We read of the devastation caused by earthquakes, fires and floods and of the abundant, luxuriant tropical vegetation that took over when the place became derelict.

Next the book describes some English children who lived there. We hear plenty of details about their clothes, their games, their cat and what he used to do (swim round the bathing pool and fight with snakes). The children's daily life and activities were very different from those of any child living in this country nowadays.

After this comes a vivid and frightening description of a tropical hurricane: fierce lightning all over the sky, cracking thunder, torrents of rain, devastating wind. The children's poor cat was chased through the house and out again by a pack of maddened wild cats. The roof collapsed and the family had to take refuge along with the negroes and the goats in the cellar. The father handed wine round and all the children went to sleep drunk.

Following this disaster the parents decided to send their children to school in England. The rest of the book is about their adventures – equally hair-raising and unusual – at sea. The children find themselves on a pirate schooner, and have many an excitement and experiences both funny and terrifying, before they finally disembark in England.

What we have done here is to *review* the book – to go over it in our mind after reading and enjoying it as a whole, in order to see more clearly what made it enjoyable and therefore memorable to us. Professional reviewers, whose job it is to do this for the 'books' columns of newspapers and magazines, know well enough that if they tell the whole story, or go into too much detail about the setting or the characters, they may be spoiling the book for other readers. Their job, after classifying the book (adventure story, thriller, autobiography etc.), is to whet appetites. If you haven't read *A High Wind in Jamaica* we hope we have whetted yours.

However, in a GCSE examination or coursework assignment your job isn't quite so straight forward, even if you are asked simply to 'write a review of a book you have enjoyed'. Your job is to prove to the examiner that you have read and responded to the book. Most people who will read a review have not read the book; they are looking for guidance as to whether it is worth buying or asking for at the library. But when you write a review, keep in mind that you will have one critical reader rather than many who haven't read the book.

We have shown you that *A High Wind in Jamaica* is easy to use as the subject of a review. It is so full of detail and variety that it would be easy to answer the sort of questions we looked at earlier, on different aspects of the story.

● A question on *the setting* (type 3 in the list of five likely topics given on pp. 40-1) would be easy; the details Richard Hughes gives of the island, the houses on it, the pirate ship, are all so vivid and memorable.

● A question about *children* (type 4) would be a gift; the novel is all about children and they are very different from one another.

● A question that asks you to describe *an important incident* (type 1) would be a walk-over. The tropical hurricane comes near the beginning, and is so well described that you can almost feel you are in it. If you want other incidents to choose from there are many memorable scenes later in the book: two unexpected and bizarre deaths, for instance, or a hilarious episode where the sailors are trying to catch a drunken monkey who has escaped up the rigging.

> . . . understanding of and response to close reading [in coursework folder]   (LEAG)

When such a book is fresh in your mind, it is like having someone by your side telling you what to write; memorable details come into your mind which will give interest and life to anything you write about the book.

It is essential that you convince the examiner you have really read the book you are talking about, not just skimmed through it, or – worse still – seen it on film or television without having read it at all. (*Warning* Nothing is easier for an experienced examiner to recognize than second-hand knowledge of a book as derived from television adaptations.) A very good way to show that you know the book well is to *quote* some of the actual words you have been reading. Let the book grip you, enter into its world, see it through the eyes of its author, and before you know where you are the words and sentences of more interesting parts will be fixed in your memory. Here are three bits we found no difficulty in remembering after putting down *A High Wind in Jamaica*:

When Lame Foot Sam the negro is tempted to steal a handkerchief someone has dropped, he suddenly remembers it is Sunday. He drops it hastily and starts covering it with sand – '*Please God I thieve you tomorrow,*' he exclaimed hopefully, '*Please God, you still there.*'

After the storm which destroys the children's house – '*The furniture was splintered into matchwood. Even the heavy mahogany dining table, which they loved, and had always kept with its legs in little glass baths of oil to defeat the ants, was spirited right away.*'

On board ship the children make friends with a black pig. They like to sit on him – *'If I was the queen,' said Emily, 'I should most certainly have a pig for a throne.'*

Quoting details like these often gives the flavour of the book better than describing it in general terms. Quoting them *accurately* – even just a few words like 'have a pig for a throne' – also proves you are a careful and observant reader.

FURTHER PRACTICE

1

Moorings

In a salt ring of moonlight
The dinghy nods at nothing.
It paws the bright water
And scatters its own shadow
In a false net of light.

A ruined chain lies reptile,
Tied to the ground by grasses.
Two oars, wet with sweet water
Filched from the air, are slanted
From a wrecked lobster creel.

The cork that can't be travels –
Nose of a dog otter.
It's piped at, screamed at, sworn at
By elegant oyster catcher
On furious red legs.

With a sort of idle swaying
The tide breathes in. Harsh seaweed
Uncrackles to its kissing;
The skin of the water glistens;
Rich fat swims on the brine.

And all night in his stable
The dinghy paws bright water,
Restless steeplechaser
Longing to clear the hurdles
That ring the point of Stoer.

(From *A Round of Applause,* by Norman MacCaig, Chatto & Windus, London.)

1 There is one central image or comparison in the poem. Say what it is. Do you think it suits the subject matter? In your answer (which should not be more than one paragraph) refer to particular things in the poem (70-100 words).

2 Comment on the use of language and the sound of the words in lines 2, 7, 8, 17-18 (50-70 words).

3 Imagine you are the boat's owner. Describe coming to use it in the early morning following the night described in the poem (100-150 words).

(Hints on answering on p. 176)

2 We have seen that questions or coursework assignments on literature are of two main kinds: either general, 'open-ended', to be answered from your own reading – like the 'review' we gave you of *A High Wind in Jamaica* on p. 86 – or directly related to a piece of writing given to you. This may be a poem, play excerpt or a fictional piece. For practice in the second kind we print below an extract from a novel by Evelyn Waugh called *Sword of Honour*. Read it carefully then answer the questions that follow. You will find our answers or suggestions on p. 176, but don't read them until after you have tried the questions for yourself. As this kind of exercise in an English examination has usually to be done within a *set* time limit, try to keep to the times suggested. They are related to the mark-scheme given here.

[Guy Crouchback, a lieutenant in the Royal Corps of Halberdiers, has been posted to the Isle of Mugg, off the west coast of Scotland, for training with the Commandos. Tommy Blackhouse, who knew Guy before the war, is Colonel of the unit.]

Tommy greeted him.
   'Guy, I've bad news. You've got to dine out tonight at the Castle. The old boy had been making a lot of complaints so I sent Angus round to make peace. He couldn't see the Laird but it turned out he was some kind of cousin, so next day I got a formal invitation to dine there with Angus. I can't chuck now. No one else wants to come.   5
You're the last to join, so go and change quick. We're off in five minutes.'
   The seat of Colonel Hector Campbell of Mugg was known locally as 'the New Castle' . . . The exterior was German in character . . . of moderate size but designed to withstand assault from all but the most modern weapons. The interior was pitch-pine throughout and owed its decoration more to the taxidermist than to the   10
sculptor or painter.
   Before Guy and Tommy had left their car, the double doors of the New Castle were thrown open. A large young butler, kilted and heavily bearded, seemed to speak some words of welcome but they were lost in a gale of music. A piper stood beside him, more ornately clothed, older and shorter; a square man, red bearded. If it had   15
come to a fight between them the money would have been on the piper. He was in fact the butler's father. The four of them marched forward and upward to the great hall.
   A candelabrum, consisting of concentric and diminishing circles of tarnished brass, hung from the rafters. A dozen or so of the numberless clusters of electric   20
bulbs were alight, disclosing the dim presence of a large circular dining table. Round the chimney-piece whose armorial decorations were obscured by smoke, the baronial severity of the rest of the furniture was mitigated by a group of chairs clothed in stained and faded chintz. Everywhere else were granite, pitch-pine, tartan

and objects of furniture constructed of antlers. Six dogs, ranging in size from a   25
couple of deerhounds to an almost hairless pomeranian, gave tongue in inverse
proportion to their size. Above all from the depths of the smoke cloud a voice roared.
    'Silence, you infernal brutes. Down, Hercules. Back, Jason. Silence, Sir.'
    There were shadowy, violent actions and sounds of whacking, kicking, snarling
and whining. Then the piper had it all to himself again. It was intensely cold in the   30
hall and Guy's eyes wept afresh in the peat fumes. Presently the piper, too, was
hushed and in the stunning silence an aged lady and gentleman emerged through
the smoke. Colonel Campbell was much bedizened with horn and cairngorms.* He
wore a velvet doublet above his kilt, stiff collar and a black bow tie. Mrs. Campbell
wore nothing memorable.   35
    The dogs fanned out beside them and advanced at the same slow pace, silent but
menacing. His probable destiny seemed manifest to Guy, to be blinded by smoke
among the armchairs, to be frozen to death in the wider spaces, or to be devoured by
the dogs where he stood. Tommy, the perfect soldier, appreciated the situation and
acted promptly. He advanced on the nearest deerhound, grasped its muzzle and   40
proceeded to rotate its head in a manner which the animal appeared to find
reassuring. The great tail began to wave in the fumes. The hushed dogs covered
their fangs and advanced to sniff first at his trousers, then at Guy's. Meanwhile
Tommy said:
    'I'm awfully sorry we couldn't let you know in time. Angus Anstruther-Kerr had   45
an accident today on the rocks. I didn't want to leave you a man short, so I've
brought Mr Crouchback instead.'
    Guy had already observed the vast distances that separated the few places at
table and thought this explanation of his presence less than adequate to the laird's
style of living. Mrs Campbell took his hand gently.   50
    'Mugg will be disappointed. We make more of kinship here than you do in the
south, you know. He's a little deaf by the way.'
    But Mugg had firmly taken his hand.
    'I never met your father,' he said. 'But I knew his uncle, Kerr of Gellioch, before
his father married Jean Anstruther of Glenaldy. You resemble neither the one nor   55
the other. Glenaldy was a fine man, though he was old when I knew him, and it was
a sorrow having no son, to pass the place of Gellioch to.'
    'This is Mr Crouchback, dear,'
    'Maybe, maybe, I don't recollect. Where's dinner?'
    'Katie's not here yet.'   60
    'Is she dining down tonight?'
    'You know she is, dear. We discussed it. Katie is Mugg's great-niece from
Edinburgh, who's paying us a visit.'
    'Visit? She's been here three years.'
    'She worked too hard for her exams,' said Mrs Campbell.   65
    'We'll not wait for her,' said Mugg.
    As they sat round the table the gulf that should have been filled by Katie lay
between Guy and his host. Tommy had at once begun a brisk conversation about
tides and beaches with Mrs Campbell. The laird looked at Guy, decided the distance
between them was insurmountable and contentedly splashed about in his soup.   70
    Presently he looked up again and said:
    'Got any gun-cotton?'
    'I'm afraid not.'
    'Halberdier?'
    'Yes.'   75
    He nodded towards Tommy.
    'Coldstreamer?'
    'Yes.'
    'Same outfit?'
    'Yes.'   80
    'Extraordinary thing.'
    'We're rather a mixed unit.'
    'Argyll myself, of course. No mixture there. They tried cross-posting at the end of
the last war. Never worked.'
    Fish appeared. Colonel Campbell was silent while he ate, got into trouble with   85
some bones, buried his head in his napkin, took out his teeth and at last got himself
to rights.
    'Mugg finds fish very difficult nowadays,' said Mrs Campbell during this process.
    The host looked at Tommy with a distinctly crafty air now, and said:

Cairngorms: semi-precious stones

'Saw some sappers the day before yesterday.'   90
'They must have been ours.'
'They got gun-cotton.'
'Yes, I think so. They've got a lot of stores marked "Danger".'
The laird looked sternly at Guy.
'Don't you think it would have been a more honest answer to admit it in the first   95
place?'
Tommy and Mrs Campbell stopped talking of landing-places and listened.
'When I asked you if you had gun-cotton, do you suppose I imagined you were
carrying it on your person now? I meant, have you brought any gun-cotton to my
island?'   100
Here Tommy intervened. 'I hope you have no complaint about it being misused,
sir?'
'Or dynamite?' continued the laird disregarding. 'Any explosive would do.'
At this moment the piper put an end to the conversation. He was followed by the
butler bearing a huge joint which he set before the host. Round and round went the   105
skirl. Colonel Campbell hacked away at the haunch of venison. The butler followed
his own devious course with a tray of redcurrant jelly and unpeeled potatoes. Not
before the din was over and a full plate before him did Guy realize that a young lady
had unobtrusively slipped into the chair beside him. He bowed as best he could from
the intricate framework of antlers which constituted his chair. She returned his   110
smile of greeting liberally.
She was, he judged, ten or twelve years younger than himself. Either she was
freckled, which seemed unlikely at this place and season, or else she had been
splashed with peaty water and had neglected to wash, which seemed still less likely
in view of the obvious care she had taken with the rest of her toilet. An hereditary   115
stain perhaps, Guy thought, suddenly appearing in Mugg to bear evidence of an
ancestral seafaring adventure long ago among the Spice Islands. Over the brown
blotches she was richly rouged, her short black curls were bound with a tartan
ribbon, held together by a brooch of the kind Guy supposed were made only for
tourists, and she wore a dress which in that hall must have exposed her to an   120
extremity of frigeration. Her features were regular as marble and her eyes were
wide and splendid and mad.

'You aren't doing very well, are you?' she remarked suddenly on a note of
triumph.
'This is Mr Crouchback, dear,' said Mrs Campbell, frowning fiercely at her   125
husband's great-niece. 'Miss Carmichael. She comes from Edinburgh.'
'And a true Scot,' said Miss Carmichael.

'Yes, of course, Kate. We all know that.'

'Her grandmother was a Campbell,' said the laird in a tone of deepest melancholy, 'my own Mother's sister.'   130

'My mother was a Meiklejohn and her mother a Dundas.'

'No one is questioning your being a true Scot, Katie,' said the great-aunt; 'eat your dinner.'

During this exchange of genealogical information, Guy had pondered on Miss Carmichael's strange preliminary challenge. He had not distinguished himself, he   135
fully realized, in the preceding conversation, though it would have taken a master, he thought, to go right. And anyway, how did this beastly girl know? Had she been hiding her freckles in the smoke, or, more likely, was she that phenomenon, quite common, he believed, in these parts – the seventh child of a seventh child? He had had a hard day. He was numb and choked and under-nourished. An endless   140
procession marched across his mind, Carmichaels, Campbells, Meiklejohns, Dundases, in columns of seven, some kilted and bonneted, others in the sober, durable garb of the Edinburgh professions, all dead.

He steadied himself with wine, which in contrast to soup or fish, was excellent. 'Doing well,' of course, was an expression of the nursery. It meant eating heavily.   145
Hitherto instinct and experience alike had held him back from the venison. Now, openly rebuked, he put a fibrous, rank lump of the stuff into his mouth and began desperately chewing. Miss Carmichael turned back to him.

(From *Sword of Honour* by Evelyn Waugh, Chapman & Hall, London.)

The following . . . forms of writing . . . will be acceptable: . . . personal responses to . . . a [literary] text, real or imagined interview with a writer, outline of a sequel to a novel or a play . . . [etc.]   (SEG)

Questions

1 Give an account of Guy's feelings during this episode, in your own words. You can write as though you were Guy if you wish.

2 How do we know that Tommy is more at his ease in these surroundings than Guy?

3 Although the circumstances are not particularly light-hearted many people find this part of the book very funny. How does Waugh achieve this by his description of the visit?

4 Write an account of a visit or a meal at which you, as guest, felt embarrassed or uncomfortable. Try to convey both your discomfort and how it might have struck another person – observer or participant.

(Answers on p. 176)

W4 LETTERS AND PRACTICAL WRITING

4.1 Writing Letters

The ability to write a good letter is a great asset. It may help you to get a job, an interview, an exam success or a chance to present your ideas in a newspaper or magazine. Later on you may need to write to an MP, a local councillor or the manager of an organization such as a bus company; and you yourself may hold a position which involves a great deal of letter writing. A good secretary writes letters for the manager, who signs them as if they were his or her own; many secretaries write better letters than their employers! Most important of all, letters are still one of the best ways of keeping in touch for people who are apart. Nearly everyone writes a love letter at some time while many older people live for letters from their grown up family.

> A variety of styles of writing will be required . . . e.g. letters, reports and instructions
>
> (SEG)

LAYOUT

Here is a letter someone wrote to his insurance company. It is a formal letter, or course, because he did not know exactly who might read it and simply needed to put in hand a business matter.

```
                                          4 The Close
                                          Battington
                                          Shropshire
                                          SY7 8JA

                                          22 January 1987

        Commercial Union Assurance Co Ltd
        1 Merridale Road
        Chapel Ash
        WOLVERHAMPTON
        WV3 9RT

        Dear Sir,

                Key Household Policy no. HA170733113

            I wish to add two named items to those already
        listed in the policy, so that they can be covered
        against fire, loss and theft under the terms of the
        policy.  The two items are:

        1  Cello bow by Cuniot-Hury (named on stick) value £1 000

        2  Camera: Ricoh 500G, body no.27315956

            Would you please let me know what additional premium
        you require?

                    Yours faithfully

                    S. Johnson.

                    (Mr) S. Johnson
```

Points to notice

The date is given in full.

The tendency nowadays is for the address to be unpunctuated. As long as it is clearly spaced, this is quite acceptable. If you do punctuate the address, use a full stop after any abbreviation (e.g. St., Lancs.), and a comma at the end of each line except the last, which has a full stop.

The subject of the letter is set out as a heading; this helps your letter to get to the right room in a large office.

If you are replying to a letter with a reference number, quote it, so as to get your letter quickly to the right person and the right department.

The whole letter should be well set out on the page; notice how the spacing makes our sample letter easy to read.

Use capital letters for the opening words (Dear Sir, Dear Madam), but for the first word only of the closing phrase (Yours faithfully).

Use your normal signature. If possible it should be easily read and roughly parallel with the rest of the letter. If you can't write your name legibly, type or write it in script or capitals below the signature. It may help your correspondent if you put Mr, Ms, Mrs or Miss in brackets after or before your signature.

The envelope

There should be a space of at least 1½ inches (5 cm) above the address on the envelope so that it is clear of the postmark. For a formal letter, write or type the address exactly as it appears at the head of your letter.

When writing to a private address, always use the number of the house if it has one, even if it has a name. Use capital letters for the name of the town and put the post-code on the last line of the address.

Beginning and ending

There are three methods, according to the type of letter.

1 Formal letters, to firms, government departments and individuals whom you may not know, start: Dear Sir (or Sirs) or Dear Madam and end Yours faithfully (note the two l's).

2 Friendly letters to people you know fairly well or have met recently, for example to a teacher at your school or someone who has employed you, start Dear Mr Jones, Dear Mrs Roberts, Dear Dr Graham, and end: Yours sincerely (note the two e's). Never use 'Dear Sir' for someone you have met personally or know well.

3 Letters to relatives and close friends start 'Dear Jane' or in any way you think suits the person you're writing to. Endings can be varied: Yours ever, Love to you both, Best wishes, etc.

Nowadays firms and government departments tend to use style 2 instead of style 1. The practice came from America, where an appearance of friendliness is thought to be suitable even in business matters.

CONTENT, TONE AND STYLE

Before writing anything, think out what you want or need to say and the best order to say it in. If the letter is an important one make rough notes first. State clearly at the beginning why the letter has been written. Use a fresh paragraph for each division of the subject. The content of the letter requires the best words for the job and the right tone of voice. The tone is sometimes more difficult to gauge than the words.

If you are writing about something for which you are going to pay, such as a holiday, or sending for a special offer of a dress, you will need a different tone from the one in a letter which is asking for a reference, applying for a job or suggesting an exchange holiday with a member of a French family.

For the first type the tone should be polite, but not too polite. You are paying; therefore 'Please send me . . .' or 'Kindly send . . .' is enough, perhaps with the ending 'I shall be glad to hear from you as soon as possible'. It is too polite to say 'I shall be very grateful . . .' You are the buyer; let the seller be grateful to you. But when you are asking for – not buying – someone's time or services, your tone should be warmer and more polite.

Thus if you invite someone to speak at your school or society or to sponsor a charitable appeal, you must choose words to show your gratitude. The phrases 'very grateful', 'much appreciate', 'generosity' would be in place.

Lastly the tone of an application for a job needs special care. It can reveal your personality more clearly than any facts about you. It will be read very closely by a prospective employer, because it is all he or she has to go on. What are the relative chances of these applicants for a post as receptionist?

1 . . . because I like lots of people, and often go to parties. They say I'm a good mixer . . .

2 . . . I understand that the receptionist will often need to put people at their ease. My experience at Smith and Hardy will help here . . .

Here is a good example of a clear, well-spaced preliminary letter. In the middle sentence 'to' should be omitted and 'of' would be better than 'concerning'.

> 14, Cranford Way,
> Beckworth,
> Derbyshire.
> DB8 2YO
>
> 8th August, 1987
>
> The Personnel Officer,
> Smart & Sons Ltd.,
> Marsh Street,
> Kiddington,
> Derbyshire.
> DB2 5KD
>
> Dear Sir,
>   I wish to apply for the post of Sales Manager, as advertised in 'The Daily Herald', 7th August, 1987.
>   Would you please send to me an application form and any further details concerning this post?
>   I enclose a stamped, addressed envelope.
>
>   Yours faithfully,
>   F.L. James.

The best words for a formal letter are often the fewest needed to state your purpose. It may well be that the person you are writing to receives a great many letters. So keep it as short as politeness and clarity allow. This should prevent the chatty approach; as in

'I know you're terribly busy but it's better to be busy than bored, isn't it?'
or the irrelevant information as in the example

'The reason I'm writing is because my handwriting is the best although I'm not so good at English as Jane. I do hope you can come, because if you do I can have a new outfit.'
Or the afterthought which should have come earlier

'P.S. We hope you will be able to stay for a cup of tea afterwards.'

If you receive a rude letter, do not reply rudely, however provocative and insulting your correspondent may be. In conversation it is easy to tone down rude remarks; it is much more difficult once they are written. If you have to complain about something, state the facts calmly; don't get worked up or abusive. Normally a polite complaint stands the best chance of success. Your letter will be read by someone whose business it is to attend to difficulties and he or she will help more willingly if you ask rather than demand, explain rather than complain.

Avoid 'business' English, which still survives in places. In these examples the right-hand column gives the preferred version.

In connection with your inquiry, we have to acquaint you that our practice is to prefer payment by cheque.

We prefer to be paid by cheque.

Such employment does not involve the necessity of obtaining a certificate of fitness.

A fitness certificate is not needed for such employment.

be good enough to advise us	tell us
the attention of your good selves	your attention
have delivered same	have delivered it
acquaint with, inform	tell
alternative	other, another, different
anticipate	expect
commence	begin
consider	think
proceed	go
a proportion of	some
purchase	buy
residence	home
to state	to say
terminate	end
utilize	use

PRACTICE

1 You have to write to a local celebrity to invite her to plant a tree for which you have helped to raise the money. What do you need to say? Jot down your ideas and then check with the list below; you may think of something we haven't included:

- Reason for writing
- Date, time, place
- Exactly what are you inviting her to do? Shovel soil? Make a speech? Meet people?
- Estimated length of ceremony
- Who and how many present
- Gratitude and appreciation
- Offer to provide any other information required

The last point is a precaution; you hope the letter has included everything necessary. (You can compare your letter with the one we wrote if you turn to p. 177.)

> The coursework folder must include: (a) *two* pieces . . . done wholly in class . . . with no help. . . . Candidates must be given opportunity to respond in a variety of ways which may include: a letter or a report; writing argumentatively; summarizing; note-making; speech writing
> (MEG)

2 An elderly widow who is a friend of your parents has complained that you were one of a group of teenagers who disturbed her sleep by noise after a party. Your parents have asked you to write a letter of apology and to offer to do something for her. Write the letter.

3 Suppose that you are a wealthy person who has been asked for money for an old people's home and a dispensary for sick animals. You favour only one of them. Write a letter to a friend explaining your preference and urging him, if he is approached, to make the same choice.

4 Recently your local paper has published letters to the Editor complaining about the behaviour of young people on the buses. Write two letters:
  (a) a typical letter of complaint
  (b) your own reply in defence of the alleged offenders

Set out the letters correctly and where necessary invent names and addresses.

Here are three letters which were sent to a manufacturer of motorcycle sprockets (toothed wheels driven by chain). Which do you think is most efficient for its purpose? Make up your mind, then turn to page 179 for the manufacturer's reactions. Re-write one of the unsatisfactory ones. Names and addresses have been changed to spare the writers' blushes!

```
                                                    22 Fairfield Drive
                                                        Fadesley
                                                          Lancs


            Dear Sir

                    Can you make me  a rear sprocket for a 1968 Ariel
            Huntmaster but not cast as the original but in steel
            same size as standard  How much

                          Arielly,
                                Alan Becking
```

```
                        98 Steep Street
                        Burton-on-Hill
                        Staffs

                            March 3rd


        Dear Sir,

            Have you a sprocket suitable for AJW Greyhound moped,
        sizes 25 teeth by 3/16.  The holes to fit the sprocket to the
        wheel can be drilled from the old sprocket which I am quite
        willing to do myself.  If you have same would you please send
        me price etc so I can forward my money on to you as I'm waiting
        for the sprocket as I need my bike to go to college on.

            Yours faithfully,


            Mr B Rider
```

```
                                                    21 Spring bank Rd
                                                        Farnsworth
                                                          LANCS



            Dear Sir,
                I am writing to enquire exactly what information you
            require when asked to make a gear box and rear wheel sprocket
            to suit a particular bike.
                I am in a position to acquire Reynold chain for no cost
            but the pitch is slightly larger than my standard chain which
            is fitted to a Suzuki 'GT. 750A' motorcycle.
                Obviously I cannot supply a pattern of either sprocket as
            it is going to be different to the standard ones due to pitch
            difference.
                Hoping you can help me.

                          Yours faithfully

                          Mr F. Wheeler
```

To end the section we have an example of a clear, vigorously expressed letter. Most of the sentences are fairly short, because brief sentences carry punch; the words used also tend to be short. A young office worker, Golding Bright, wanted to become a drama critic, so he applied for advice to Bernard Shaw, a famous critic and playwright. This is part of Shaw's reply. It was written on 2nd December 1894.

Dear Sir,

. . . You have not at all taken in my recommendation to you to write a book. You say you are scarcely competent to write books just yet. That is just why I recommend you to learn. If I advised you to learn to skate, you would not reply that your balance was scarcely good enough yet. A man learns to skate by staggering about and making a fool of himself. You will never write a good book until you have written some bad ones . . . I began by writing some abominably bad criticisms. I wrote five long books before I started again on press work . . . You must go through the mill too; and you can't possibly start too soon. Write a thousand words a day for the next five years for at least nine months every year. Read all the great critics . . . Get a ticket for the British Museum reading room, and live there as much as you can. Go to all the first-rate orchestral concerts and to the opera, as well as to the theatre. Join debating societies and learn to speak in public. Haunt little Sunday evening political meetings and exercise that accomplishment.

Study men and politics in this way. As long as you stay in the office, try and be the smartest hand in it; I spent four and a half years in an office before I was twenty. Be a teetotaller; don't gamble; don't lend; don't borrow; don't for your life get married; make the attainment of EFFICIENCY your sole object for the next fifteen years; and if the City can teach you nothing more, or demands more time than you can spare from your apprenticeship, tell your father that you prefer to cut loose and starve, and *do it*. But it will take you at least a year or two of tough work before you will be able to build up for yourself either the courage or the right to take heroic measures. Finally, since I have given you all this advice, I add this crowning precept, the most valuable of all. NEVER TAKE ANYBODY'S ADVICE.

(From *Advice to a young critic* by George Bernard Shaw, Peter Owen, London.)

4.2 Reports; Practical Writing; Making Notes

Making notes is a first step towards the making of a summary or a report. These three things – a summary, note-making and reports – are closely linked skills. They may relate to a complete passage or to one particular part.

These skills need few words but plenty of thought. Remember Bernard Shaw's apology to a correspondent for writing a long letter; 'I didn't have time to write a shorter one'. In note-making especially, time for thought is needed to

– grasp the main points of an argument or story;

– sort out the points that matter from those that don't;

– decide the best way of setting out the notes.

Really good note-making needs a lot of practice; but from the start you can make the notes look good.

It should be possible to read notes at a glance, that is the way they are used in real life – for instance by journalists, people delivering speeches that have been made up for them and those engaged in research of various kinds. Page layout is therefore very important. DON'T be miserly over space! Cramped writing with no room for the eye to rest makes for difficult reading. Here are some notes one of us wrote for himself while making preparations for a concert he had to arrange as one of the events in a local gala week.

Points to notice

1 Give each new item a fresh line.

2 Number the items. If there are subsidiary points use letters (a, b, c, etc.) or Roman numbers (i, ii, iii etc.). Indent these (as illustrated).

3 You do not need to write continuous prose. Leave out any words you can as long as the meaning is clear to you (and to the examiner, if you are doing an exam).

4 Use shortened forms of words where possible and initials for names. Remember, again, the examiner who does not want to be held up by misunderstandings.

5 Use figures for numbers, not words: 8, 64, etc.

Gala Concert   Wed. 20th. Aug.

Light classical — single movts. not whole
works — variety of instruments, singers etc
(check last year's programme)

To be done before 1st. Aug.

1 Contact performers
  (a) singers (Fred, Mary, Michael + ?)
  (b) instruments
    i) piano (David, Hilary)
      (n.b. arrange to move piano into hall)
    ii) strings (Peter, Steve, + ?)
    iii) others? (horn? clarinet?)
2 Arrange rehearsals
  (a) dates + times
  (b) places
3 Book hall

6 Emphasize by <u>underlining</u> or CAPITAL LETTERS.

A piece of writing like the following could well appear in your examination paper. We shall use it to show how to prepare a set of notes for the writer of a gardening book on the topic 'What causes weed seeds to spread?'.

Most gardeners, faced by the abundance of weeds that take root in any patch of newly turned soil that has been allowed to lie fallow for a few weeks, have asked themselves where on earth weeds come from. The answer, of course, is that each has grown from a seed that could have been deposited in the soil in one of an astonishing variety of ways.

The biggest culprit when it comes to spreading weeds is the bird. Whether it is the humble sparrow or the exotic waxwing, almost every bird eats seeds in large quantities. Some of these seeds pass right through the bird's body; those which fall on suitable ground germinate readily.

Secondly we must blame the wind. Apart from seeds adapted for windborne travel, like the familiar dandelion 'parachute', a lot of seeds are tiny enough to blow about on their own. The minute, soot-like spores of ferns are an extreme example. Water, too, must take its share of the responsibility – and not just the sea water which deposits coconut shells around the fringes of tropical islands. Streams, rivers and the tiny rivulets which flow everywhere after heavy rain, all carry seed and deposit it on their banks or where they dry up.

Wild animals pick up seeds on their feet and transport them this way. Some seeds are covered with spines which adhere to animal fur and wool and are later rubbed off. Smaller animals (the squirrel is one) collect edible seeds such as acorns and stockpile them for winter foodstuff, or carry them back to an underground lair. If the animal is killed in the meantime, the seeds may eventually sprout. Certain insects, including ants, frequently carry seeds about.

As if all this were not enough, many plants have their own unusual ways of spreading seed. Quite a number do it by exploding their seed capsules violently, scattering their contents far and wide. Others, such as sycamore, fit wings to their seed so that it flutters well away from its source.

Notes

Sources of weeds

1 birds'
   (a) feet
   (b) droppings

2 wind blowing
   (a) v. small seeds
   (b) seeds evolved for flight

3 water: sea, streams (esp. after rain)

4 animals (feet, fur, hoarding) and
      insects, e.g. ants

5 plants self-spreading by exploding
      pods and winged seeds

You will notice that we have used some abbreviations. If the notes were solely for your own use, you could use more, such as 'ss.' for the plural of seeds.

Test yourself

It is easy to test your own note-making skill. Prepare notes on a passage in this book or on any subject that interests you, perhaps in an encyclopaedia. Put them aside for a day or two. Then, without referring to the source, try expanding your notes into a piece of continuous prose. Check this with the original, or get a friend to check it. If you have forgotten important points in your re-write or got the wrong idea, your notes were not clear enough. Decide what went wrong, and try again later.

You may get practice in other subjects. History, Geography and English Literature *always* involve finding some ways of condensing a mass of material, and so also do other school subjects.

Final hints

If the piece you are making notes on has key words or names that are unfamiliar, make a spelling list of them as part of your set of notes.

It is worth remembering that making notes, a report or a summary is a useful skill not only for examinations. If you want information about a holiday place, or a do-it-yourself activity, you can find plenty of books or helpful advice. But not all that you hear may be relevant to your needs, so train your mind to pick out the necessary bits.

PRACTICE

The new GCSE continues the practice of setting a passage and then asking a variety of questions on it. You may be asked to summarize, write notes, produce a report, extract information on a particular point or for a special purpose, write a letter or show your understanding of the piece. Again you may be invited to study a map or a diagram in order to extract information from it.

With the two passages below here are some typical questions. Study each passage and then answer them.

Passage 1 – Red Deer

A landowner is planning to stock a large tract of moorland with red deer. This has provoked much discussion in the district and the editor of the local newspaper invites you to use the following extract from a book to write informative notes on the red deer, its habitat, names and mating habits. Many people welcome the landowner's idea; others fear the animals may be a danger to pedestrians. Write the notes.

> . . . demonstrate the ability to re-present material effectively for a particular purpose, audience or medium
>
> (LEAG)

Finding and Photographing the Red Deer

We have two indigenous species of red deer in Britain. The Red Deer, large and handsome, and the Roe Deer, diminutive and dainty. Of the other species which are to be found in the wild state, Fallow Deer are said to have been introduced from the continent and the rest, Sika, Mountjac and Chinese Water Deer, are escapees from captivity.

The Red Deer is our largest wild mammal and outside of Scotland the largest concentration is to be found, though not easily, on Exmoor. Inspired local guesswork puts the total number of Exmoor deer at between five hundred and one thousand. Exmoor National Park covers some two hundred and sixty-five square miles. Discounting the area around the perimeter of the Park which is also used by the deer, it soon becomes apparent that the chances of stumbling across many of these shy animals by chance are pretty remote. I live a short distance from the edge of Exmoor and for the past ten years or so finding the deer and making a photographic record of their way of life has accounted for much of my spare time.

Male red deer are known as stags, females hinds and youngsters calves. The stag has been described as noble, regal and indeed as a monarch. It may come as a surprise to some to learn that for a part of each and every year a full grown stag is by no means either of these, for sometimes between mid-March and mid-April he must shed the antlers which give him his kingly appearance. For a few days after shedding or casting, as it is called locally, he presents a sorry sight.

The process of renewal or growing a new set of antlers is strange indeed. The new growth which commences a matter of days after shedding the old is made under cover of living tissue remarkably velvet like in appearance and at which time the stag is said to be 'in velvet'. During the summer months the new antlers grow rapidly until about mid-August when they are complete. The blood supply to the antlers having dried up, the velvet also dries and commences to peel off, the process being speeded up by the animals themselves thrashing or rubbing their new adornments on whatever bush or sapling takes their fancy. By the end of September most of the Exmoor stags have a new set of antlers entirely free from velvet and are then said to be clean.

At birth both sexes are alike, with big dark eyes and creamy spotted russet coats—a red deer calf is appealingly attractive. During the male calf's second year the first signs of antler growth appear. It can be very little or might be as much as a foot at which time he becomes known as a pricket. In each successive year as the antlers are shed and renewed, branches or points are added from the main stem or beam until the stag reaches his prime. These additional points are all named. The lower two jut forwards above the brow and not unreasonably are known as the 'brow' points. These are closely followed by the 'bay' points and then some distance further up the beam come the 'tray' points. These six points are known as the animal's 'rights'. Those points above the rights which form in a cluster like the fingers on your hand are merely counted, two, three, four and rarely five or more. Thus a stag can be described as having all his rights and three a' top each side or, in the case of odd numbers, two and three, three and four and so on. This is much more difficult to explain in print than it is to use. Confusingly stags often fail to produce perfect sets of antlers, sometimes lacking one or both bay points and less frequently a tray point. On the other hand it is extremely rare for a mature stag to be without his brow points and to the best of my knowledge my photograph of such an animal is unique as far as Exmoor deer are concerned.

High point of the deer watchers' year is the 'rut' or mating time which occurs during October and November when the stags are in peak condition. Normally silent, retiring and tolerant towards one another, they become vociferous and belligerent. The woods echo to their roaring whilst out on the forest I have heard the clashing of antlers before I've seen the combatants tussling fully a half a mile distant. Each stag's aim is to attract as large a group of hinds as possible and thereafter keep all rivals at bay by force if necessary. The rut is possibly the best time of year for watching the deer at close quarters since the stags not only advertise their presence by their roaring but additionally are much preoccupied by the business in hand. At any other time of year the deers' highly developed senses will defeat all but the most carefully planned and executed approach.

Crawling through rain-soaked heather or peat bog, perhaps lying still for an hour to avoid detection may not be everyone's ideal leisure-time pursuit. I'm often asked why I do it, and one reason must be curiosity but that's not all. I've shown all my four daughters the deer at longish distances and last year I judged my sixteen year old ready to take on a serious stalking 'day out'. Her reaction upon seeing the animals are close quarters for the first time suggests another reason. She remarked 'aren't they beautiful?' They are.

(From *'Finding and Photographing the Red Deer'*, by David Doble.)

Obviously much of the passage is about antlers, but since the editor does not want anything about these, your notes will be along these lines (when you have used your dictionary for **indigenous, vociferous** and **belligerent**).

Notes

1 Largest indigenous wild mammal, found on Exmoor. Adult males are stags, females hinds, and young, calves. Only adult males have antlers.

2 Mating
   (a) occurs Oct.-Nov.
   (b) stags in peak condition
   (c) stags normally quiet now noisy and aggressive
   (d) stags aim to attract and keep large group of hinds – fights off other stags
   (e) best time for deer-watching

Passage 2 – Sharks

Even in fresh water, sharks hunt and kill. The Thresher shark, capable of lifting a small boat out of the water, has been sighted a mile inland on the Fowey River in Cornwall. Killer sharks swim rivers to reach Lake Nicaragua in Central America; they average one human victim each year.

Sewage and garbage attract sharks inland. When floods carry garbage to the rivers they provide a rich diet which sometimes stimulates an epidemic of shark attacks. Warm water generally provides shark food and a rich diet inflames the shark's aggression.

In British waters sharks usually swim peacefully between ten and twenty miles offshore where warm water currents fatten mackerel for their food. But the shark is terrifyingly unpredictable. One seaman was severely mauled as far north as Wick in Scotland. Small boats have been attacked in the English Channel, Irish Sea and North Sea.

Most of the legends about sharks are founded in ugly fact. Even a relatively small shark – a 200 lb Zambesi – can sever a man's leg in one bite. Sharks have up to seven rows of teeth and as one front tooth is damaged or lost another moves forward to take its place.

The shark never sleeps. Unlike most fish, it has no air bladder and it must move constantly to avoid sinking. It is a primitive creature, unchanged for 60 million

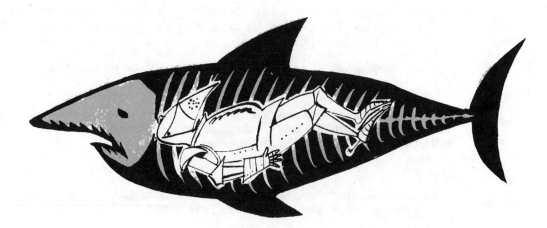

years of evolution. Its skin is without the specialized scales of a fish. Fully grown, it still has five pairs of separate gills like a three-week human embryo.

However, the shark is a brilliantly efficient machine. Its skin carries nerve endings which can detect vibrations from fish moving several miles away. Its sense of smell, the function of most of its brain, can detect one part in 600 000 of tuna fish juice in water or the blood of a fish or animal from a quarter of a mile away. It is colour blind and sees best in deep water, but it can distinguish shapes and patterns of light easily. Once vibration and smell have placed its prey, the shark sees well enough to home in by vision for the last 50 feet.

The shark eats almost anything. It will gobble old tin cans and broken bottles as well as fish, animals and humans. Beer bottles, shoes, wristwatches, car number plates, overcoats and other sharks have been found inside dead sharks. Medieval records tell of entire human corpses still encased in armour!

The United States military advice on repelling sharks is to stay clothed – sharks go for exposed flesh, especially the feet. Smooth swimming at the surface is essential. Frantic splashing will simply attract sharks and dropping below the surface makes the swimmer an easy target. If the sharks gets close then is the time to kick, thrash and hit out. A direct hit on the snout, gill or eyes will drive away most sharks. The exception is the Great White Shark. It simply kills you.

1 What evidence is supplied to show that sharks have been, and still are, a great danger to man? (About 80 words)

2 Write a brief letter to the press on the danger to bathers after a shark has been sighted about 15 miles offshore from an English seaside resort.

or

3 Write a brief reply from the chairman of the local hotels association, reassuring visitors. In each case, omit address and date.

(Answers, p. 179)

Other items on which you may be asked questions are: maps and diagrams (we provide examples of these), notices and advertisements.

Here is a notice at a hospital:

Applicants are requested to state the reasons for any exceptional treatment they require.
This says the same but more briefly:
Say why you need special treatment.

Now try your hand at improving these notices:

1   READ THIS

Civilian personnel will halt here and report their presence at the guard room. They will on no account proceed further till vetted and granted clearance by the security officer on duty. Offenders are warned that any failure to observe these regulations will result in detention and prosecution.

2 All drivers and visitors to the hospital are strictly forbidden to park in or on the verge of this road. Attention is drawn to the fact that a public car park is available in Avon Street.

3 In cases where the school day is terminated earlier than the normal time owing to the necessity to get pupils home before the onset of severe frost conditions, a careful note of the relevant circumstances must be made and transmitted to the Education Office at the earliest possible opportunity.

[From a circular to a country school.]

(Answers, p. 180.)

Much advertising is successful because it hits below the belt. That is to say, it flatters us or frightens us, or appeals to human characteristics and weaknesses, such as snobbery, greed, vanity, sex and the desire to be like other people. Here are half-a-dozen advertisements. Imagine yourself, or someone else, responding to four of them in the way you guess the advertisers wish. In each case say why a person might reply favourably to the advertisement. Pick out the key words.

(1) Speedicol is the first and only British manufacturer to make over 2 000 000 refrigerators – solid proof that they are the most popular choice in Britain today. Don't miss out on Speedicol!

(2) Don't be ashamed of your lavatory. Even in the cleanest home, harmful germs can multiply at an incredible rate. Why expose your family to unnecessary risks, when a bottle of Sann . . .

(3) *If you have two cars in your garage* . . . you'll enjoy the spaciousness, luxury, atmosphere and character of individually built-in furnishings by Chesterfield. The choice of top people.

(4) Girls of good taste go for Gloss, the rinse with the extra sheen that's guaranteed to transform any hair.

For Monday morning in the office or Thursday afternoon at Ascot, gleaming Gloss is the choice of girls who know. For all those occasions when a girl must look her best.

(5) Your good taste will tell you . . . Bluff's Beer is beer as it should be. Traditionally triple brewed from finest malt for extra flavour, it is diamond-clear, yet soft as velvet. True, Bluff's will cost you more than ordinary beers, but it's the appreciated choice of those who know.

(6) In this, the age of strain, you owe it to yourself to stay at the top. But as stress takes its toll, you begin to feel – and the boss notices it too – just a little under par, listless . . .

What you need is not a crude painkiller, but a pick-me-up with a built-in algocide to keep away the ache till the tonic your body demands begins to work. That, quite frankly, is why we want you to know about Nervax 172 . . .

(Answers, p. 180.)

FURTHER PRACTICE

Read the following piece on the household water supply.

The Domestic Water Supply

When you turn on a tap, you expect the water (hot or cold) to come out, and it nearly always does. However, it is as well to know something about the things that actually cause this to happen so that you can decide what to do on the millionth occasion when it doesn't.

As a rule, the householder's responsibility for the water arrangements begins at the point where the service pipe from the mains crosses the boundary of his land. There may be a stop-cock in the garden here, but if not there will certainly be a stop-cock or main tap just inside your house.

The usual place is under the kitchen sink, since the cold tap (for drinking water, etc.) here is connected to the rising cold main. When this stop-cock or main tap is turned off, no more water from the main will come into your house. Consequently it is the tap to make for and turn off if there is a burst anywhere. In many houses the cold water (drinking water) tap is taken direct from the incoming rising main, as it is called: this makes it easy to check whether you have found the right stop-cock and whether it is in working order or not. Simply turn on the cold-water tap and then screw down the stop-cock. The flow from the cold-water tap should quickly cease. If it does not, it may be because the stop-cock is defective or it may be (in the older houses) because the cold-water supply to the tap is taken from a storage cistern and not from the rising main. Whatever the reason, you must find out why the water still runs. You must stop the water in order to check it, so look for an external stop-valve that can be closed. If you can't discover one yourself ask the water company to send someone round to explain things.

Next in importance to the inside stop-cock is the 'draw-off' tap. Somewhere in your house is a tap which, if you turn it on after the stop-cock has been closed, will draw off all the water left in the rising cold-water main. This is often the cold-water tap at the kitchen sink. It is important to be able to do this, not only for full protection when the house is unoccupied in the winter, but also to enable repairs to be made.

The common water supply arrangements are usually as follows: there is a mains cold supply to the kitchen for cooking and drinking purposes, and to a storage tank or cistern in the loft. The storage tank supplies the cistern in the w.c. and also provides the cold water for the hot-water system, if any. The cold-water supply to bath and wash-basin is almost invariably taken from the storage tank and not direct from the main.

(From *The Awful Handyman's Book*, by J. Wheeler, Wolfe Publishing, London.)

Either (a) you have to explain how to turn off the water because you are going away for Christmas, or (b) a course for plumbing apprentices refers to: rising main; stop-cock; storage tank.
Make notes to explain the three terms accordingly.

(Answers, p. 180)

> Expression may be in a variety of modes such as . . . objective description or explanation of processes from knowledge and experience   (LEAG)

Additives Ban in Children's Food Urged

Seventy MPs have backed a motion urging the Government to ban unnecessary additives from foods liable to be consumed by children under five.

The MPs have called for an urgent government debate on additives, particularly Tartrazine, one of the most common artificial colouring agents, which has been banned from foods in Birmingham schools.

Two of the campaigners, Sir Geoffrey Johnson Smith, Conservative MP for Wealdon and Mr Michael Meadowcroft, Liberal MP for West Leeds, said that the Government could no longer ignore the growing evidence against additives.

'MPs are increasingly concerned about the effects of these additives, particularly

Tartrazine, on babies and young children,' Mr Meadowcroft said. 'The Government can start by removing all unnecessary additives from foods which children eat and more money must be spent on research.'

Nutritionists and consumer groups have campaigned against additives for the past nine years in Britain and there have been similar moves in Europe, the United States and Australia.

Last year leading supermarkets such as Tesco, Safeway and Sainsbury banned a wide range of additives, including Tartrazine, from their 'own-label' lines and other manufacturers have followed suit. But many products containing Tartrazine are still being sold.

Tartrazine, a yellow colouring from a group of synthetic chemicals called azo dyes, originally derived from coal tar, is suspected of affecting children's behaviour. Dieticians in Birmingham are studying other food additives to see if they should be banned from school foods after two reports published last week. Tartrazine leads a list of additives investigated by the London Food Commission during the past three years. According to a report published by the commission last October, a number of azo dyes are suspected of causing cancer.

Dr John Hunter, a consultant physician and gastro-enterologist at Addenbrookes Hospital, Cambridge, said that the Government should inject more money into research. 'Tartrazine is certainly harmful, but only in a small percentage of people. It has been shown to be related to hyperactivity in children, and other problems such as skin rashes, migraines and bowel upsets,' Dr Hunter said.

The Hyperactive Children's Support Group believes that at least one in 30 children in Britain is hyperactive. Mrs Vicky Colquhoun, its chairman, said, 'We have thousands of worried parents contacting us every month for advice on diet'. She also believes that pregnant women should eliminate unnecessary additives from their diet.

(From *The Times*, 30th June 1986.)

Your mother is on a committee that is worried about additives in children's food. You notice in a newspaper the heading of the news item above and show it to her. As she is very busy she asks if you would extract information on the following points and prepare a brief circular to parents:

–What is Tartrazine?
–Should it be used in children's diet?
–What has already been done?
–What more should be done?

(Answer, p. 180)

Writing Detective Stories

What about the business of throwing dust in the reader's eye? First, there is one rule the conscientious detective story writer never breaks: he is not required to tell you everything that goes on in the detective's or murderer's mind, but he must not conceal any material clue found by the detective. Apart from this pretty well anything goes in the great game of reader-baffling. If he is an artist as well as a craftsman, the writer will try to avoid irrelevant red herrings. This sounds like a contradiction in terms: but what I mean is that the false trails and misleading clues should all stem naturally from the story itself, not be superimposed upon it merely for the sake of deception. Whether they are material or psychological, these false clues and trails should be the result of the murderer's trying to shake off the detective, or of other suspects trying to conceal skeletons in their own cupboards, or of some apparently accidental turn of events which is nevertheless brought about by the main action.

Technically, the placing of genuine and false clues is perhaps the most fascinating part of a detective writer's work. A genuine clue–one, that is, pointing to the murderer–may be slipped in unobtrusively in a passage of dialogue or description: on the other hand, it may be positively hurled at the reader (this is double bluff) so that he is convinced it must be a false one, intended to mislead. Similarly a false clue is sometimes made to loom large, sometimes played down so that the warier type of reader may be induced to take the bait. There is always a danger of the detective novelist's being too clever: not too clever for his readers–this he should always aim to be–but too clever for his characters. It is absurd, for instance, if a suspect who has previously been shown as of only average intelligence should turn into a brilliant, audacious liar under police examination.

As with clues, so with the murderer himself. It is an unwritten law of detection-writing that he should be one of the more prominent characters in the story: you mustn't smuggle him in, halfway through, as an apparent supernumerary. But here again you can use bluff or double bluff on your reader: you can do everything to persuade him that X is innocent; or you can call attention to X, subtly yet persistently, so as to make the wary reader believe you *want* him to believe X is the murderer. On the whole, though, it is unwise to think a great deal about foxing the reader. Let X do his best to fox the police, and the reader will find himself perplexed enough.

The classic qualities of the detective novel proper are bafflement and suspense. If, when he gets to the end of the penultimate chapter, the reader is unable to pick out the murderer, or has been led to pick out the wrong suspect; and if, when he closes the book, he exclaims 'What a fool I am! Of course it was X. I should have seen it long ago'–then the writer has done a good job. But if, though baffled, the reader is also past caring *who* committed the crime, there has been a failure of suspense. The most effective method of maintaining suspense is to toss suspicion like a ball from one character to another, never allowing anyone to hold it too long: this game can only be played if each character has a practical motive, and/or appears at first not to be disqualified psychologically, for the given murder.

The pattern of a detective novel, which is something more than a mere puzzle, may resemble that of an inverted family tree: at first, a whole line of suspects; then a gradual elimination, until only two are left–the elimination being worked not only through factual evidence (Y couldn't have done it, because three independent witnesses saw him fifty miles away at the time of the murder), but also through psychological evidence (the reader arriving at the legitimate conclusion, 'However much appearances may be against him, I am now convinced that Z simply is not the sort of person who could have committed this particular crime'). In one of my books I made the experiment of eliminating all but two of my suspects some way before the end, and of throwing suspicion back and forth between these two for the rest of the story.

In real life, police investigation is a long-drawn, cumulative and undramatic affair, which would make tedious reading for any but a professional criminologist. In our novels, the detection process must be foreshortened and dramatised. For this purpose, certain conventions have become established–the multiple-killing convention, for instance.

It is uncommon for a real murderer to cover up his initial crime with further killings: multiple murders are nearly always the work of a homicidal maniac. Homicidal maniacs are barred from detective fiction, however, because its very existence depends upon a logic of cause and effect inconsistent with the schizophrenic personality. So detective writers lean–often, I think, too heavily–on the convention that a murderer will attempt further killings, in self-preservation.

On the credit side, this convention creates suspense, since the reader is always wondering which of the characters will be knocked off next; and it contributes to the essential element of fantasy. On the other hand, multiple killing may over-complicate the plot, is sometimes no more than a facile method of eliminating some of the suspects, and too often seems a confession of failure–failure to maintain excitement without infusions, so to say, of fresh blood.

This convention, however, was given an original twist in Agatha Christie's *The ABC Murders*. Here, a succession of apparently motiveless murders was committed, the victims being killed off in alphabetical order, the locale of each crime being announced beforehand by the murderer, and a copy of the railway ABC left beside each body. Since no connection could be established between any of them, the choice of victims appeared to be quite arbitrary and the murders were therefore assumed to be the work of a homicidal maniac with a bizarre sense of humour. The murderer got some way down the alphabet before he was stopped. But, in the final solution, it came out that the murderer had committed a number of motiveless murders in order to cover up the fact that, for one of the crimes, he had a perfectly good motive. *The ABC Murders* is a classic example of the pure detective novel–the novel, that is, in which an unbroken and absolutely reasonable thread of consequence has been spun from a wildly fantastic premise: it gives us make-believe carried to its logical conclusion.

(From 'School of Red Herrings', by Nicholas Blake in *Diversion*, edited by John Sutro, Macdonald and Jane's, London.)

Choose one of these questions:

1 Nicholas Blake is due to come to your school or organization to talk on 'Writing Detective Stories – Advice from an Expert', but is prevented by a sore throat. He sends you a copy of his talk and asks if you would read out a shortened version of about 200 words. Prepare this.

2 You are collecting first-hand accounts of writing methods for a project on 'How writers work'. Prepare a set of notes on detective story writing that will help you to write up your project.

(Answers, p. 181.)

Read the following passage carefully and then answer the questions set on it.

Compensation for Victims of Road Accidents

Everyone injured in a road accident will get compensation from an official fund, irrespective of who was to blame, if the Government adopts a recommendation in a Royal Commission report due this week.

The basis of the scheme is that, by amending the law to introduce 'no fault liability', someone injured in a road accident need no longer go to court to prove negligence in order to get compensation.

Under the present, much-criticized system, there are countless instances of cases that have taken years to come to court and of awards considered either ridiculously low or ridiculously high. The Loach case, reported in 1976, is one not unusual example. It followed a car crash on the M1 in May 1971, which killed Ken Loach's five-year-old son, seriously injured his wife and killed her 84-year-old grandmother, broke Loach's jaw, and emotionally injured his other small son. Everyone agreed that the accident was caused by a wheel falling off another car and that the Loaches were blameless. But, after five years of litigation, the family was left not only without any hope of compensation, but with a bill of nearly £1,000 for legal costs.

Under the Pearson scheme, compensation in all accident cases would be automatic, prompt and paid at regular intervals, as long as the victim needed it. Payments could be adjusted as the victim improved or deteriorated and also to take account of inflation.

The Commission's view is that the cost of the scheme should be borne by the motorist; there are two main ways the Government could collect the money. It could set up its own third party insurance office and make it compulsory for motorists to insure with it; or it could simply add a new tax to the price of petrol, on the ground that this would be the most equitable way of sharing the cost – because the more miles a motorist covers, the greater the risk of an accident.

The Government is expected to favour the second course because it would complement the energy conservation policy both by discouraging inessential motoring and making it more attractive for motorists to use smaller and more economical cars.

Opposition to the scheme will be led by organizations representing motorists and lawyers. Since it will no longer be necessary to sue for compensation, lawyers will lose a large and lucrative part of their business. It has been estimated that from one fifth to one third of all the money involved in the present accident compensation systems goes in lawyers' fees.

Motorists' organizations will see the Pearson recommendation as yet another blow to an already over-taxed section of the community. But the Government will view this protest against the fact that the cost to the country for caring for road accident victims is more than £400 million a year. Transferring some of that cost directly to the motorist would greatly relieve this burden on the National Health Service.

1 What, according to the writer, is the present procedure if one wishes to claim damages for injuries received in a road accident? **Use your own words.**

2 What changes are envisaged in the new recommendation?

3 After reading about the Loach case, what appear to you to be the faults in the present system?

4 How might the scheme be paid for?

5 Why does the Government prefer the second of these?

6 Outline the opening part of a letter to an MP from a motoring organization which opposes the scheme.

7 How might the Government answer this protest?

(Answers, p. 181)

Geo-thermal Unit

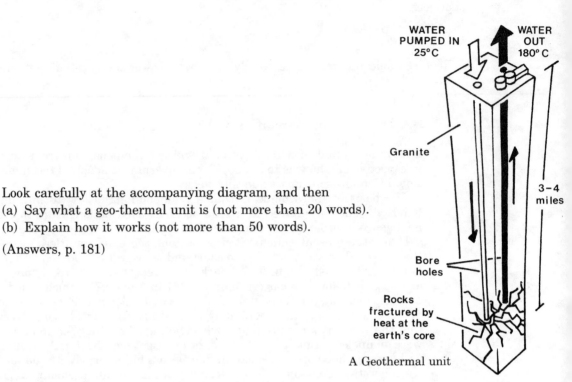

Look carefully at the accompanying diagram, and then
(a) Say what a geo-thermal unit is (not more than 20 words).
(b) Explain how it works (not more than 50 words).

(Answers, p. 181)

A Geothermal unit

The M25

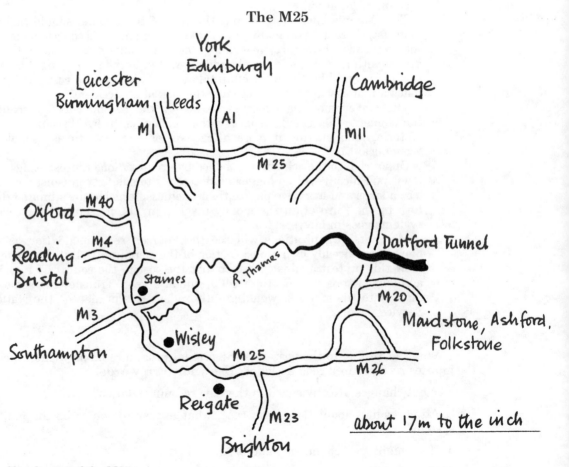

Sketch map of the M25

Consider the sketch map of the M25 and the accompanying news item and then answer the questions below.

(from specimen examination paper) Look carefully at Map A . . .   (SEG)

The Government faces bills of up to £500 million during the next 10 years to cope with serious overcrowding already evident on the M25 motorway even before it is finished.

Traffic on the £1000 million London orbital road has so exceeded ministry forecasts that on the busiest stretches it is running at up to 115 000 vehicles a day compared with an expected 75 000. This is causing daily queues several miles long and compares with an average of 40 000 vehicles on Britain's six-lane motorways and a design maximum of 85 000.

The M25 itself is a six-lane motorway throughout its 120-mile length, except for a short stretch near Heathrow where there are eight lanes and through the Dartford Tunnel, where there are four. This has already been shown to be a serious underestimate and substantial widening is essential unless the motorway is to become a massive bottleneck at peak times, driving traffic back on to the surrounding local roads it was intended to relieve, experts say.

Extra lanes are needed round the west and north-east sides, at a probable cost of £420 million in 1986 terms, £520 million in 1993 values. The most urgent needs are: Staines to Wisley, the busiest stretch of the entire motorway; the Dartford Tunnel, where traffic has already reached 85 000 vehicles a day, compared with a forecast of 60 000; A1 to M4; Leatherhead to Reigate; and M11 to M20: if the Channel Tunnel goes ahead, extra lanes will be needed.

1 What appears to have been the main purpose in building the M25? (10 words maximum)

2 Give instructions and any needed warnings to drivers wishing to travel
   (a) from Brighton to Cambridge, and
   (b) from Oxford to Ashford.

3 Why is there likely to be further heavy spending on the M25?

(Answers, p. 181)

The following passage is an extract from *Roadcraft*–the police drivers' manual. Read it carefully and answer the questions which are printed after it, using your own words as far as possible. Note that the numbering of the paragraphs is that used in the manual.

How Vision is Affected by Speed

6 Crowds of pedestrians can move about on the pavements of a busy shopping thoroughfare without colliding with one another, not so much because they are all the time looking out for obstructions, but mainly because their speed of movement is so slow that they can change their pace and direction in time to avoid collision. The length and breadth of their view may be short when they move slowly. If, however, one of them wishes to get along quickly he begins to look further ahead, to pick out the places where the crowd is thinnest and to direct his course and increase his speed accordingly. He then finds that his view of other pedestrians at close quarters deteriorates, so that quite often, if one of them comes into his path suddenly, he narrowly avoids collision.

7   The driver of a motor vehicle adjusts the length and breadth of his view in a similar way, but of course, over greater distances, because his speed is a good deal more than that of the pedestrian. When driving at 60 mph the focal point is a considerable distance ahead and stationary objects there appear clear and well defined, whereas the foreground becomes blurred. At this speed a distinct effort is required to pick out foreground details, and if more than occasional glances are directed at them there will be a natural tendency for the driver to reduce his road speed.

8   When road speed must be kept low owing to traffic conditions, the focal point naturally shortens and the driver observes details. These often indicate that a danger situation is developing and he then has time, owing to his slow speed, to take the precautions which will prevent him from becoming involved.

9   From this natural tendency of the eyes to focus according to speed, it is clearly dangerous to drive fast in the wrong places. If traffic is medium to heavy, foreground details must be seen, and to enable the eyes to do this and the brain to function as a result of the stimulus received, speed must be kept within reasonable limits.

10   Fatigue brought about by continuous driving over long periods is first felt as eye strain and lack of concentration, and although special efforts may be made by the driver to maintain his normal standard of observation, he will find the task becomes increasingly difficult, his speed will slacken and his recognition and assessment of danger situations become late and inaccurate.

1 Why do pedestrians not collide? (10-15 words.)

2 When, and in what way, is fast driving dangerous? (About 60 words.)

3 A traffic officer is going to give a talk to school leavers on 'What drivers need to know', using the manual quoted above. Set down the notes he made for the part of his talk taken from the extract quoted above.

(Answers, p. 182)

W5 ESSENTIAL SKILLS

5.1 Spelling

English spelling used to be much more free and easy than it is now. Great writers like Shakespeare did not bother about 'correctness' and Milton tended to spell phonetically, i.e. writing down words as they sounded, as in 'vigor', 'dout', and writing 'mee' when he wanted to emphasize the word 'me'.

Things are different now. When half a dozen newspapers selling millions daily all spell the same, we've come to think that spelling is standardized, so we accept only one form for most words. Therefore it's not surprising that some of us find we cannot remember how to spell every one of the 8000 words of an educated person's vocabulary. You won't need that number just yet, but if you need to improve your spelling you will certainly be able to get up to the standard expected in examinations. There are various methods to improve your spelling, all of which work well.

VISUAL MEMORY

If you see a word frequently, you tend to remember what it looks like; so take in the spelling of words on posters, television and newspapers. Reading aloud also helps, therefore take every opportunity of reading, for example to children and poorly-sighted people.

RULES

English has few rules, but many habits that are useful guides. For instance vowels (a,e,i,o,u and sometimes y) have long and short forms:

short	long
fat	fate
mat	mate
mop	mope
rat	rate
win	wine

Note how the added 'e' (on the right) lengthens the short vowels. But if you double the consonant after the first vowel, you make it short again: fatted, matted, winner. These changes are a matter of habit rather than absolute rules, because we can have the same spelling with different pronunciations: d*oll*y (short o), p*oll*ing (long o).

FAMILIES

Groups of words with something in common form themselves into families. Here are two examples of these families: the first groups share similar endings:

average, courage, damage, sausage, village,
captain, certain, curtain, fountain, mountain

And two groups with unsounded letters, c and h:

ascent, discipline, scene, scientist, scissors
ache, character, chemistry, scheme, stomach

There is more about these families and the ways they help in *Spelling and Punctuation* by D. Thompson (Oxford University Press). We mention two more families, the first because it helps to decide the spelling of 'two'. Link it with the rest of the 'tribe', all containing the idea of two: twain, twenty, twice, twin, twig (where a branch divides into two). Then, as an example, there is the 'fin' family of words: fine, final, finish, definite, infinite, etc. – all from the Latin 'finis' meaning 'end' or 'boundary'.

If the next group counts as a family, it is a quarrelsome one. Are these correctly spelled: receive, siege, believe, niece? There is a rule to decide whether they have IE or EI:

I before E

(except after C)

If the sound is Ee

Make sure which part of the rule settles the IE or EI in our four words and think why these words do not come under the rule: eight, feign, weight. There is an exception to the rule: **seize** hold of it!

BUILDING UP WORDS: AT THE FRONT

Additions at the beginning of words (prefixes) are usually made without alterations:

> dis +appear = disappear
>
> mis +spell = misspell
>
> anti+freeze = antifreeze
>
> ex +terminate = exterminate

When this leads to double letters, remember *why* they are doubled and you will never go wrong:

> dissatisfy, innocent, unnatural

When the addition of a prefix makes the new word difficult to say, we merge the awkward letters:

> ad+tract becomes attract
>
> con+lapse becomes collapse
>
> in+legal becomes illegal
>
> in+responsible becomes irresponsible
>
> When *all* is added to the front of a word and units with it, it loses an *l*:
>
> almost   already   although   altogether   always

But – for no good reason whatever – we are not allowed to join *all* and *right*. We must write them as separate words.

BUILDING UP WORDS: AT THE END

The commonest additions (called suffixes) are *ing* and *ed*; and with most people the right changes become a matter of habit. Note the dropping of the *e*:

> bite+ing becomes biting
>
> drive+ing becomes driving
>
> write+ing becomes writing

And note the double letter when *ed* or *ing* is added:

> begin+ing becomes beginning
>
> excel+ing becomes excelling
>
> run+ing becomes running
>
> occur+ed becomes occurred
>
> propel+ed becomes propelled
>
> transmit+ed becomes transmitted

The doubling makes sure of the pronunciation and takes the stress: beGINNing, transMITTed. But if the syllable before the *ed* is not stressed, there is no doubling. In these words the stress is on the first syllable:

> benefited
>
> bracketed
>
> frightening

These changes are made as a matter of habit, rather than by an absolute rule; there are some exceptions.

er, or, ise The doer of an action is usually expressed by adding er: adviser, runner, scanner. However a number of words coming from Latin or French end in *or*: accelerator, radiator, supervisor, tractor.

Civilise or civilize? realise or realize? Either will do.

Plural forms

-y to -i	babies	territories		
-y kept	alloys	chimneys	donkeys	valleys

The letter before the -y decides the plural:
vowel = no change; consonant = change to -i.

-f to -ves	calves	knives	lives	shelves	wives
-fs	chiefs	proofs	reliefs	roofs	
-oes	potatoes	tomatoes	mosquitoes	cargoes	volcanoes
-os	commandos	curios	dynamos	photos	radios solos

The -os endings tend to be fairly recent additions to the language.

THE AWKWARD SQUAD

Below is a list of commonly misspelled words. In most of them the difficulty vanishes when you think about them. 'Believe' for example follows the I before E rule; 'certain' and 'definite' need to be linked with their families; get the pronunciation of 'separate' and 'similar' perfect. Long words like 'incidentally' and 'independent' must be said syllable by syllable, preferably aloud. Do not try to learn the list by heart. Take four or five at a time, and think why they are spelled as they are.

accidentally	gauge	quarrelling
accommodation	government	quietly
across		
address	happened	receive
affect	height	recognize
appearance		recommend
approach	immediate	
	incidentally	safety
beautiful	independent	science
beginning	interrupt	sense
believe		separate
	knowledge	stopped
cemetery		studying
certain	leisurely	succeed
changeable	library	
committee	lose	their
conceivable		there
	manner	
definite	medicine	until
desperate	minute	usually
develop		
disappointed	necessary	vegetable
	noticeable	
effect		weather
embarrassing	obedient	whether
everyone	occurred	whose
except		woman
existence	parallel	worrying
	people	writing
February	possession	
finally	precede	you're
fulfil	privilege	

FINAL HINTS

Mnemonics (pronounced 'neemonix') are jingles and easily remembered sentences. Make them up to fix the spelling of awkward words: Compa*rat*ively free from rats; acco*mm*odation is in double rooms; don't *lose* your nose dose.

Pronunciation helps with words like: athletic, business, competition, fuel, naturally, remember, surprise.

Syllabication does too: knock the stuffing out of long words by saying them aloud, syllable by syllable: environmentally, hospitalization, intercontinental, semi-articulated vehicles, telecommunication.

Look, cover, say

1 Write the word down and look at it
2 Say it aloud; repeat, bringing out the syllables
3 Cover it
4 Write it down; check for accuracy.

Revision, little and often, is a great help.
Persevere and you will succeed.

5.2 Mind the Stop

Here are some words spoken casually to a friend:

I went into the town to do some shopping, and met Jean coming back – she'd gone early to avoid the crush.

In turning the sounds into signs on paper we have used three marks of punctuation:

.	full stop	at the end, to show the speaker had finished.
,	comma	to mark the pause between two connected statements: 'I went . . .' and '. . . met Jean . . .'
–	dash	because the speaker broke off to explain the second statement straightaway, before continuing.

For hundreds of years after the invention of writing there were no punctuation marks and no difference between capital and ordinary letters. Readers had to supply their own, so reading was a slow process and most people had to read aloud. Alfred the Great used a pointer to keep his place and when one man (St Ambrose) took to reading silently, people came from far away to see him. We now use punctuation to show how the *parts* of a sentence fit into the *whole*, how the words were spoken and how fast or slowly the speaker went. If the writing has never been heard, punctuation tells us how a passage should be read.

PAUSES; SOUNDS OF SURPRISE! A QUESTIONING TONE?

These are the kinds of thing punctuation was invented to deal with. Now that writing is no longer restricted to specialists, punctuation is indispensable. It helps the reader to understand more exactly what is written. It helps the writer to put his thoughts and ideas in order.

After a reasonable amount of practice in reading and writing, most people punctuate almost automatically. If you feel uncertain where to use punctuation, try first saying aloud what you want to write (with the 'voice' inside your head if you are in an examination) and notice where you pause, and why.

PRACTICE

Use a tape recorder. Describe something straightforward – the cat settling down to sleep, the wind, your clothing – for not more than a minute. Then write down what you said, putting punctuation where you paused or changed your pace or tone. Check your written version by following it closely during a playback of your recording. Another way of checking is to give your script to a friend who is willing to read it into a tape recorder; then compare the two recorded versions.

MARKS OF PUNCTUATION

Full stops

These punctuation marks are the most important of all; get them rightly placed and you will not go far wrong. They come after any complete unit of expression: a sentence or sentences, even a single word. Anything that follows such full stops must start with a capital letter. They are also used after abbreviations: etc., O.B.E.; but in modern usage the full stop is commonly dropped when an abbreviation consists only of capital letters: UK, BBC, GCSE. When the abbreviation ends with the same letter as the complete word, as in Dr, Mr, etc. there is no need for a stop.

Commas

● divide a sentence so as to make it easy to take in and understand. (There are plenty of examples in this book.)

● separate the items in a list: Shoes, socks, shirts, jeans and an anorak. Note that *and* replaces the comma between the last two items.

● used in pairs, they mark off words or phrases or quotations: 'Stamford, formerly on the Great North Road, has become quieter since the by-pass.'

N.B. Commas must not be used between two separate statements, unless they are linked by a conjunction:

1 Mum has a filthy cold, *so* she spent the day in bed. (RIGHT)
2 Mum had a filthy cold, she spent the day in bed. (WRONG)

Semi-colons

These are used between statements which are complete in themselves, but deal with the same subject. We could have used them instead of commas in the examples immediately above. Here is another example from a Science Fiction story:

. . . around her, the Machine hummed eternally; she did not notice the noise, for she had been born with it in her ears.

Colons

These are often placed before lists, quotations and examples:
If you're taking the Pennine Way, you'll need at least the following: a really good map, a compass, a sleeping bag, a torch and an emergency ration quite separate from your food for the day.

Colons mark a close connection (but not close enough to justify the use of a semi-colon) between two sentences that might otherwise be separated by a full stop. The second sentence is often an expansion of the first.

An old rule about these four stops can still act as a rough guide to their relative 'value': one for a comma, two for a semi-colon, three for a colon, and four for a full stop.

We have given the standard rules for these marks of punctuation because examiners expect candidates to follow them. Some professional writers punctuate in a very personal way, but our advice is to follow the rules.

Question marks

These are placed after direct questions:
I asked him whether he was coming to the sale.
   'I don't know yet,' he replied. 'Will you be there?'

There are two questions here, but only one is direct, so only one question mark is needed. In the piece below there are three questions, but only one requires a question mark. Which one?

It was difficult to decide what to wear. Would I look out of place in a long dress. I asked Jean what she would be wearing, but she had no more idea than I had.

Exclamation marks

These (sometimes nicknamed 'shriek marks!') indicate tone and are effective if they are used rarely and *one at a time*! They are like full stops in that the word after an exclamation mark must start with a capital letter.

The Dashes

● act like brackets, placed round an insertion into a statement:
There was no one about—we'd forgotten it was Boxing Day—and we couldn't find a garage open anywhere.

● indicate a surprise or abrupt change:
We thought someone was ill in the next room—but it was only an owl, snoring on the chimney top.

Below are: a plain statement, a surprising statement and one that is both surprising and alarming. How do you know from the punctuation which is which?

1 I opened my briefcase, but the money was not there.
2 I opened my briefcase – but the money was not there.
3 I opened my briefcase – but the money was not there!

Hyphen

This is not really a mark of punctuation. It is a short dash used to link words that are thought of as one word; red-hot poker, happy-go-lucky. If the words can be united (wheelbarrow, classroom) it is neater to do so. A good dictionary will decide. If the word means the same without a hyphen, do without.

Quotation marks

These are also called 'inverted commas'. Single quotes ('. . .') are now commoner than double (". . ."). They are normally placed outside the punctuation – the comma and full stop in the following examples:

'It's time we started,' Robert remarked.

An ancient proverb is: 'Early to bed and early to rise makes a man healthy, wealthy and wise.'

The mark (') is also called an apostrophe when it:

● indicates an abbreviation: can't, I've, they're.
Think why the repeated word is correct in: It's lost its bone.

● indicates possession. With singular words the apostrophe + s is added, as in: Jennifer's handbag. With plural words, the method is to put the apostrophe after the s that shows the word is plural: employees' cars only, visitors' entrance.

But when, as in a very few old English words, the plural ends with n (men, women, children) an apostrophe + s is added: women's shoes, etc.

PUNCTUATION FOR DIRECT SPEECH

In writing, *direct speech* is the term given to a written version of words actually spoken, for instance in a conversation that is part of a story. The rules already given for quotation marks are the most important things to remember, but there are one or two additional points worth making. Layout and punctuation are fairly standard, the aim being to make the passage easy and unambiguous to read.

The best way to revise speech punctuation methods is to look closely at examples ready to hand, and check your own writing from them. Almost any printed work of fiction will do for this. For our example here we need go no further than the story on p. 40.

River Afternoon

'D'you want to go home?' she asked.
'We only just got here.'
'If you didn't want to fish we could bathe. It's hot.'
'It's too bloody bright; we need a bit of wind. If you hadn't have shouted at me up there – I nearly had a bite –'
'It's no fun if you can't talk.'
'You better bloody go home then.'
A bathe, she thought, A lovely cool bathe.
'Hey, look,' said Peter, 'there's that big 'un again!'
'He's too wily; you'll never catch him.'
'Want to bet?'
She clenched her fists and stared at the line . . .

Points to note:

● Other marks of punctuation *inside* the closing quotation marks at the end of a speech, e.g. *. . . home?' . . . a bite –' . . . that big 'un again!'*

● Change of paragraph for each change of speaker, however short the speech.

● Words indicating who the speaker is – *she asked, said Peter* – only put in when necessary to avoid confusion. When it is obvious who is speaking, leave them out. In this extract the change of paragraph makes it clear most of the time.

● Notice how the punctuation is placed when a speech is interrupted in order to indicate the speaker: *'hey, look,' said Peter, 'there's* . . . (Here an exclamation mark could have been placed after *look*, but the writer chose to save it for the end of Peter's remark.) The comma after *look* comes before the quotation marks; *said* has a small letter, because it is within a sentence, not starting a fresh one. Similarly *there's* has a small letter, being a continuation of Peter's remark. Without the interruption it would have read: *'*. . . *look, there's that big 'un again!'*

With practice and with constant careful checking of your writing, punctuation, even of speech, soon becomes automatic.

5.3 Grammar and Usage

Grammar is the word used for the study of words and the rules that apply to their working. It includes the parts of speech, the way words change or inflect their forms and how these forms are used and the combining of words into sentences. Here are some examples of inflexions:

he	him	she	her	they	them
do	does	doing	did	done	
happier	happier	happiest	happily		

Because any living language is constantly in use it is bound to be constantly changing— growing, developing, shedding words and adding new ones, responding to the changing demands made on it by its users. For this reason, no account of the grammar of a living language can ever be complete and final. (For this we need what is called a 'dead' language, like Latin.) The rules are always changing and what was marked wrong yesterday will pass today.

SOME USEFUL GRAMMATICAL TERMS

Parts of Speech

In traditional grammar this is the term for the eight types of word usage. Here they are, with examples:

noun	chair house idea London
pronoun	I you ourselves
adjective	comfortable (chair) big (house) bright (idea) busy (London)
verb	hear explore agree be
adverb	(hear) clearly quite (busy) sometimes (agree) well (done!)
preposition	at in with
conjunction	and but although if
interjection	hullo ah

These terms relate to *the way words are used* rather than to the words in isolation. Often the same word is used in different ways:

The magistrate may *fine* you. (verb)

I've paid my *fine*. (noun)

He soon acquired a *London* accent. (adjective)

London has several theatres. (noun)

Adjective or adverb?

Adjectives help (or qualify) nouns and pronouns. Adverbs help (or modify) verbs, adjectives and other adverbs. The *-ly* ending is a common way to form adverbs from adjectives, but look at these:

real adj./*really* adv.
loud adj. or adv./*loudly* adv.

You look real smart. (WRONG) ('Smart' is an adjective, and needs the adverb 'really' to modify it.)
'Am I talking too loud?' 'No, I like loud voices.' (RIGHT)
(The first 'loud' is an adverb, the second an adjective.)

Subject, Object, Main Verb

The miner (subject) strikes (main verb) one (object) of his few remaining dry matches with extreme caution.

There must be a main verb in every complete sentence and the verb agrees with the subject. If the sentence above had *miners* the verb would become 'strike'.
Pronouns change their form (inflect) according to their job in a sentence:

Nominative I he she we   I shot the albatross
He/She was making cakes   Are we too soon?
Accusative me him her us   He hit me. (etc.)

VERBS

Present, Past and Future

These are different forms of **verbs**:

I *make/am making* bread (present)
I *made/was making* bread (past)
I *shall make* bread   (future)

Active and Passive

This concerns the way **verb** and **subject** are related:

	bites	
The dog	*bit*	the man. (active)
	will bite	

	is bitten	
The man	*was bitten*	by the dog. (passive)
	has/had been bitten	
	will be bitten	

Transitive and Intransitive

Verbs are said to be transitive when their action or state is transmitted to an **object** (which will be a noun, pronoun or its equivalent):

He *was driving* the car. (transitive, 'the car' being the object)
The great day *has come*. (intransitive)

Some verbs are used both transitively and intransitively, e.g.:

That girl *plays* the trumpet. (transitive)
That girl *plays* happily by herself. (intransitive, the words after the verb being adverbial)

Agreement

1 However extended the sentence may be, subject and main verb must always agree:

The old fellow, silver-haired and decrepit, and his daughter, well-known locally for her skill as a tennis player, *was* seen enjoying the morning sunshine. WRONG
(The sentence should read '*were* seen' because there are two subjects, 'fellow' and 'daughter'.)

Sometimes the subject word refers to a collection or group (e.g. committee, board, team, herd). If they form a single unit the verb is singular:
The team is (*not* are) flying to Moscow for the Olympic Games.

If the context makes it clear that they are a number of individuals, the verb is plural:
The committee *were* a long time making up *their minds* about the candidate. (The plural must then apply throughout.)

2 In any continuous writing tenses of verbs should agree:
When I *arrived* (past) he *greeted* me warmly and *took* my coat.

Every time I *sleep* (present) here I *feel* uneasy, although the proprietor *does* all he *can* to make me comfortable.
(See the notes on *Direct and Indirect Speech* opposite.)

3 *This/that* (singular) *these/those* (plural)
Make sure that you are consistent:

This thing is ⎱
These things are ⎰ obvious. RIGHT

These kind of things always cause trouble. WRONG

This kind ⎱ of thing always ⎰causes trouble.
These kinds ⎰ ⎱cause trouble. RIGHT

4 *Anybody anyone everyone nobody no one none nothing*
All these words (and others like them) are singular, and should be followed appropriately:

No one *is* expected to wash up today.
If anybody *makes* a move, I'll shoot.
None of the people here *is* too fat.

(The last example may sound unnatural; the plural words 'people' makes the ear expect a plural verb.)

Everyone in the plane had *his* hands up.

(The problem here is that 'everyone' may include both male and female. If the sentence begins to sound awkward it is best to change the wording, e.g. 'They all had their hands up.')

FURTHER POINTS OF GRAMMAR

Pronoun Inflexions

1 Linked pronouns can sometimes cause confusion:
You and I (=we) *are* invited.   RIGHT
('I' is in the nominative because it is the subject.) *But*
They asked you and I to come.   WRONG
Here 'you and –' forms the object, so the accusative is needed:
They asked you and me (=us) to come.   RIGHT

2 Pronouns following a preposition are in the accusative:
Between *you and me*, I think he is a liar.   RIGHT

3 *Who* (nominative)/*whom* (accusative)/*whose* (possessive)
The accusative 'whom' can sound pedantic and is used less often nowadays than it used to be, e.g. *Who did you want?* sounds better than *Whom did you want?* even though as the object it should be in the accusative.

Comparison of Adjectives and Adverbs

Many adjectives and adverbs have different forms for *comparing* two people, things or states (**comparative**), and for the *highest* degree (**superlative**):

	comparative	*superlative*
happy	happier	happiest
miserable	more miserable	most miserable
good	better	best

1 It is wrong to double the comparative:
I couldn't be more happier.   WRONG

2 Some adjectives and adverbs, because of their meaning, have no comparative or superlative degrees, e.g. *unique* (it is impossible to be more unique than unique).

Other Doubles

1 Negatives: He never gave me no book.   WRONG
(Logically this means he *did* give a book.)

2 Past Tense: I would have loved to have gone.   WRONG
I would have loved to go.   RIGHT

3 'The reason is because . . .'   WRONG
The word 'because' itself contains the idea of 'reason'. The correct form is *either* 'the reason is that . . .' *or* 'because . . .'.

Direct and Indirect (Reported) Speech

Because any language starts and is sustained by its spoken (oral) forms, we find the need to record speech in various ways when we write. In stories or narrative essays, which are often the easiest kinds of continuous writing in examinations, two chief ways are used.

This short piece came from a paperback version of a popular television series. Jamieson, a detective, has been hiding on board a berthed ship, listening to a group of criminals.

> As he neared the outside vent, he reminded himself that he ought to be thankful he had at least overheard the plotters, even though he couldn't see them. It was the first break of any kind he had gotten* in three weeks of investigation. He emerged from the shaft without being seen, screwed the wire mesh cover back in place and hurried to join his work crew. When the quitting whistle blew at five-thirty, there was a general exodus from the dock area. Jamieson headed for a nearby pay phone. He dialled, then asked for an extension number.
>
> 'Dobey,' a male voice said.
>
> The undercover officer said, 'Jamieson here, Captain. Glad I caught you before you left.'

Here are alternative ways of writing three parts of the extract:

1 ... he reminded himself that he ought to be thankful he had at least overheard the plotters, even though he couldn't see them.
(**Alternative**) *'I ought to be thankful,' he said to himself, 'I have at least overheard them. Pity I couldn't see their faces, though.'*

2 He dialled, then asked for an extension number.
(**Alternative**) *He dialled. 'Put me through to extension 34, please.'*

3 The undercover officer said, 'Jamieson here, Captain. Glad I caught you before you left.'
(**Alternative**) *After giving his name, Jamieson told the captain he was glad he had caught him before he left.*

What we have done is to change a report of the words into the actual words thought or spoken (1 and 2), and vice versa (3). It is useful to have both these methods at your fingertips. In general, indirect speech is more formal, less lively than direct speech. Notice how it works. Indirect speech doesn't need the quotation marks needed for direct speech. Other changes are:

		direct	*indirect*
(*a*) Verbs change tense	1	I have	he had
	2	Put me ...	he asked
	3	I caught	he had caught
(*b*) Pronouns change	4	I caught you	he caught him

(*Note* Because both first and second person pronouns change to third person, you need to make sure that no confusion arises, e.g. 'He told him that he thought he was coming with him.' This could mean EITHER 'I thought you were coming with me.' OR 'I thought I was coming with you.' To avoid confusion you may need to use nouns: 'He told John that he thought he, Peter, was coming with him.'

		direct	*indirect*
(*c*) Colloquial turns of phrase are avoided	1	Pity I ...	–
	2	Put me through	asked for

(*d*) References to time are changed (e.g. today/that day; tomorrow/the next day etc.)

(*e*) 'this' becomes 'that' etc.

Practice

Try it for yourself on the story *River Afternoon*. Use the part which begins on p. 41 (see p. 182 for the rest of our version):

'You ought to hold it still.'   She said that he ought to hold it still.
'I know what I'm doing ...'   He retorted that he knew what he was doing ...

STYLE

We talk of a friend's *style* in clothes. More generally, we may say 'I like her style', meaning her way of carrying herself, choosing what clothes suit her best, how she will face the world each day. 'Now, that boy (or girl) has real style!' Here we are concerned as much with *personality* as with clothes or appearance. We often hear the expression 'lifestyle'. In this term the ideas we have already noticed are drawn together, so that we see a person's whole way of life as an expression of his or her individual personality.

Style is a useful term to describe writing and the idea of style can, once we have fully grasped it, help with our own writing. Here too it starts with personality – the writer's personality, his individual outlook and his particular reasons for writing. The style of a piece of writing is the *way* in which a writer gives written expression to what he has to say. But it goes further than this: because *how* he writes depends on two other factors: *content* (i.e. what is to be said) and *audience* (i.e. who the writing is for).

* *Note* 'gotten' is American usage. British English-speakers would use 'got'.

An example

A report written for a scientific journal on rainfall and flooding in a particular area will be written in a different style from a journalist's eyewitness account of the same floods in the local paper. A flood victim's letter to his relatives abroad would be in a different style again.

In all those three cases the writer adapts the way he or she writes to suit his or her audience and the particular circumstances. We do the same in our own speech and writing; we try to choose the most effective *manner* of speaking. This is sometimes called the *register* we employ.

When it comes to English for examination purposes, register is an important matter. If you are writing a story, slang and colloquialisms may be needed in the direct speech, but should be avoided in the background narrative. In *River Afternoon* the girl, holding the tin of bait, says 'Yuk!...ugh, horrible!' but the adjective used to describe the maggots is not 'yukky' but 'nauseating'.

In conversation we may use the expression 'dead nice' to express approval, but it would add less than nothing to a description of a dress, a book or a person in a written essay. 'Moan' is a popular alternative to 'complain'; it might fit into a conversation in a story. But no examiner would like to read that Juliet 'moaned' when Romeo was banished, or that Heathcliff (in *Wuthering Heights*) was 'a bit of a moaner'.

It is not always slang that is inappropriate. An examination candidate once wrote that Macbeth was 'upset' after the murder of King Duncan (which he had in fact committed himself). The word is too feeble; 'appalled' comes nearer to the scale of Macbeth's feelings.

Peter, in *River Afternoon,* is quarrelling with the girl for disturbing the fish by throwing stones. His feelings boil up, and lead to his order: '. . . keep your hands in your bloody pockets.' The swearword here is a fitting measure of his anger, but earlier in the story, even before the quarrel, he uses it frequently. Why? What does it tell us about him? In what sense is it *appropriate* in the context of the story?

A word of warning finally: however friendly you feel – or want them to think you feel! – towards the examiners, avoid too personal and chatty an approach. Here are three openings that make this mistake and would earn poorer marks as a result.

The Funfair
Ever been on the Big Wheel? No? You don't know what you're missing! . . .

Childhood Fears
I was a bit of a coward as a child really. I don't usually like admitting it but you won't tell anyone, will you?

The Waxworks
You go in through this doorway that looks real spooky . . .

Only *practice* will allow you to develop your own style, but we can give you some helpful hints to follow and show you how others succeed or fail in finding good writing style.

DO'S AND DON'TS

Things to do	Things to avoid
1 Try to be brief, simple and sincere.	Avoid longwindedness and affectation.
2 Take trouble always to choose the right word.	Steer clear of commonplace words and phrases and of clichés.
3 Keep your sentences clear in construction and use active verbs where there is a choice.	Avoid clumsy or confused sentence structure; avoid excessive use of passive verbal constructions.
4 Aim for variety of construction between one sentence and the next.	Avoid making your writing monotonous; beware of repeated sentence patterns.

All the following examples were written by 15- and 16-year-olds, in answers to examination questions.

Confused sentence structure (3)

I was to be one of the noisy gossips in the opera, a character that did not cause me great difficulty in putting forward, according to my father!

Commonplace words and phrases (2)

June 4th *dawned bright* with *not a cloud in the sky*, but just after midday, when preparations were *in full swing*, dark clouds *raced across the sky* and the wind picked up tremendously. (The only memorable group of words in this example is 'the wind picked up tremendously'.)

Monotonous sentence patterns (4)

Local factories usually prepare floats on which their employees can enter the Carnival, schools prepare floats, Brownies prepare floats, Guides prepare floats, and so the list goes on . . .

Affectation (1)

A fleecy cloud, a rich ploughed field . . . We have been moved by the beauty of spinning, dancing toes, we have touched St Paul's with reverence, and laughed at the audacity of the wind.

(In spite of the writer's grasp of *vocabulary* this is affected, insincere writing. It does not ring true; the writer is trying to make us have feelings that are faked.)

Longwindedness (1)

The stately home was much more restricted; the course for you to take was plotted out, there were people watching you continuously, although I realize that this was to make sure nothing was stolen. Only certain areas were open to the public, and these were specially picked, decorated and furnished in a way to make people interested. Nothing there was really surprising and if I went again it would probably be almost exactly the same.

Brevity (1)

The pit is a way of life . . . hot, dry, dusty summers and dreary winters.

(These two examples of brevity are taken from an essay about a coal mine. They are dramatically economical compared with the previous example. Not a word is wasted.)

Simplicity (2)

Coal has been tipped in the gutter and left so you can't get in the gate until Joe comes to shift it.

(From the same essay. Look how much we are told in these 20 words: that coal has been tipped in the gutter; that it shouldn't have been left there because it obstructs the gate; that people using the gate will have to wait for a man to shift it; that the man is called Joe, and it is his job to shift the coal.)

The right word (2)

The air was damp with spray from the firemen's hoses, which lay across the road *like spaghetti*.

Passive verbal constructions (3)

Saturday is when most people do things they would be too idle to do on a Sunday. Lawns are mowed and gardens are dug; most of the shopping is normally done on a Saturday.

(The passive verbs *'are mowed'*, *'are dug'*, *'is done'* take away from the purposefulness and continuity of the Saturday activities.)

Active verbs, varied sentence structure (3)

'That'll make you my boss then, won't it?' said David, and he walked over to the big red fire-engine, leaving Daniel alone with his thoughts.

(Here the writer wants to keep the initiative with David. The active verbs help him to do so. It is David who spoke, walked, left Daniel.)

BEGINNINGS AND ENDINGS

The opening sentence of a piece of writing has to attract the reader's attention, interest and curiosity. Here are four good examples:

- A crowd of people had turned out to watch the blazing building.
- The pit is a way of life.
- The trouble began when the masters started getting a £10 bonus for each boy who passed the exam.
- As I look back on that night I still shudder with fear.

Each of these clearly refers to the main subject of the essay. Each leaves the writer free to develop this primary idea, without confusing it with others less important. Now look at this opening sentence to an essay entitled *A Day to Remember*:

We had all been looking forward to this day for a long time, not only the young ones, but also the older ones who may have taken part in similar occasions before.

'We', 'this day', 'young ones', 'older ones', 'similar occasions' – there are too many loose ends here. Only the first two were in fact developed in the essay that followed. A better opening might have been

> We had all been looking forward to this day for a long time.

The reader thinks 'what day?'. The writer has left himself free to develop the subject as it suits him; he may answer the reader's question, or leave it and first describe his anticipation of the day, or the preparation, keeping the reader guessing for a while.

● Keep your opening sentence simple and clear. *Don't* introduce ideas that you cannot, or don't want to follow up.

Your closing sentence needs to round off the piece of writing. It must not start any new ideas. It is often possible to draw together the main ideas in the piece of writing. The closing sentence can refer back to the opening, or to the piece's title. The writer of *A Day to Remember* ended better than he began, like this:

> The dancing continued until twelve o'clock, when everyone returned home happy and contented that we had all made this a day that we would remember.

5.4 Using a Dictionary

Anyone who is serious about improving his or her English should own a dictionary. Most bookshops stock some good ones such as:

The Pocket Oxford Dictionary (Oxford University Press)
Chambers Twentieth Century Dictionary (R. and W. Chambers)
The Heinemann English Dictionary (Heinemann Educational Books)

A dictionary supplies a great deal of information: what part of speech a word is; its spelling, pronunciation, main meanings and sometimes its derivation. It also gives the meanings of various special uses; under 'dog' for instance, you will learn the meaning of 'dog in the manger' and other 'dog' expressions.

Here is a Heinemann entry that concentrates on the main meanings and is spaciously set out.

> **particular** (*say* partik-yoolar) *adjective*
> 1. relating to one person, group, of thing rather than to all: 'in this *particular* case I have no sympathy for the accused'.
> 2. special: 'she is a *particular* friend of mine'.
> 3. careful or attentive to details: 'she is very *particular* about what she eats.
> **particular** *noun*
> a point: 'you are correct in every *particular*'.
> in **particular,** '*in particular* I think the photography in the film was excellent'
>
> (= especially).
> *Word Family:* **particularly,** *adverb,* especially; **particularity** (*say* partik-yoo-larra-tee), *noun* **particularize, particularise,** *verb,* to mention or deal with separately or in detail.
>
> **particularism** *noun*
> an exclusive concern for one's *own* interests, etc.
> *Word Family:* **particularist,** *noun, adjective.*

And here is another, from *The Pocket Oxford Dictionary*. It gives more information, especially examples, but has to pack it in more tightly.

> **partic′ūlar,** 1. adj. Relating to one as distinguished from others, peculiar, (*whatever his p. hobby may be*); considered apart from others, individual, (*this p. tax is no worse than others*); worth notice, special, (*took p. trouble; for no p. reason*); minute (*a full & p. account*); scrupulously exact; fastidious (*about, what* or *as to what* one eats &c.); in *p.*, especially (*mentioned one case in p.*). 2. n. Detail, item (pl.) detailed account. **partic′ūlarism** n., exclusive devotion to a party, sect, &c., principle of leaving political independence to each State of an empire &c.; **partic′ūlarist** n. **particū′lă′ritў** n., (esp.) fullness of minuteness of detail in description. **partic′ū′larīze** v.t. &. i. (*-zable*), mention one by one, name individually, go into pp.; **particūlarīză′tion** n. **partic′ūlarlў** adv., (esp.) very (*am particularly, not particularly, sorry to hear it*), to an especial extent (*they are very poisonous, & particularly when green*), in detail (*cannot go into it particularly now*), in p. (*generally & particularly*). [PART]

To get in so much, it uses abbreviations (adj. for adjective, n. for noun. pl. for plural), numbers and signs and different styles of type. Such items are explained at the beginning of the dictionary.

TO FIND THE WORD YOU WANT

The words are arranged in alphabetical order, so that

bit come before **bite**
fascinate comes before **fascism**

In the first example it is the fourth letter of the second word that decides. But in the second it is the sixth letter that decides.

Practice

Set out the following words in the order they would appear in a dictionary.

impediment	impassive	impetuous	impenetrable
impasse	impeach	impartial	imperial
impetigo	impel	impedance	impetus

Check your order by your dictionary; all the words appear on two successive pages. If you find you are slow at this, work with a friend.

The difference between the sound of a word and its spelling may cause trouble: 'pneumonia' sounds as if it begins with 'new'. Here are a dozen of these misleading frontal sounds:

ek	eccentric	new	knew, pneumonia
fiz	physical, physics	nyf	knife
fo	phone, photo	on	honest
jel	jealous	ri	wrist, write
kem	chemist	sin	cinema, synthetic
kw	quality, quick, etc.	sy	science, psychology
nay	neighbour	way	weight

Dictionaries help you to find what you want by printing guide words at the top of each page – the first and the last words:

plant	plaster	plastic	platinum

If you are looking for 'planetarium' you know you have gone too far, because 'e' comes before 't'. You are in the right place for 'plateau' ('te' before 'ti'), but if you want 'platypus' turn over.

Combined words are given under the main part. In this list the part in italics shows you where to find them in the *Chambers Twentieth Century Dictionary*:

*bar*maid	invisible *imports*	*parallel* bars
faith-healer	*level*-crossing	special *pleading*

Sometimes, when both parts of a word are prominent, it will appear under each part. If in doubt, look up both; *universal joint* appears in Chambers under both parts, but is more fully explained under *joint*.

Practice

Look up: bookworm, cheese-mite, song-thrush.

HOW TO USE WORDS

Some words are very versatile. For instance, the simple word 'plant' has at least five meanings as a noun, and six as a verb. A dictionary will sort them out, usually numbering the meanings 1, 2, 3 etc. This makes cross-referencing easier if the word is referred to elsewhere in the dictionary.

Most dictionaries will tell you what part of speech the word is; or, if it can be used in different ways, will indicate the parts of speech together with the meanings. Can you complete the abbreviations for the eight parts of speech?

a.   int.   pron.   adv.   n.   v.   conj.   prep.

Verbs are often listed as *transitive* (v.t. *or* tr.) or *intransitive* (v. i. *or* intr.).

Dictionaries can also help you to use linked words accurately. Many words are normally related to others by *prepositions*:

worthy of reward

eligible for promotion

When words can be used with more than one preposition, the one to be used is normally settled by the context.

Practice

Decide the prepositions for these words, and check with your dictionary (Answers on p. 182):

complimented	different	immune
contrary	exempt	liable
deficient	identical	persevere

HOW TO SAY WORDS

Before the days of cheap printing, spelling depended more on the sound of the spoken word than it does now. The sounds have varied from one part of the country to another according to local speech habits. But nowadays our pronunciation as well as our spelling has been standardized by radio and television and with English crossing so many national boundaries it is a help to have accepted pronunciations recorded by dictionaries and shown by a system of signs.

There are three important points to do with the way words sound when we say them:

(a) the vowel sounds (particularly whether *long* (–) or *short* (˘), (see below);

(b) the consonants (whether singly, or in clusters of two or more);

(c) the placing of accent or stress.

1 Vowels

Most dictionaries give a key to standard vowel sounds either at the beginning of the book or at the foot of each page. Here is one such key:

> māte, mēte, mīte, mōte, mūte, mōōt; răck, rĕck, rĭck,
>
> rŏck, rŭck, rŏŏk; caw, cow; bah, boil

Look for the key in your own dictionary. It will establish the way all vowel pronunciations are shown in the rest of the dictionary.

Practice

Find our from your dictionary whether the vowel sounds indicated by italics are long or short:

c*a*nine	*e*difice	li*th*ograph	dr*o*ll	j*u*gular
b*a*rony	pl*e*nary	sp*i*ral	R*o*many	al*u*minium

Not all vowel sounds are simple. Where more guidance is needed a dictionary will often given a phonetic spelling of the whole word, or the difficult bit, in brackets after the word:

> none (nŭn)   rucksack (rŏŏ)   jaunty (jaw-, jah–)   rough (rŭf)

2 Consonants

All except four of our consonants have only one accepted pronunciation each when used singly. The four exceptions are c, f, g, and s, which each have two:

*c*astle,	*c*entre	*g*rand,	*g*iant
*f*ox,	o*f*	*s*ample,	a*s*

The dictionary will always indicate which of these is needed if there is likely to be any doubt. It will also help with variable-sounding consonant pairs or groups, like –gh:

> laugh (lahf)   bough (bow)

and with difficulties brought about by the phonetic inconsistencies of English spelling, like these:

orchard (–tsh)	rouse (rowz)
orchestra(–k–)	route (rōōt)

3 Accent/stress

English is a strongly stressed language and it is often important to know where the stress is placed in normal usage. Here are some easy examples:

> tradition   umbrella   murderous

It is not difficult to recognize that the stress falls on the second, the second and the first syllables respectively. But which syllables would you stress in these words?

> controversy   foreboding   bamboo   rosemary

Find out how your dictionary marks accented syllables; it is often by a raised comma ('), an acute sign (´) or a raised stop (·) after the stressed syllable.

Remember that no dictionary claims to be always right. Its job is to record *normal* usage, and this varies from year to year. If you enter into controversy over the way 'controversy' should be stressed, don't expect the dictionary to settle the argument. It may well give both pronunciations.

O6 LISTENING AND TALKING

6.1 Introduction

So far, we have concentrated on written English, because so much of what you do in school and in other educational settings depends on it. Yet we all know that our main medium of communication, most of the contact we make with other people, depends on *spoken* English. We

- convey or receive information,
- express our feelings,
- set up and develop relationships

in speech. We acquire and pass on knowledge by listening to and speaking *oral English*. The new GCSE syllabuses recognize this by insisting on a grade in oral English as part of the certificate.

As a general guide to what will be expected of you, here are *five key criteria,* i.e. points that will be considered in all parts of the oral assessment and which all relate to all four of the units in this particular section:

CONTENT
LANGUAGE
AUDIENCE
GESTURE
CLARITY

Each of these is explained below. Try to memorize them, as a check when you are involved in oral work. Invent a sentence to help you remember them. Ours is **C**ougars and **L**eopards **A**re **G**iant **C**ats.

CONTENT Unless you have something worth saying there is no point in speaking at all. Whatever the situation – a conversation between two, a group discussion, a talk or speech – you need to decide on the *content* of what you will say.

LANGUAGE This covers the words you use (your grasp of *vocabulary*), whether you speak grammatically, any accent or dialect you may have. (This last is no drawback as long as it does not lead to indistinct or unfamiliar expressions.) The point also links with the next one, because a good speaker will adapt his or her tone and language according to the person being spoken to.

AUDIENCE Any speaker, to be effective, needs to be aware of and to respond to his or her audience. Often this is only one person – a friend or colleague, your teacher or examiner – but you still need to suit what you say to her or him. You will realize that sometimes this may affect both *content* and *language.*

GESTURE British people are traditionally reluctant to support their words with gestures; indeed, they have a reputation for being undemonstrative. But many who use English these days – no doubt including many of you using this book – have other roots, and gestures, movement in support of speech, come naturally to you. This term can include all nonverbal signals like facial expression, stance, even the way you wear your clothes.

CLARITY Finally, however good your *content,* accurate and wide-ranging your *language,* perceptive your recognition of your *audience* and eloquent your *gestures,* if you can't be heard it is all wasted! Clarity includes audibility and volume, clear enunciation and articulation, variety of intonation – the way your voice rises and falls according to the meaning, and lack of hesitation and 'fill-in' noises (e.g. 'er', 'um').

In one form or another these are to be found in every GCSE oral syllabus, because they summarize the main points of the *national* criteria for oral English published by the Schools Examinations Council for the Department of Education and Science.

How many of these forms of *spoken English* have you used or heard in the last week or so?

'U–nit–ed!'

Telling a friend how to reach your house

Weather report on radio

'What's for breakfast?'

Answering the telephone in someone else's house

Asking a parent or friend to help you find something

'Tickets please! Move right down the car!'

'Have you got a bus pass?'

'Oh blast! It's raining!'

Asking how to do something – feed the cat, light the gas fire or geyser

Explaining to a small child why not to touch a hot iron or stove

'Paper! Standard! Read all about it!'

'Anyone in?'

Your opinion of a pop tune/singer/athlete

Deciding what to buy for the weekend

'Mmm! Darling, that's amazing!'

Finding out whether the loaf was baked today

'Where does it hurt?'

'Mind the gap! Stand clear of the doors please!'

'If the litmus paper changes colour . . .'

You could easily make a similar length list for yourself and not exhaust the subject. Try it!

This demonstrates well that 'oral English' is not just another part of the school timetable, but is involved in almost everything we do. However, not all of the examples we listed lend themselves to being tested or assessed for an examination. We must also remember that no *book*, which is in its essentials a carefully thought out form of *written* English, can hope by itself to give all the detailed guidance you may need on how best to achieve a good standard in speaking and listening. That must come from *sound*, and through your ears. What we can do is to give you some pointers, and to draw attention to some of the problems you are likely to encounter.

TAPE RECORDERS

We shall not apologize for stressing once again the value of using your own or a borrowed cassette tape recorder to help prepare yourself for the compulsory oral part of GCSE and SCE English. It can help with so many different kinds of oral English. Use it

● to record speech from television. (It is good practice to hear what was said without looking and see how much was dependent on non-verbal elements – gesture, facial expression, movements etc.)

● to record speech from radio – news, commentaries, DJs, talks, plays. The experts are always worth listening to even if you hate the sound of their voices! Get into the habit of *listening critically* to newscasters, announcers, DJs. Do they pronounce everything 'properly'? How wide a range (low to high) has their intonation? Compare it with your own or a friend's

● to record and playback your own attempts

● to monitor discussions – between two (you and a friend, you and the person you are interviewing, etc.), or in a group

● to exchange tapes with a friend so that you can assess and discuss each other's progress.

> The 'playback' facility of the tape recorder is a useful tool, since it . . . helps to give the listener something of the analytic power that the reader has over his printed text   (SCE)

Many of the ideas we shall give you in the following pages can be helped with a tape recorder and for some a tape recorder is essential. Oral (speaking) and aural (listening) English are two sides of the same coin, so we shall be considering them together. We have grouped the points in four categories: just as we grouped written English into units W1-W5, so here we group oral English into units O6 to O9 (O for oral).

6.2 Oral Expression

In unit W1 we dealt with a wide range of writing; this unit draws attention to the many kinds of oral expression and communication. If you want to develop your ability to communicate effectively on a personal level you need practice, as with any other acquired skill. You may think that talking 'comes so naturally' that there is no need for this. Perhaps your parents – or even your teachers! – think you get too much practice already. What is needed is consciously thought out and directed practice – something very different from the casual chat that fills so much of our day. To get our ideas, opinions or convictions listened to we need

- good planning beforehand,
- clear thinking while we are speaking,
- a sensitive awareness of our audience,

so that we can adapt our style and tone accordingly.

A good indication of the various kinds of oral practice needed is given by the list of 'speech activities' recommended in the syllabus of the Midland Examining Group, which we listed in the Introduction. As you see, we divided these into *group* and *individual* activities. Quite often you need to sustain a two-way conversation on a topic chosen by you. This requires forethought and planning to do well. If the person you are talking to – or with – is a teacher, perhaps even a total stranger, you need to have enough *confidence* in yourself and your ideas not to be put off by shyness, selfconsciousness or nerves. The best antidote for all these is the assurance gained from familiarity with and enthusiasm for your subject matter. Most of us have had the experience of hearing someone – it may even be oneself – suddenly 'find his tongue' once the conversation turns to a topic on which he is knowledgeable, whether it's train-spotting, cycle-racing, snooker, falconry or tropical fish. Whoever you are talking to, you also need to be interested in him or her, because talking and listening in this situation are to-and-fro activities, like tennis. Here are two examples:

(a) *Teacher:* What have you chosen to talk about?

Student: My dog.

(pause)

Teacher: Tell me about him.

Student: Well – er – actually, I haven't got a dog now.

Teacher: No?

Student: No.

(pause)

Teacher: Can you tell me what happened?

Student: My married sister's got him.

(b) *Teacher:* What have you chosen to talk about?

Student: My dog – at least he used to be mine, but he's gone to my married sister now.

Teacher: Oh. How do you feel about that?

Student: Well, I was a bit upset at first and I still miss him, but I can see why it's better he should be with my sister . . .

It is not difficult to see which of these conversations is likely to last longer and develop more interestingly. Notice how the second candidate volunteers information in her first reply. This gives the teacher an opportunity to respond with another lead, making the student's job easier.

> [Candidates] will generally be expected to . . . listen to others and show awareness of both verbal and non-verbal communication (LEAG)

It is possible to prepare yourself by guessing at some of the more obvious questions beforehand, and by being aware of how the conversation may develop.

TOPIC DIAGRAM

Try drawing a diagram starting from your topic in the centre and exploring the ways in which your answers could be used by you or by the other person to keep the conversation flowing. Here is one such diagram based on a typical conversation subject, 'My Holiday in France':

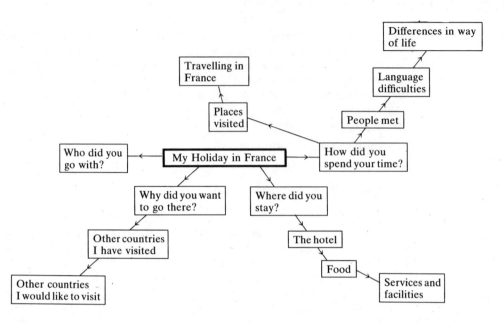

In that kind of conversation the emphasis is on your right handling of the *process* of talking. Sometimes the emphasis is shifted to a *product*—a formal speech, a report, an account of a particular event, and so on. You need practice in this more closed kind of oral exercise as well. Let's take an example from a written examination paper. It reminds us that speech and writing can be mutually supportive.

> At times their [i.e. the candidates'] work will be directed towards producing a performance, such as a talk, a reading, a role-play . . . a narration of an anecdote . . . etc. These may be described as *products* as this distinguishes these occasions from situations where oral work occurs in the context of other activities. This *process* work might include exploring a poem or story . . .
>
> (NEA)

Question

A group of fifth-formers is organizing a campaign to reduce litter in the school buildings and grounds. Write the speech in which the campaign is explained to the school by a senior student in an Assembly.

A speech has a hard job to do: it must catch and hold the attention of the audience, which may be a very mixed one; at the same time it has to get its meaning over to every individual in that audience, ideally at a single hearing. The question helps, in that it tells you exactly who your audience will be; but there is also a special problem, because you have to hold the attention of a wide age-range. Keep the sentences simple in structure. Try to use humour—people listen better if they can smile—but show that you are personally convinced of the importance of your subject. Be polite to your audience: remember they didn't ask to hear you. If you leave them with a good opinion of you they are more likely to remember your words. One of us tried a 'role-play' exercise and came up with this short speech:

We *love* litter—when it's in the bin!

This week the fifth-years begin their 'Clean up the school' campaign. 5A, B and C will be watching you in the corridors and classrooms, 5X, Y and Z in the grounds.[*] We have bought in—at vast expense—lots of plastic sacks. If anyone is seen to drop litter, even a single sweetpaper or crisp packet, the penalty is filling one of them with litter from the grounds *after* school—wet or fine.[*]

Classes whose rooms have the least litter on their corridor for three consecutive days will be awarded one of our Credit Posters, like this (hold up poster). If you win more than one, there are other treats in store. Watch this space, as they say!

As you might expect in a well-run establishment like ours, this campaign has the backing of the Head and all the staff. It is not just a gimmick, it's a highly educational operation aimed at improving the quality of school life for all of us. We are putting a 'Suggestions Box' in the entrance hall, next to the founder's portrait. Each week we shall read out at this Assembly the best ideas we get. Please make sure that your suggestion papers go right into the box, and don't litter the entrance hall.

Next week Martin Milton of 5Y will announce details of 'Litter Lines', a poetry and essay competition, with startling prizes.[*]

Thank you for your attention. Get litter-picking!

That takes only one and a half minutes to say, so should probably be a bit longer. We have put asterisks[*] at three places where the speech could usefully be expanded. Try your hand at doing this, either by writing it, or – better – by delivering the speech into your tape recorder and 'ad-libbing' extra bits at these points. Afterwards, try making a similar length speech on a topic of your own choice. Instead of writing it in full, make a set of notes and use them to record the full speech on tape. Get a friend to listen to it with you, and listen *critically*. We are not suggesting this joint listening just for company. It is surprising how much more you notice when you are conscious of someone else listening with you.

However, a tape recorder can help even when you have to work on your own. Don't believe anyone who tells you you can't practise oral English by yourself. You can! Here is a good method, which can also be enjoyable because it involves watching your favourite television programmes.

Record

(*a*) a sports programme on television. Turn down the sound and record your own commentary for two to five minutes of play;

(*b*) part of a favourite drama serial (*Dallas, East Enders,* etc.). Turn down the sound and record your own commentary on what is happening. Include descriptions of characters, clothes, settings etc. (If you are lucky enough to have the use of a video recorder, it is interesting to record the same pieces simultaneously with your own tape recording. This gives you a check on your own work when you play it back.)

Playback

Points to note: Did you speak audibly? Were there any places when you stumbled or repeated yourself? Did you use slang, or sloppy, casual expressions? Did your commentary succeed in getting across your own feelings or opinions? Did you forget or overlook any important details?

> . . . some listening assignments should deal with matters such as standard and non-standard language forms, accent and dialect (SCE)

That was a self-help exercise. Much of your oral/aural coursework – and in most syllabuses this is what determines your oral grade – is likely to take place in groups. You don't need a classroom and a teacher to practise group discussion, as long as you have three or four others prepared to join you, and a tape recorder.

Here is one way of setting to work:

Before the recording each chooses a topic to introduce to the others, e.g. a holiday, favourite film/music/sport, what annoys you about your parents/school etc., something you feel strongly about, e.g. censorship, nuclear power, pollution, and prepares a set of notes on his or her topic.

Another method is for the group first to choose a *theme,* e.g. sport, hairstyles, teaching methods, outdoor pursuits, weather – and then for each member to decide on a particular topic related to the theme. Here is an example:

	1st member: clothes for all weathers
	2nd member: farming *or* gardening *or* holidays
THEME: **weather**	3rd member: sounds and sight of different weathers
	4th member: caught in bad weather (describe)
	5th member: weather predictions/forecasts

Record

Each member introduces his or her topic (3-4 minutes). The group first ask questions, then discuss generally the points raised. Both talks and questions/discussions should be taped.

Playback

All listen critically, then discuss to bring out the following:

Did you respond to talks? If not, whose fault?

How could talks be developed to get more/better focused response?

Are there any places where the conversation/discussion could have developed but failed to?

Did everyone take part in discussions? If not, why not?

Was any one member dominating? Why?

Were any points misunderstood? Whose fault?

Sometimes oral English has a more humdrum task to perform – giving instructions, explaining a process or a technique, passing on information accurately. Often carelessness can lead to embarrassing mistakes. One of us remembers a particular such piece of carelessness that taught him a lesson. He wanted his son to arrange a rendezvous with a foreign friend, as the son was visiting the friend's town but had never met him, though they were both professional musicians. The son contacted his father's friend and they arranged to meet in the hotel foyer. Each waited patiently for 45 minutes before returning, the son to his room, the friend to his home. A phone call proved that they had both been at the appointed place as arranged. Thanks to the father's carelessness neither had a correct idea of the other's age and each had overlooked the other, although they had both been in the same place at the same time. Half the evening had been wasted!

Not all oral descriptions are tested so directly, but it is easy for two people working together to practise accuracy of this sort. The following method is almost a game, but it has more than entertainment value. Each works out in private a sequence of actions for the other to do. It should involve movement within a known environment – a room at home, the garden, your immediate town neighbourhood, the school playground even – and specific things to do at named points. The whole sequence should take about five minutes. Try it out by yourself first, then record your instructions. Exchange tapes, and each watches while the other follows his/her partner's instructions. It is important for the watcher to stay silent and note down any mistakes. When both have finished, compare notes and find out what led to any errors there might have been. Your first attempt may well be too easy or too complicated, so try it several times.

In such uses of language no feelings are involved. If you giggled or otherwise betrayed how you were feeling as you recorded the instructions it would have distracted your 'subject'. Often, however, language is used to persuade, and to do this successfully the speaker needs to involve his or her listeners' feelings. Our final exercises are concerned with this more loaded kind of oral communication.

Practice

1 Compile a radio advertisement for a new product – chocolate bar, casual shirt, after-shave, hair conditioner – including a jingle (rhyming verse) to fix the name in the minds of your 'consumers'.

2 You have been offered two minutes of radio time to make an appeal for your favourite charity. Prepare notes and tape your appeal. (If this is done as part of group work, the group can establish a merit order for the results after discussion.)

3 (Group work) List the six most memorable television advertisements, then (a) decide what makes them memorable, (b) note how much use they make of language. Notice particularly the speaker's intonation, (c) discuss whether they could increase the sales of their products, and if so why.

O7 LISTENING IN RELATION TO SPEAKING

This unit pays special attention to listening and its relation to speaking.

'Did you go to London?'   'No, we went on Tuesday.'

Not hearing or not listening can lead to anything from a comedy series to an international incident – and miles away from a good GCSE grade!

Hearing and listening are not the same.

Hearing depends on good ears – in the hearer – and clear speech from the speaker or clearly recognizable sounds from other sources. Hearing someone or something tells us nothing about the hearer beyond that. We all know how easy it is to 'hear' but not to 'heed', e.g. an alarm clock, or an unwelcome piece of news.

Listening, on the other hand, requires concentration and a willingness to hear, even when the source is obscure.

> People seem to listen most successfully when . . . they are given a clear purpose for listening . . . they are able to engage or interact in some way with the speaker . . .   (SCE)

School sometimes demands too much concentration in listening – teachers talk so much – and then in come the 'defence mechanisms' – switching off, daydreaming, doodling. Part of our oral education must be to extend our listening span, our capacity for concentrated and prolonged listening. Television and, to a lesser extent, radio, often tend to contract it. They dole out entertainment, news, information in small, predigested portions for so much of their air space.

'**A good listener**' – these words point to oral/aural skills similar to those described in unit W2 on pp. 59 and 60. Good listening can help you to

- extract information,
- marshal facts,
- summarize,
- draw inferences from what you hear.

The Midlands Examining Group syllabus includes a formal listening or aural test. Candidates listen to a pre-recorded cassette and then, after an opportunity to make notes and read a transcript with the second hearing, answer in writing the printed questions on the passage recorded. Candidates are required to respond 'both to what is said *and the way in which it is said*' (our italics) i.e. an exacting listening test. In unit W2 we pointed out how tone of voice can affect meaning. Try to train yourself to recognize changes of *tone*. A good exercise is to think of a common phrase like 'Do you like chocolate?' By stressing first one then another word you can change the meaning through a change of tone. Then try adding a word – 'really' ('Do you really . . .') or 'all' ('. . . all chocolate') and so on. If you do this with a friend and a tape recorder it can be fun as well as being instructive.

        concentration   willingness   selectivity

These are the three ingredients for successful listening. We have already spoken about the first two. No one can be a receptive listener all the time, so it is worth practising the skill of *selecting* what we want or need to attend to out of what we hear.

Practice

1 In unit W2 (p. 66) we gave an example of a boy listening to a weather forecast for a particular purpose. Read it again, then try this for yourself. Decide first what kind of weather you want for a chosen purpose – fishing, cross-country running, revising – then switch on a forecast (radio is better than television for this exercise) and select for concentrated listening only the relevant bits.

2 Check the area covered by your Examining Group (it will be one of the following: Scotland, N. Ireland, Wales, N. England, Midlands, London/E.Anglia, S. England). Now listen to a national news and weather broadcast and pick out only the items connected with that area. Jot down notes as you listen. If you tape the broadcast at the same time you can check your accuracy.

3 Using the same area pattern, note whether any area was not covered either by news or by weather, or which received the most attention.

Selective listening in group work

A group leader who listens carefully is more capable of keeping the discussion going and sticking to the point. She or he can intervene when they hear group members repeating points. Even as an 'ordinary' group member, if you can remember what has been said you can ask a question or volunteer a comment which will move the discussion on. If your job is to report back, you can do justice to the group as a whole by concentrating on the most interesting and original points and noting how the discussion develops.

> ...candidates [need] to develop the skills of oral communication in situations where individuals are both listeners and speakers. Emphasis must be placed on the inter-relatedness of listening and speaking   (MEG)

To be a good listener your concentration must include the speaker as well as the words spoken. 'I can concentrate better with my eyes closed' may be true for listening to music or even poetry (though you will miss much if the poetry reading is really skilled). It does *not* make for sharp listening to a particular speaker.

'Non-verbal' points

Your whole posture – the way you sit or stand, hold your head, look at the speaker – helps to signal your attentive interest and establish that mysterious thing called *rapport* with the speaker and also helps him or her to be a better speaker too. Whether in conversation one-to-one, in group discussion or as a solo speaker, try to sit or stand comfortably, look relaxed but not sloppy. Listen with your eyes as well as your ears. Ask yourself: What does that look of his mean? Is he afraid, aggressive, smug, anxious? Does he seem friendly? What you observe like this will help you to decide what to say when your turn comes.

It is a good idea to practise improving your powers of concentration by giving yourself aural memory tests. This sounds daunting, but isn't if you choose your raw material well. Do you listen to or watch *Top of the Pops?* How many of the top twenty can you remember ten minutes later? Or next morning? After a radio news broadcast try to see how many headlines you can remember before the announcer says 'Here are the headlines again'.

Further practice

Passing on messages, instructions, information

Ask a friend to work with you and take it in turns. Here are some 'role-play' exercises which will provide useful practice.

1 (*a*) A explains how to get to the Post Office; tells B to buy two first class, three second class stamps, two television licence stamps and to ask what time the post goes on a Saturday. B repeats the route back and what he or she is to do.

(*b*) A has a Spanish friend B to stay. B wants to telephone home. A looks up international dialling in the Phone Book and explains to B the code for Madrid, the charge band and the cheapest times to phone. B does not fully understand, so A has to find other ways of putting it.

(*c*) A is the teacher giving instructions for English homework. B doesn't understand and asks for more details.

2 Think of something that you know how to do but your partner does not, e.g. making a paper model, playing a card game. Tape your teaching attempts and your partner's questions and responses. Reverse roles and try with another subject. (Use the playback session to find out where you wasted words, did not make yourself clear, lost patience, etc.)

3 Give your partner directions for a journey, by a route she or he does not know. Tape the directions. Your partner then listens to the tape and draws a map of the route. Now compare this with a correct map and discuss why mistakes were made if there were any. Change roles and do it again with a different route.

Just as we speak before we write, so creative oral arts come before written ones. We have a problem here. We have got so used to the idea that all creative use of words is 'literature', i.e. words written down (and usually printed in books), that we don't even have an equivalent word representing spoken poetry, plays, stories and so on. But a play*wright* need not be a play-*writer* and – particularly outside what is sometimes called 'Western' culture – much poetry is still composed orally (e.g. in African countries, and amongst Eskimos, American Indians, Maoris), like the bards used to do in Britain. They are, and were, 'makers' of poetry – poem-*wrights* not poem writers.

So we welcome the parts of GCSE oral English syllabuses which remind us that creative 'literature' is matter for talking and listening as well as for reading and writing. (We shall leave out the quotation marks round 'literature' in this unit now we have made our point.)

It is useful to separate two aspects of oral literature as it features in the English (rather than the *English Literature*) course for GCSE: *process* and *product*.

Process includes conduct of a group discussion on a book, the way a play is read and entered into, the actual reading of or quoting from a poem as part of a spoken appreciation of it. The emphasis here will be on the way you cope with it while it is taking place – your audience awareness, expressiveness of delivery, responsiveness to the text or to other creative verbal material (it could be a recorded play excerpt, for example) and to the other people involved.

The *products* of oral and aural work in literature might be a performance of a rehearsed play-reading, the prepared reading of a poem, an improvized role-play episode. Here the emphasis is not so much on the manner and conduct of the performance, more on an assessment of its total effectiveness and how fully it achieves its aims.

The suggestions that follow are arranged in these two categories of *process* and *product*. You will recognize that it is not always possible to allocate a piece of oral work exclusively to one or the other; often a process will lead to a product, and both can be tested and assessed in the same assignment.

PRACTICE (with the emphasis on *process*)

1 (on your own) Choose a favourite poem from one of the books you have been reading or that you have written yourself. *Tape* yourself reading it *three times*, the first two immediately after one another, the third on the following day and at a different time of day if possible. Don't listen to the first two until you have completed the third reading. Try to aim at improving with each successive reading. It is a great help if you know the poem by heart and do not rely on the printed text. *Playback:* listen closely, with paper and pen handy, and jot down any points you notice – monotony or variety, emphasis, speed and pauses, etc. If you are working with a friend, each of you do the exercise on your own then exchange tapes, make notes on the other's recording and compare notes.

2 (in pairs) *Endings* You know how television and radio serials ('soap operas') try to build up and hold their captive audience by ending each episode with what used to be called a 'cliffhanger' – a moment of tension or some unsolved problem. Tape or make notes on several successive endings (e.g. of *Coronation Street* or *East Enders*). About two minutes of each should be plenty. Listen together to, or compare notes on, the whole series of endings, then both together try planning and recording an 'ending' of your own.

3 (group work) Take a book or short story you have all been reading. Each group member chooses to be one of the characters. If there are not as many characters as there are group members, two can represent the same character. Discuss together a particular event or climax in the book, each speaking from the point of view of her or his chosen character. If you can tape the discussion and another group does likewise for a different book or story this is also a good way of getting to know the texts better.

4 (two or more) Work out the front page contents of a newspaper, imagining it to be published in the setting of a book or play being studied, e.g. 'In fair Verona where we lay our scene' for *Romeo and Juliet,* in Port Elizabeth for Fugard's *'Master Harold' . . . and the boys* (p. 78), or the future in John Christopher's *The Guardians.* Discuss layout, headlines, chief news items etc.

PRACTICE (with the emphasis on *product*)

5 (on your own) Prepare and tape a 'reading performance' of a particular episode in a book being read in your course. (Some actors have specialized in such solo performances, e.g. Roy Dotrice as Aubrey in *Aubrey's Brief Lives,* and Emlyn Williams, who has toured the world as 'Charles Dickens' giving readings from his own books.) Choose a piece lasting about six or seven minutes, which is self-explanatory and comes to a clear conclusion. Tape yourself doing it, listen to and note your 'performance' and prepare a final taped version for a more public hearing–to your class or group, to your parents. If necessary prepare a few words of introduction to the episode on the lines of ours introducing the piece from *River Afternoon* (p. 40).

6 (group work) Each group member prepare on his or her own a passage from a novel, short story or play, or an extract from a long poem, for reading aloud. Think out four questions that can be answered from your chosen piece. Read the passage to the group, then put each question in turn to the group, who must answer from what they have just heard without the help of the written text. Their answers will indicate both whether you read the passage well and whether they listened properly.

> The group oral test will take the form of discussions which develop from short talks given by members of the group in turn. Candidates will be examined in groups of either five or six . . . The talk should last between three and four minutes and must not be read from a prepared script . . . A group discussion will follow each talk, lasting about five minutes   (LEAG)

7 (in pairs) Each choose to be a character from a play, novel or short story read recently. The two should be from different stories. Imagine a meeting between the two characters–it may be in heaven or hell!–and record the conversation that takes place. An interesting way of using the *product* from this exercise is to play the tape to others in the course and ask them to identify the characters. Examples of suitable pairs might be:

Elizabeth Bennet (*Pride and Prejudice*) and Portia (*The Merchant of Venice*)
Laurie Lee (*Cider with Rosie*) and Anne Frank (*Diary of Anne Frank*)
Billy Caspar (*A Kestrel for a Knave* or *Kes*) and Billy Liar (*Billy Liar*)

8 (debate speech) Prepare and tape a 5-minute speech either *for* (pro) or *against* (con) the motion that 'reading, writing and listening to poetry is a waste of time'. Whichever side you choose, you will need to base your argument on particular poems.

9 (on your own) Prepare and tape a story–real or fictional–in such a way that your audience will (a) be attentive because they want to know what happens as the story is being told, (b) have their curiosity satisfied by the time the story ends. (This is more difficult than it sounds. Try out your first attempts on parents or friends before you give the final 'performance'.)

Postscript to unit 08: We have chosen to make most of this unit actual work suggestions rather than instructions or advice. This is because you learn more about oral English in this connection by practising it than by reading about it.

This unit corresponds to unit W5. It is concerned with speaking and listening techniques – language, clarity, variety, pace, tone, gesture. The spoken language is so much more fluid and changeable than the written that it is less satisfactory to try to isolate 'techniques' from other aspects. You will find that many of the points and work suggestions we have given you already in units O6 to O8 are also connected with technical skills as dealt with here. Nevertheless, it is worth trying to draw some of these skills together. When you speak you want to be heard and understood. If people say 'Pardon?' or 'Speak up!' you probably talk too quietly or indistinctly. If people seem hurt or insulted by what you say you may have got the wrong *tone*.

What you say must suit the occasion – formal speech for a formal situation (a speech at a wedding, introducing a distinguished guest at a meeting), more casual words and tone for a friendly gathering, or amongst people of your own age. Ask yourself: What am I aiming to achieve in this bit of talk – inform my audience, get a friendly response, touch the hearers' feelings? Is what I am planning to say appropriate to the person addressed and to the occasion? Thus, at a funeral one would *not* strike up a casual conversation with someone in the next seat by saying 'A funny thing happened to me on the way to church'. Nor at a rugby victory celebration would one have much success by trying to engage a neighbour's interest in your passion for crochetwork.

The following exercises will help you to identify and correct your own particular weaknesses. Choose ones that you know you will find hard to do, don't stick to the ones that seem easy.

PREPARATION (for 1-5 below)

Record yourself speaking in as many different settings as possible, e.g. at a family meal (with the others' permission), during telephone conversations with a friend, a parent, a younger child, reading a poem or a part in a play, practising a formal speech.

Playback

1 (Speaking clearly) Listen carefully. Can every word be heard clearly? Replay to check which words, or which kinds of words, are indistinct. Are vowels or consonants at fault? Beginnings or endings of words? Do you drop your voice at the end of a sentence (a common fault)?

2 (Choice of words) Is your vocabulary wide enough for the subject and the occasion? Have you repeated words so often as to become noticeable? Are the words suited to your listener? (A good way to measure your ability in this last is to practise describing complicated things to a younger child.)

3 (Pace) Do you talk too fast? or too slowly? Do you vary the pace according to the subject? (It is particularly helpful for this point to compare your performance with the experts – television or radio commentators, disc-jockeys etc.)

4 (Intonation) Do you raise and lower the pitch of your voice enough? (A common fault is to speak in a level monotone, which is difficult to listen to with concentration even when all the words are clearly enunciated.) How many notes of the scale do you use when you speak? If it is only two or three – get a musical friend to help if you are tone-deaf! – practise increasing the number by at least two. Listen to a group of happy smaller children; you can often measure their happiness by their range of intonation.

5 (Tone) Does your tone match the occasion each time? Whenever you speak try to decide what note you want to strike – friendly, courteous, deferential, dignified, respectful, casual, authoritative, intimate, cool, stand-offish . . . ? Remember that often the tone needs to change as a conversation, discussion, talk or speech develops.

6 (Gesture) A tape recorder can't help with this important aspect of oral English. (See the Introduction). It is worth asking a friend to tell you of any unconscious mannerisms you betray when speaking – twisting your hair, pulling one ear, fiddling with a chain or bangle, swaying or moving about unnecessarily. Actors learn the value of controlled gesture and movement, and of its opposite, controlled stillness. Sometimes absolute stillness can be more riveting than the most extravagant gesture—just as something said very quietly can sometimes be more effective than something bellowed at the top of your voice. Practise reading an exciting episode in a book, (a) without any physical movement but with maximum tonal variety; (b) with one, two or at most three carefully chosen gestures or movements to bring out the meaning more clearly. Next time you watch a television interviewer (e.g. Terry Wogan, Michael Parkinson) look for the 'body language'—smiles, grimaces, head and hand movements, etc.—that is used to supplement their words. It is instructive to turn the sound off so that you can concentrate on this aspect. How much of the 'message' do you get even without sound? Comedians are often expert at this. Have you ever wondered why the audience in a radio comedy show are laughing when nothing has been said? Notice how a skilled comedian watches his audience closely and responds to it.

Reading aloud

Some examining groups recommend as part of the oral English course reading aloud in prose and verse, or in role-play, e.g. as a newscaster. Such exercises may be used to assess your GCSE grade, and in any case are worth practising for their own sake. There are plenty of experts easily to be found—on radio or television, or on records and cassettes—and careful listening to them can help you with this aspect of oral skill.

Your teacher may ask you to read a passage aloud as part of your coursework oral assessment, either a piece you have chosen or one set as a test piece. If you choose your own piece, try to find one with plenty of variety—perhaps with some direct speech, or with more than one narrative 'voice'. Here is what to do in the time given you for a read-through:

- Get the gist of the passage (what it is about) as quickly as possible.

- Look for unfamiliar words and try saying them to yourself—mouthing the words if you can. Remember! A confident mispronunciation of an unknown word is better than a gap, which could destroy the whole sense of the passage.

- Notice where the sentences end (marked by stops, question marks, or exclamation marks) so that you can indicate these and other pauses in your reading.

- If there is time, skim through it all again. You may be able to decide on one or two places for special emphasis this time.

FURTHER PRACTICE (oral)

The following suggestions do not relate to any of the oral units in particular, but will provide you with general practice for the oral English GCSE and SCE assessment.

1 *A game* (2 people) *A* begins a conversation with a question. *B* must answer with another question. The first one who fails to use a question loses a point. See how long you can keep it up. (*Aim:* to prevent 'yes' and 'no' and other blocking answers in conversation.)

2 (Group work) Tape (sound or video) a discussion programme or chat show from radio or television. After listening and/or watching the playback (together) with the following questions in mind, discuss it between yourselves.
Questions: Was the interviewer good at his job? Which questions helped the guest most? Was/were there any particular remark(s) that hindered the progress of the discussion? If so, why and how? Did all the participants listen to each other?

3 (Group work) The group plans a crime. Work out details of time, place etc. Each group member needs an alibi. Other group members test each alibi in turn to try and break it. This can all be taped, then played back in the group for further evaluation, both of the alibis and of the way the questioners set about trying to break them.

4 (Role-play) Two contrasted meals out, e.g. in a fashionable restaurant and in a transport cafe. Note the behaviour and language required in each situation.

5 (Role-play) In a shop: complaining about a faulty garment/shoddy piece of hardware/stale food to an assistant, then to the manager.

6 (Role-play) In a hospital out-patients department: accompanying a grandparent, and complaining at long wait. Parts could be Gran, you, hospital receptionist.

7 (Story-telling) Tell a familiar story, e.g. a fairy story, folk tale or fable, from a biased or one-sided perspective. Examples might be Cinderella from a feminist viewpoint, Red Riding Hood from the point of view of the police, etc.

> [Participants] should draw up a set of ground rules for civilized behaviour in group discussions
> (SCE)

The tests in this section are designed to give you more practice in written English. They are planned so that you can test yourself. Answers (where provided) are on pages 182-9; and a checklist of the tests is printed after the last one (p. 157).

Test 1 (General)

20 minutes
(32 marks)

ACCURACY

See how many marks you can score in this self-measurement test.

1 Here is a statement:

In a mixed class the girls who are cleverer soon get bored

This means that the girls in the class who are cleverer than the others soon get bored. By adding *two* marks of punctuation you can make it mean that *all* the girls are cleverer. What are the marks and where do they go? (2)

2 Re-write this statement so as to remove the doubt:
The marksmanship of the company is highly satisfactory and the shooting of the sergeant-major was especially praiseworthy. (3)

3 Here are two phrases: (a) *John and I* (b) *John and me*
Decide which of them, (a) or (b), would fit better in each blank space:

When   come to your party we shall bring our presents with us. Mum and Dad gave   a bike each, so we can ride to your house.   ride everywhere these days. (4)

4 Punctuation again! comma (,) semi-colon (;) colon (:) dash (–)
Decide which of these four marks of punctuation fits best where the box is:

For this job you need the following □ drawing pins, paste, brown paper (2)

5 lay   laid   lain
These words are often confused. Which of them belongs in the space?
Do you know how long you have   there snoring? (1)

6 Match the five abbreviations below to their meanings:
   n.b.   compare
   etc.   note well
   cf.   that is
   e.g.   and other things
   i.e.   for example (4)

7 There are standard ways of ending letters. Which of these would you use in a letter to the retiring head of your primary school? (Some are wrong for any letter!)
   (a) yours truely   (e) Yours sincerely
   (b) Yours Sincerly   (f) yours Faithfully
   (c) Your sincere ex-pupil (g) yours Sincerely
   (d) Yours faithfully   (h) Yours truly   (2)

8 Here is a longer test of your skill in punctuation. To set out the passage below you will need to use the following kinds of marks: two full stops (.) an exclamation mark (!) a question mark (?) three sets of inverted commas ('. . . ') an apostrophe (') and three capital letters.

you know I cant do I of course you do she said scornfully. (10)

9 Now set out the piece given for question 8 correctly, deciding where to place the words in *three* different lines (or paragraphs). (3)

10 Each of the three sentences below contains one faulty word. Choose one sentence and correct the fault in it. (If you can find the other faults as well, award yourself two bonus marks.)

(a) Without his having to say so openly his tone of voice inferred that he was bored.

(b) They told me I had past with a few marks to spare.

(c) She didn't do history because she was completely disinterested in the subject (1)

When you have done your best, turn to p. 182 and find out how many you have scored. Don't worry if you got some of the questions wrong, or even if they were all wrong. This book will help you put right your mistakes.

Test 2 (See Unit W5)

15 minutes
(40 marks)

SPELLING

1 These words are correctly spelt:

reign niece receipt piece siege

What is the rule that applies to all of them? (3)

2 The word *incarnate* has three syllables (in-car-nate). How many syllables are there in these words?

contemporary originally responsibility criticism occasionally similar

(When you are spelling long or unfamiliar words, it is a good idea to split them up into their syllables.) (6)

3 Fill in the blanks in

If you are ill you may have a d-------

Two people not in the same room are se-------

Two people arguing are having an a-------

If you keep a shop you are running a b-------s

If you have a job for four weeks you are a t-------y employee

If you fail when you expect to succeed you are d-------d (6)

4 These words are correctly spelt:

achievement believe chief deceit height

What would you say to people who argue that they are wrongly spelt? (3)

5 What has the spelling of these words in common? When you have decided, write down four more in the same family.

guarantee guess guide guitar brogue guy (5)
3+2

6 The past of *kill* is *killed*; the past of *eat* is *ate*. Write down the past of:

rise submit prefer remember dispel occur (6)

7 These words are correctly spelt. How does the rule work that gets them right?

conceit feign relieve foreign ceiling (3)

8 What has the spelling of these words in common? Write down four more in the same family

jealous treasure pleasant health (5)
3+2

9 What is noticeable about the spelling of this group of words

resign gnaw design consignment (3)

(Answers on p 183)

Test 3 (See Unit W4)

25 minutes
(22 marks)

MAKING NOTES

Read the passage below and answer the question that follows.

Round about 1975 the price of oil greatly increased and this gave a powerful stimulus to research into alternative methods of producing energy, one of which was to harness wind. As a result, firms all over the world have been making wind turbines that are both reliable and able to produce energy at prices that can compete with other generators.

Some of the manufacturers of these wind turbines are British, turning out mainly 3 ft.-diameter machines for private use. Much larger are the wind energy projects favoured by the generating boards. For instance, there is a 25-metre-diameter wind turbine, producing 200 kilowatts, on trial at Carmarthen Bay, South Wales, and a huge 60-metre turbine is under construction on Burgar Hill, in the Orkneys, to generate 3 megawatts. So far as Europe is concerned, Denmark has been the pioneer and hundreds of farmers use wind turbines with individual outputs up to about 100 kilowatts to provide most of their electricity needs, selling their surplus on days of abundant wind to the local utility. However it is in America that most progress has been made with the development of 'wind farms'. In California for example the past four years have seen the installation of privately managed 'farms' with a total generating capacity of over 1000 megawatts, and more are planned.

Much more could and should be done in Britain. Research by the CEGB and Department of Energy has shown that a fifth of our electrical needs could be

A wind turbine at Burgar Hill

provided by wind systems – more than we get from nuclear power stations. Wind farms would be sited in windy and thinly populated areas, where they would provide the income and employment needed to compensate for job losses in agriculture. With this potential – using no irreplaceable fuel, wasting no space, and never polluting the atmosphere – it is surprising that the Government is so noncommittal and unhelpful. It spends £250 million a year on nuclear development, but in 1985 devoted only £14 million on developing alternative forms of energy – and this comparatively small sum has now been cut.

Next Friday there is to be a Fifth Year debate: 'That energy is not necessarily nuclear'. Make notes from this article so that you could speak in favour of wind power:

(a) its advantages over other forms of energy

(b) present achievements.

(Answers, p. 183)

Test 4 (General)

10 minutes
(12 marks)

VOCABULARY

1 Think of a word or phrase meaning the same as:
  lenient incentive redundant
  relinquish grotesque synthetic

2 Think of a word or phrase meaning the opposite of:
  impudent opaque tranquil
  destitute deciduous acquiesce

(Answers on p. 183)

Test 5 (See Unit W2)

30 minutes
(20 marks)

You have applied for a job with Marks and Spencer, and have been called for interview.

(a) To prepare for the interview, you have been reading the Chairman's statement from the company's Annual Report (see p. 145). In about 100 words make a summary for yourself of their policy in purchasing and store development.   (*14 marks*)

(b) Look at the picture of furniture alongside the statement. Suppose your interviewer were to ask whether you thought selling furniture at M & S would be successful. Jot down a brief reply.   (*6 marks*)

(Answers, p. 184)

Test 6 (General)

5 minutes
(11 marks)

ACCURACY

Proof-reading is one of the best means of developing accuracy and any time left over at the end of a written test should always be spent in this way. Correct the 11 mistakes in the paragraph below; one of them is the omission of a word.

Drivers of the nest generalion of trains will not have to sit the front cad, potentally the most damgerous place, because they will be tranelling too fast.

At more than 190 mqh it would be inpossible for a driver to step a train within the tange of vision.

(Answer, p. 184)

MARKS AND SPENCER p.l.c.

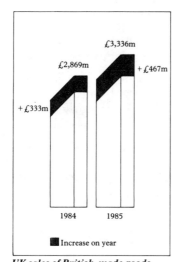

UK sales of British-made goods.

Legend: ■ Increase on year

Bars: 1984 £2,869m (+£333m); 1985 £3,336m (+£467m)

Purchasing policy

Last year we sold £3·3 billion worth of British-made goods, £467 million more than in the previous year. This commitment to buying British-made goods whenever they are available encouraged our British suppliers to invest £135 million in new plant and machinery for the production of St. Michael goods last year.

Store development in the UK

We opened a new store in Dunfermline and increased the selling space in a further 18 stores. We successfully opened additional stores in three locations where we were unable to increase the footage of our existing premises. As a result of these developments selling space was increased by 271,000 square feet.

The modernisation programme is proceeding vigorously and 44 stores have been converted. The new layout includes walkways and more space for customers to select their purchases. We believe this modernisation has resulted in a more attractive, comfortable and convenient shopping environment and in all the stores which have been modernised sales have increased substantially.

The capital investment programme last year was over £140 million and plans made during the year will enable a significant acceleration of investment in the year ahead. This will add a further 500,000 square feet of selling space and include the first out-of-town development at the Metro Centre near Gateshead which will open in the autumn.

During the year we will open a further eight satellite stores including Edinburgh, Croydon and Oxford Street, London. We will modernise a further 2·7 million square feet of selling space and plan capital expenditure for the year 1986/87 of over £300 million.

In the four years ahead to 1990, we are planning a total capital expenditure of over £1,500 million which will be invested in further developing stores in established city centres and opening out-of-town stores where we believe there are additional sales to be achieved. We have already announced that, subject to planning permission, we will develop three out-of-town sites jointly with Tesco PLC at Broxbourne (Cheshunt), Handforth (Wilmslow) and Cambridge and with ASDA-MFI GROUP PLC at South Gyle near Edinburgh. Negotiations are well advanced for a number of similar out-of-town developments.

Good shopping facilities are becoming increasingly important to customers and we welcome the fact that many local authorities are taking steps to improve town centres and are responding to the needs of shoppers who wish to use their cars.

Below: Furniture – newest addition to the homeware catalogue.

Test 7 (See Unit W4)

15 minutes
(10 marks)

In reply to an advertisement by a firm called Maylow of Fishpond Lane, Middlefield, Yorkshire, you have sent for a dress (or anorak). It arrives; the material is very good, but the garment is seriously faulty. Two buttons have no buttonholes to match them and one seam has a half-inch gap between the two edges that should be sewn together. Write a letter to the firm describing the faults and asking for a replacement.

(Answers on p. 184)

Test 8 (See Unit W3)

20 minutes
(20 marks)

Read the poem below carefully, then answer the questions that follow. (Try timing this test accurately. The marks give you a guide to how long to spend on each question.)

The Planster's Vision

Cut down that timber! Bells, too many and strong,
   Pouring their music through the branches bare,
   From moon-white church towers down the windy air
Have pealed the centuries out with Evensong.

Remove those cottages, a huddled throng!   5
   Too many babies have been born in there,
   Too many coffins, bumping down the stair,
Carried the old their garden paths along.

I have a Vision of the Future, chum,
   The workers' flats in fields of soya beans   10
     Tower up like silver pencils, score on score:
And Surging Millions hear the Challenge come
   From microphones in communal canteens
     'No Right! No Wrong! All's perfect, evermore.'

John Betjeman

Questions

1 We must suppose that a 'planster' is a person who believes in planning rather than random development. The word seems to have been invented by the poet. He does not share 'the planster's vision'. Quote evidence for this from the first four lines and explain your choice.

(4 marks)

2 There is an obvious contrast between the bells which the planster wishes to destroy and the microphones he wants to replace them with. Point out other similar contrasts in the poem.

(6 marks)

3 Write your own 'vision of the future', either approvingly or ironically. You can write it in verse if you wish, or as a conversation. *(10 marks)*

(Answers on p. 184.)

Test 9 (General)

10 minutes
(10 marks)

Make a list of all clichés, slang expressions and colloquialisms in the following piece. Then re-write the piece without using any of them, in your own clear words.

If I am for the high jump I'd rather the headmaster got straight down to the nitty-gritty and didn't beat about the bush. If I've been in the wrong and I know I've got it coming to me I'd rather just be given a thrashing and no messing about. That way it's all over and done with and no hard feelings.

(Answers on p. 184)

For instructions about the next two tests and Test 21, turn to unit W2 (p. 60). Make an intelligent guess at finding an appropriate word for each space.

Test 10 (See Unit W2)

15 minutes
(16 marks)

During the day – which is rainy, so the children are inside most of the time – there are a number of small bickerings between Joe and Mary, which arise either when Mary says the children can do something which Joe has already refused, or when

Joe refuses them something which Mary has said they could do or have. Generally arguments about the children take place in their ____ ; but today the bickering went on whether the children ____ there or not. Both Mary and Joe tend to ____ in to the children when they cry; so all ____ children cry very quickly when what they want is ____ them, and sob loudly until one or other parent ____ in. For instance: Joe says Elizabeth cannot have a ____ that Chris is looking at. Elizabeth starts to cry. ____ insists that Chris gives her the book. Or: Chris ____ an ice-cream, and is told by Joe that he ____ have one in this weather. Chris starts to cry. ____ comes back into the room and shouts at him, ____ that if he doesn't stop he'll have to go ____ bed. Chris's crying increases in volume. Mary dare not ____ directly against Joe's directions in a matter as major ____ ice cream but she finds Chris some sweets, and a ____ to play with, to console him in his loss.

During the morning I produced a simple reading book and asked Chris how much of it he could read.

(From *Wellington Road,* by Margaret Lassell, Routledge & Kegan Paul, London.)

(Answers on p. 185)

Test 11 (See Unit W2)

15 minutes
(*15 marks*)

There were no more speeches. Rabbits have their own conventions and formalities, but these ____ few and short by human standards. If Hazel had ____ a human being he would have been expected to ____ his companions one by one and no doubt each ____ have been taken in charge as a guest by ____ of their hosts. In the great burrow, however, things ____ differently. The rabbits mingled naturally. They did not talk ____ talking's sake, in the artificial manner that human beings ____ sometimes even their dogs and cats – do. But this ____ not mean that they were not communicating; merely that ____ were not communicating by talking. All over the burrow, ____ the newcomers and those who were at home were ____ themselves to each other in their own way and ____ own time; getting to know what the strangers smelt ____ , how they moved, how they breathed, how they scratched, ____ feel of their rhythms and pulses. These were their topics and subjects of discussion, carried on without the need of speech.

(From *Watership Down,* by Richard Adams, Rex Collings, London.)

(Answers on p. 185)

Test 12 (See Unit W4)

30 minutes
(*25 marks*)

UNDERSTANDING AND MAKING NOTES

Read the passage and then answer all these questions:

1 Give the meaning in the passage of: privation (para. 1); mortality (para. 3); fluctuations (para. 4); decade (para. 7); wreak havoc (para. 9); not more than five words each.   (*5 marks*)

2 Quote the words from the passage which say:
 (i) Weather changes seriously affect the survival chances of the birds.
 (ii) The birds which weren't almost wiped out escaped in several ways.
 (iii) There may be no real reason for us to worry about birds in winter.

(*2 marks each*)

3 What is natural selection, according to this passage?   (*5 marks*)

4 Give the two 'strategies' referred to in para. 4   (*4 marks*)

5 Someone has written to a newspaper about the likely extinction of some bird species as a result of very hard winter weather. From the passage note points to include in a consoling letter.   (*5 marks*)

(Answers, p. 185)

A Bird's Cold Comfort

Few things are more distressing during a prolonged cold spell such as the present one than the privation of birds. Puffed up to twice their natural size they strip the berries in our gardens and lose all sense of fear in their frantic search for food.

The plight of wildlife has evoked considerable comment over the centuries. The Anglo Saxon Chronicles note that in the severe winter of 1047 'birds and fish perished from the great cold and through hunger', while Thomas Walsingham records that in the great winter of 1408, when the frost was said to have lasted fifteen weeks, 'birds such as thrushes and blackbirds perished almost entirely through hunger and cold'.

Gilbert White makes many observations in his journal about the mortality of birds and other creatures in the frequent cold winters of the late 18th century.

More important, Charles Darwin noted in his work, *On the Origin of Species,* that in his own garden an estimated four-fifths of the birds died in the bitter winter of 1855. He concluded that climatic fluctuations were an important feature in the struggle for existence of any species.

The way in which freezing weather contributes to natural selection – the strongest individuals survive – can be examined in statistics collected by bird-watchers. These show clearly how vulnerable certain species are. In particular small songbirds such as the wren, long-tailed tits and gold-crests, waders and birds that hunt fish such as redshank, heron and kingfisher.

Statistics have been kept on heron since the 1920s, and in the coldest winters, for example 1947 and 1963, more than half the population died. But in subsequent mild years the numbers returned to former levels and during the past 60 years the overall picture is one of considerable long-term stability.

A similar story is found with other vulnerable species. After being almost wiped out in the cold of 1963, the population of wrens increased some tenfold in the following decade. Kingfishers, moorhen and mistlethrush also made remarkable recoveries both from this record-breaking winter and from lesser setbacks in the cold weather of 1971 and 1981-82. The species that survived more easily used a variety of strategies. Many simply fled south and westwards driven by the bitter north and east winds. The lapwing is known as the *ave fria* (the bird of the cold) in Spain. Here we recognize the arrival of Scandinavian species such as the fieldfare and the redwing as a warning of impending cold weather.

Other birds change their feeding habits. In one extreme case it was reported in January 1963 that a flock of starving pigeons attacked a woman carrying a basket of bread rolls and stole her wares.

So our concerns may be misplaced. The most extreme winters wreak awful havoc but the effect is relatively short-lived. Usually only the weakest stocks are weeded out. While feeding helps, the evidence of centuries shows that our birds can come through the worst our climate throws at us.

(From an article written by Bill Burroughs in *The Times,* on 25 January 1985.)

■ Test 13 (See Unit W5) ■

20 minutes
(30 marks)

SPELLING AND USAGE

Many of the points tested here are discussed elsewhere in the book. If you get a low score the book will help you to improve.

(3 marks each question)

1 *Road* is singular: the word *roads* is plural. Give the plurals of:
 recess   spoonful   tomato

2 We make *helpful* negative by adding *un – unhelpful*. What are the negative forms of:
 definite   legal   satisfied

3 In the sentence *He's finishing the work* we say the verb is in the present. In *He finished the work yesterday* the verb is in the past. Now put the verb in these examples into the past
 He is beginning
 She is doing very well
 I always choose nylon bearings

4 In *Sue performs that work on the guitar* we say the verb is active. In *That work is often performed on the guitar* the verb is passive. Put the verbs in these sentences into the passive:

   He transmits the message
   She speaks the words clearly
   She lays her bag on the counter.

Your answer should begin with *The message ...., The words ...., The bag ....*

5 In the group of words *knew, knotted, knife, khan* the first three have a *k* which is not sounded. *Khan* is the odd one out because the *k* is sounded. Say the following groups of words aloud and in each pick out the word which sounds different compared to the other three words in the same group.

   average   wastage   engage   courage
(Listen to the final syllables in each case.)

   access   occur   excess   succeed
(Listen to the c's.)

   reason   jealous   health   weather
(Listen to the first syllable in each word.)

6 Correct the italicized word in each of these sentences:
   He never did *nothing* of the kind.
   I *can't* hardly stand on this surface.
   She hadn't *never* seen a squirrel.

7 Fill in the gaps in these words:
   ar   ment (energetic discussion) *fa   y* (group of relatives) *o   t* (leave out) *ath   ic* (connected with sport) *misch   ous* (full of mischief) *sim   ar* (alike).

8 A letter has been omitted in each of these words. Rewrite them correctly.
   accomodate   Febuary   imediately   exept   goverment   suprise

9 Fill in the one-letter gaps in these words:
   math–matics   defin–tely   rep–tition

10 Each of these three misspellings is caused by bad pronunciation. Say and write the words correctly.
   buisness   interduce   feul

(Answers on p. 185)

Test 14 (See Unit W2)

30 minutes
(10 marks)

SUMMARY

Read Mary Coe's account on p. 23. In not more than 50 words, summarize the contrasts which she points out between past and present.

(Answer, p. 185)

Test 15 (See Unit 1.3)

10 minutes

Either: Write three different opening sentences to describe an occasion when you might have thought: 'I have never felt so cheap'.
Or: Complete these words in three different ways: The first time I . . .

(There are no right answers to these tests. Ask a friend to choose which would interest him or her enough to read on.)

Test 16 (See Unit W4)

20 minutes
(9 marks)

MAKING NOTES

Read this newspaper report and answer all the questions below.

It is difficult to understand the complacency of government ministers on alcohol when so much effort is exerted over illicit drugs, Mr Derek Rutherford, a director of the Institute of Alcohol Studies told a conference in Westminster Abbey yesterday.

He criticized the Government for its unwillingness to publish before the late autumn a survey of young people's drinking habits although it had been completed and delivered to the Minister of Health in October last year.

The report, he said, would confirm that, of all chemical substances, alcohol was the main threat to the young.

The number of young people who die each year with alcohol as the main contributory factor was roughly equal to the toll in three jumbo jet crashes a year, he added.

Mr Rutherford said that the most common cause of death for young people was alcohol-related injury, which he estimated killed at least 1000 young people a year.

The rise in drunkenness offences among people aged under 18 had risen more than threefold during the past 20 years and among girls under 18 the rise had been 610 per cent.

(From *The Times,* 10 June 1986.)

1 Very briefly, what is Mr Rutherford's objection to alcohol? Write your answer in the form of a headline for the report. *(3)*

2 What piece of evidence does the speaker mention in support of his criticism of the Government as self-satisfied and slack? *(3)*

3 Is alcohol a direct or indirect cause of death among young people? Answer in one word; then give your reason for your choice. *(3)*

(Answers, p. 186)

Test 17 (See Units 1.2 and 1.3)

5 minutes

Some of the tools a carpenter uses are for *knocking* one thing into another, or for *cutting* and *biting,* or for *smoothing* rough timber. Words can be used in the same way, e.g.

'Say it, go on, say it – you're thick! Dumb, ignorant, stupid – plain thick!' The speaker here is trying to *hammer* home the message by using words in a plain, rough, disjointed manner – like a hammer.

Write two sentences

   (i) to smooth over somebody's bad temper, by using calming, soothing words:

   (ii) to make a person feel uncomfortable for having made a mistake, by using biting, unkind, sarcastic words.

(We cannot provide an answer to this test; many different ones could be equally good.)

Test 18 (See Unit 1.3)

30 minutes
(12 marks)

Read the following passage from a book called *The Mouse and his Child,* and answer the question that follows.

'Be tramps'

Early the next morning the tramp came through the town, as he did each winter. With the little dog still at his heels he walked the snowy street past the house where the children and the grown-ups lived. He looked into the dustbin to see what he might be able to use, took an empty coffee can and a bundle of newspapers, and went back to the junkyard where he had slept the night before in a wrecked car. Only then did he find the mouse and his child inside the papers, crushed almost flat

but still holding fast to each other. The tramp looked at the battered wrecks around him in the cold, clear sunlight. He looked down at himself in his ragged clothes. Then he sat down in the car he had slept in, and reached into his pocket for a little screwdriver. While the dog watched quietly, he took the mouse and his child apart to see if he could make them dance again. The junkyard lay silent, its wrecks upheaved like rusty islands in the sparkling snow; the only sounds were the bells of Christmas ringing in the town and the cawing of some crows, hoarse and sharp in the cold air.

All that day the tramp sat in the junkyard labouring over the broken toy, stopping to eat some bread and meat that he took from his pocket and shared with the dog. He was able to bend the tin bodies almost back into their original shapes, but he had a great deal of trouble with the clockwork motor. When he wound it up, the mechanism jammed, and in trying to clear it he broke some of the little cogs and bars that had made the mouse father dance in a circle and swing the child up and down. The tramp removed those parts and put the toy together as well as he could. Their patent leather shoes had been lost in the dustbin; their blue velveteen trousers hung wrinkled and awry; their fur had come unglued in several places, but the mouse and his child were whole again.

Now when it was wound up the motor worked without jamming, but the mouse and his child danced no more. The father, his legs somewhat bent, lurched straight ahead with a rolling stride, pushing the child backwards before him. The little dog sat and watched them with his head cocked to one side. The ragged man smiled and threw away the leftover parts. Then he put the toy in his pocket and walked out to the highway.

High on a ridge above the town where snowy fields sloped off on either side, the road crossed a bridge over the railway tracks, went past the town rubbish dump, and stretched away to the horizon. The tramp set the mouse and his child down at the end of the road and wound up the father.

'Be tramps,' he said, and turned and walked away with the dog at his heels.

(From *The Mouse and his Child* by Russell Hoban, Faber & Faber, London.)

Question

This story is told in the third person (i.e. the tramp is 'he' not 'I').
Either: (a) Re-write this incident more briefly in the first person ('I', 'me' etc.), including some of your feelings about your surroundings and what you are doing.
Or: (b) Continue the story as though you were either the mouse or his child, until they meet someone or something new.

(Answers and hints, p. 186)

Test 19 (See Unit W2)

25 minutes
(33 marks)

BBC APPOINTMENTS

DEPUTY EDITOR Current Affairs Television, Northern Ireland	Could you edit *Spotlight*, a current affairs programme in one of the most challenging environments for a journalist? We're looking for a self-starter who can lead confidently a small production team and manage resources effectively. You'll need to know a lot about Ireland, North and South, and have a good track record in current affairs at a senior level. Based in Belfast, but may have to travel at short notice. Salary in the range £15,976-£20,747 p.a. (according to age and experience), plus an allowance of £971 p.a. (Ref. 7631/LI)
PRODUCER/ ASSISTANT PRODUCER Information Technology Open University Production Centre	Open University Production Centre produces broadcast output and an increasing amount of video-cassette and audio-cassette based material, both for the Open University and also for outside agencies involved in education and training. We seek an additional member of production staff to work initially in the area of Information Technology. You should have a good degree in an appropriate subject area and significant relevant experience in industry or education. While there are no formal age qualifications, it is unlikely that those younger than 25 would have appropriate experience. The nature of the department's output is such that you will need to be able to demonstrate an informed interest in, and commitment to, adult education and distance learning. The most important characteristic sought is the potential to visualise while working under pressure as a member of a team. Production training will be provided where necessary. Salary £9,910-£18,205 p.a. negotiable depending on age and experience. A payment of £971 p.a. is given to compensate for unsocial hours. Based Milton Keynes. (Ref. 7643/LI)
SENIOR ASSISTANT Topical Talks African Service £13,341-£17,006* Central London	To be responsible for the output of Topical Talks — on a wide variety of subjects — for transmission into Hausa, Swahili and Somali, and for the provision of talks material, on African affairs, for general use on External Services. You will be required to write and participate in current affairs output and to organise the management of resource and background materials. We look for extensive knowledge of international and African affairs, proven ability as a writer, mature editorial judgement, and a special knowledge of Africa acquired by residence or travel is essential. (Ref. 9872/LI)
REPORTER Radio Cambridgeshire £8,528-£10,581*	Are you a young, ambitious reporter with at least three years' journalistic experience? If so, Radio Cambridgeshire has a vacancy that may interest you. The work is primarily reporting, interviewing, bulletin writing and newsreading. Good microphone voice and current driving licence essential. (Ref. 9890/LI)
REGIONAL RESEARCHER Television Arts Magazine Leeds £8,168-£10,581	*Northern Lights* is BBC TV Leeds regional arts magazine. We now need a Researcher to work on this programme, and other output as required, on a contract basis until April 1987. Essentially you will need to be a journalist with plenty of initiative. Familiarity with television production procedure should ideally be combined with a working knowledge of, and interest in, the arts of the North. (Ref. 7621/LI)
SECRETARIES Central and West London	If you are interested in broadcasting, have excellent secretarial skills and the confidence to use initiative and discretion, we need you now to work in administration areas providing essential back-up for our programmes. (Ref. 86.50/LI)
We are an equal opportunities employer	*Plus allowance of £569 p.a. **Relocation expenses considered for permanent posts.** **Contact us immediately for application form (quote appropriate ref. and enclose s.a.e.) BBC Appointments, London W1A 1AA. Tel. 01-927 5799.**

(From *The Listener*, 6 June 1986.)

Answer the following questions about the BBC APPOINTMENTS advertisement:

1 Quote the two highest salaries, including allowances, i.e. those that might be considered to offer the best career prospects, and give the jobs for which they are offered. *(4 marks)*

2 The six advertisements offer jobs based in six different places. Name the places. *(3 marks)*

3 The SENIOR ASSISTANT must have a special knowledge of Africa. How is this knowledge to be gained? Answer in your own words. *(4 marks)*

4 (i) Explain briefly what you understand by 'Information Technology'. (see PRODUCER/ASSISTANT PRODUCER). *(3 marks)*
(ii) From the same advertisement, explain 'unsocial hours' for which extra payment is given. *(3 marks)*

5 Two of the advertisements are written in a less formal tone than the others. Which are they? What difference does it make? *(4 marks)*

6 SECRETARIES: Why is a secretary with no initiative and no discretion no good? Answer briefly and without anecdotes. (*4 marks*)

7 What is the purpose of the sentence at the end: 'We are an equal opportunities employer'? (*3 marks*)

8 Choose one of the jobs advertised and write for the application form. (See unit W4 for guidance on letterwriting.) (*5 marks*)

Test 20 (General)

30 minutes
(*40 marks*)

VOCABULARY

1 Does *spurious* mean fast, false or sharp?

2 Think of a seven-letter word beginning with *l* meaning handwriting that is easy to read.

3 From the 10 words in italics below choose 5 which best fit these meanings:
   (a) notched like the cutting edge of a saw;
   (b) (mark) that cannot be blotted out or erased;
   (c) at the point of death;
   (d) proud, overbearing, haughty;
   (e) capable of more than one meaning.
   moribund   corrugated   ambiguous   biennial   arrogant
   innate   indelible   morbid   serrated   prodigious

4 What is the meaning of the prefixes in the words *impossible, illegal, inessential*?

5 *Into* or *in to*
   (a) There's the bell; we must hurry   get our satchels.
   (b) John dived   the water.

6 *Upon* or *up on*
   (a) The ornament was high   the shelf.
   (b) She lay   the sofa pretending to read.

7 Which is more likely: *crossroads* or *cross roads*?

8 Would you sooner learn dancing from a *dancing teacher* or a *dancing-teacher*?

9 If you are *cadaverous,* are you like a cad, a corpse or a caveman?

10 Which words are not needed in the following sentences?
   (a) From where did the smell come from?
   (b) I can't tell the difference between the dark-haired pair of twins.
   (c) My collection of glass animals is absolutely unique.
   (d) They returned back home tired and hungry.
   (e) John met up with his friend after work.

11 What is the singular of *media*?

12 What is the plural of *neurosis*?

13 Which of the words in brackets makes sense in the following sentences?
   (a) The best writers are (imaginary/imaginative)
   (b) Cartoons are not trying to give the (allusion/illusion/delusion) of reality.
   (c) 'I must (have/of) put my keys somewhere,' said Jane.
   (d) The (effect/affect) of the drug (effected/affected) the athletes' performance.
   (e) 'It's the (principle/principal) of the thing', said the teacher.

14 Which study is to do with words: *entomology* or *etymology*?

15 If you are *ingenuous* are you more likely to be innocent or guilty?

16 Is *sporadic* very fast, very slow or occasional?

17 Sort the following 20 words into two groups of 10, one with the heading *True,* the other *False.*

frank perjury candour forgery fallacious verity paragon fraud duplicity sincere deceive guileless spurious honest lie distortion unfeigned fidelity irreproachable sham

18 Sort the following 20 words into two groups of 10, one with the heading *Speaking,* the other *Writing.*

signature drawl mute stationery shorthand discourse manuscript raucous intonation hieroglyphic inscribe eloquence utter brochure audible index orator essay journal recite

(Answers on p. 186)

Test 21 (See Unit W2)

<u>15 minutes</u>
(*16 marks*)

(Instructions for doing this test are on p. 76)

Sadie and Kevin sat on the top of Cave Hill with the city spread out below them. They looked down at the great sprawl of factories,   and houses that were gradually eating further and further   the green countryside beyond. Into the midst of the   came Belfast Lough. It was blue this evening, under   blue, nearly cloudless sky, speckled with ships and spiked   the shipyard gantries.

'I like looking down on the   ,' said Kevin.

'Me too,' said Sadie. 'It looks so   , I wish it were!'

It was peaceful up there   the hill with the wind playing round their faces   tousling their hair. Sadie sat with her knees up   her chin, hugging her legs. She felt at ease   Kevin, though of course it was seldom she felt   with anybody, but she also felt a sort of   that she was unused to.

(From *Across the Barricades*, by Joan Lingard, Hamish Hamilton, London.)

(Answers on p. 187).

Test 22 (See Unit W4)

<u>30 minutes</u>
(*30 marks*)

LETTERWRITING

You are buying a bicycle by instalments spread over 12 months and you receive a letter from the firm concerned stating that the seventh instalment is now overdue. You reply explaining that you sent the money in the form of a postal order or cheque signed by a parent on the appropriate date; and invite the firm to take the matter up with the Post Office.

Write three brief letters: the firm's; your reply; your letter to the Post Office.

(Answers on p. 187)

Test 23 (See Unit W5)

<u>5 minutes</u>

PARAGRAPHS

A paragraph is a piece of writing containing one or more sentences (rarely more than five) dealing with one particular part of the subject or one stage of the story being told. It will start on a fresh line, the opening word usually set in from the margin.

Find two, or if possible three, successive paragraphs in whatever reading matter is handy – book, newspaper, magazine – and decide whether the writer uses any particular words to link one paragraph to another. If so, underline them or write them down. If not, re-write one of the sentences in each paragraph so as to make a natural link with the following or preceding paragraph.

(No answer can be provided for this test. Ask a friend, teacher, or parent to read and comment on your work.)

Test 24 (See Unit W3)

(No time limit.
It should take at
least 1 hour)

Look again at the passage from *Sword of Honour* (pp. 89-92). You have been asked to arrange this episode for performance as a play (radio, television or stage). Give a list of characters with brief details (age, appearance etc.) and indicate the stage or studio set, then write the script. Remember that there is no 'narrator'; the story must be made clear from what the characters say and do. You may need to make cuts in the story to adapt it for dramatization and to hold the interest of an audience.

(Hints on answering, p. 188.)

Test 25 (See Unit W5)

10 minutes
(10 marks)

DICTIONARY WORK

1 Decide which part of each of the following words will help you find the word in a good dictionary (e.g. *book* or *worm*?)

bookworm   newsprint   floating rib   floating kidney   bench-mark
goodwill   good taste   polar bear

2 The following words appear on two consecutive pages of *Chambers Twentieth Century Dictionary*. List them in the order they could be placed in the dictionary.

cognition   cocky   coelacanth   coffin   codicil   cognoscente
cocoa   cogent   co-exist   cocoon   coerce   coherence

(Answers on p. 189)

Test 26 (See Unit W3)

40 minutes
(40 marks)

The passage below comes from an adventure story. Read it, then answer the questions that follow.

[*The story so far*: Phillip, a ten-year-old white boy, and Timothy, an old West Indian black man, are the only survivors of a torpedo attack on the ship they were travelling in. Phillip has slowly gone completely blind as a result of a severe blow on the head when the ship sank. Since they landed on a deserted island Phillip has been teaching Timothy to read and write by scratching letters in the sand.]

In the afternoon, Timothy said we'd make a rope.

On the north end of the island, tough vines, almost as large as a pencil, were laced over the sand. It took us several hours to tear out a big pile of them. Then Timothy began weaving a rope that would stretch all the way down the hill to the beach and fire pile. After we'd torn the vines out, and he was weaving the rope, he said,

'Young Bahss, you mus' begin to help wid d'udder wark.'

We were sitting up by the hut. I had my back to a palm and was thinking that back in Willemstad, at this moment, I'd probably be sitting in a classroom, three desks away from Henrik, listening to Herr Jonckheer talk about European history. I'd been tutored in Dutch the first year in Willemstad so I could attend the regular school. Now I could speak it and understand it.

My hands were tired from pulling the vines and I just wanted to sit and think. I didn't want to work. I said, 'Timothy, I'm blind, I can't see to work.'

I heard him cutting something with his sharp knife. He replied softly, 'D'han' is no blin'.'

Didn't the old man understand? To work, aside from pulling up vines or drawing something in the sand, you must be able to see. Stubbornly, he said 'Young bahss, we need sleepin' mats. You can make d'mats.'

I looked over in his direction. 'You do it,' I said.

He sighed back, saying, 'D'best matmaker in Charlotte Amalie, down in French-town, b'total blin'.'

'But he's a man, and he has to do that to make a living.'

'B'true', Timothy said quietly.

But in a few minutes, he placed several lengths of palm fibre across my lap. He really was a black mule. 'D'palm mat is veree easy. Jus' ovah an' under . . .'

Becoming angry with him, I said, 'I tell you, I can't see.' He paid no attention to me. 'Take dis han' d'palm like dis; den ovah an' under, like d'mahn in Frenchtown; den more palm.'

I could feel him standing there watching me as I tried to reeve the lengths, but I knew they weren't fitting together. He said, 'Like dis, I tell you,' and reached down to guide my hand. 'Ovah an' under . . .' I tried again, but it didn't work. I stood up, threw the palm fibres at him, and screamed, 'You ugly black man! I won't do it! You're stupid, you can't even spell . . .'

Timothy's heavy hand struck my face sharply.

Stunned, I touched my face where he'd hit me. Then I turned away from where I thought he was. My cheek stung, but I wouldn't let him see me with tears in my eyes.

I heard him saying very gently, 'B'getting' back to wark, my own self.'

I sat down again.

He began to sing that 'fungee and feesh' song in a low voice, and I could picture him sitting on the sand in front of the hut; that tangled grey hair, the ugly black face with the thick lips, those great horny hands winding the strands of vine.

The rope, I thought. It wasn't for him. It was for me.

After a while I said, 'Timothy . . .'

He did not answer, but walked over to me, pressing more palm fronds into my hands. He murmured, 'Tis veree easy, ovah an' under . . .' Then he went back to singing about fungee and fish.

Something happened to me that day on the cay. I'm not quite sure what it was even now, but I had begun to change.

I said to Timothy, 'I want to be your friend.'

He said softly, 'Young bahss, you 'ave always been my friend.'

I said, 'Can you call me Phillip instead of young boss?'

'Phill-eep,' he said warmly.

(From *The Cay*, by Theodore Taylor, The Bodley Head, London.)

Questions

1 Phillip says 'Didn't the old man understand?' What is your opinion on this? Give a reason for your answer.   (*6 marks*)

2 Both of them lost their tempers. Explain why, and whether either of them was justified in doing so.   (*10 marks*)

3 . What part did the rope play in this episode?   (*10 marks*)

4 Describe an occasion when you lost your temper with someone, and how the episode ended.   (*14 marks*)

(Answers, p. 189)

Check List of Tests

Test no.	Subject	Time (mins)	Marks	Unit
1	Accuracy	20	32	–
2	Spelling	15	40	W5
3	Making notes	25	22	W4
4	Vocabulary	10	12	–
5	Summary: interpretation	30	20	W2
6	Accuracy	5	11	–
7	Letterwriting	15	10	W4
8	Poetry	20	20	W3
9	Style	10	10	–
10	Vocabulary	15	16	W2
11	Vocabulary	15	15	W2
12	Understanding: making notes	30	25	W4
13	Spelling and usage	20	30	W5
14	Summary	30	10	W2
15	Expression	10	–	1.3
16	Making notes	20	9	W4
17	Expression	5	–	1.2/1.3
18	Appreciation: expression	30	12	1.3
19	Interpretation	25	33	W2
20	Vocabulary	30	40	–
21	Vocabulary	15	16	W2
22	Letterwriting	30	30	W4
23	Paragraphing	5	–	W5
24	Playscript	–	–	W3
25	Dictionary work	10	10	W5
26	Appreciation	40	40	W3

11 GENERAL ADVICE FOR THE WRITTEN EXAMINATION

We have planned and written this book to help you with the new GCSE and SCE Standard examinations. As you will have discovered, one of the big differences between these new examinations and the old GCE, CSE Mode 1 and SCE is the reduced emphasis on the written examination paper at the end of the course. There is only one examining body, the one for Wales, that offers an option giving more than half the marks for the final written papers (see syllabus summary p. 10). The normal level is 50 per cent, and most boards offer a 100 per cent coursework option with no final external examination at all. (There is a note on coursework on p. 162.) This means that last-minute advice for 'exam day' does not loom so large and we shall not overburden you with it here.

Another reason for not doing so is that no past papers are available. Detailed references to the actual written examination papers you will be facing can rely only on specimen papers issued by some (not all) boards in advance of the first GCSE examinations in 1988. This evidence suggests that most English written papers will be on similar lines to the *composition, comprehension* and *appreciation* questions that used to be central to GCE and CSE papers, but that there are likely to be more 'open-ended' questions, i.e. ones that give you more chance to express your own views and to give more genuinely personal responses to the material you are presented with. This may be literary – a passage or passages from fiction, or from a play or poem – or in some other form – pictures, diagrams, tables, advertisements etc.

BEFORE THE EXAMINATION

In an examination you face questions set by examiners. All of them have been and most of them still are teachers. They do not like to penalize candidates and often do all they can to find the extra marks that mean a better grade for you. Exams share with other strenuous contests the possibility that you may actually enjoy the challenge. Some people can work right up to the last moment, but for most it is better to take a day off and start the examination completely fresh. This is especially so in English, where what matters is freshness and the skill gained by practice. After a day off you should be both relaxed and energetic; it does not help to be tensed up and worried. If you have used this book well you should be confident that you will do as well as you can. Unlike subjects where you have principally to demonstrate your grasp of facts, English gives you the chance to express *yourself*. This is why your physical condition on exam day is as important as your mental alertness. Go to bed early the night before. Collect anything you will need in the examination room on the evening before: pens, pencil, ruler etc.

THE PAPERS – FIRST IMPRESSIONS

Such evidence as is available suggests that GCSE and SCE Standard papers will be less formal in manner than their predecessors and more helpful to candidates. Here are three samples of instructions taken from specimen GCSE papers. First a very plain one:

Northern Ireland Schools Examination Council

GCSE ENGLISH

PAPER I

Time allowed: 1 hour 15 minutes

Candidates are advised to spend 10 minutes on reading time

This paper carries 20 per cent of the total marks

The next example gives more guidance:

London and East Anglian Group

GCSE EXAMINATION – ENGLISH

Paper 2 – Understanding and Response

Part I of this examination consists of two extracts about which you will be asked to do some writing in Part II

15 minutes is allowed for reading the extracts and for making any notes you wish, after which you will be given Part II with the questions based on the extracts.

Part I

Read the following passages. Both give accounts of teenagers meeting some old people. As you read, you should consider the following:

> *each person's behaviour, feelings and attitudes towards the old people;*
> *the old people's feelings about them;*
> *and the ways in which things are described.*

> *You will be asked questions on these points in Part II.*
> *You have fifteen minutes' reading time. You may make notes on details of the passages in your answer book.*

> *After fifteen minutes you will be given* **Part II**. *This will give you the questions to answer on the passages.*

The third example is more detailed again. We give it in facsimile, to give you a better idea of what may be in store for you.

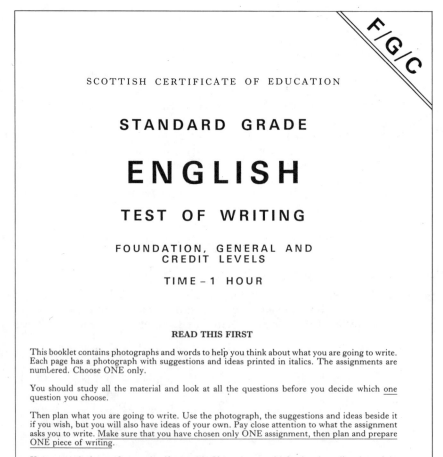

SCOTTISH CERTIFICATE OF EDUCATION

STANDARD GRADE

ENGLISH

TEST OF WRITING

FOUNDATION, GENERAL AND
CREDIT LEVELS

TIME – 1 HOUR

READ THIS FIRST

This booklet contains photographs and words to help you think about what you are going to write. Each page has a photograph with suggestions and ideas printed in italics. The assignments are numbered. Choose ONE only.

You should study all the material and look at all the questions before you decide which <u>one</u> question you choose.

Then plan what you are going to write. Use the photograph, the suggestions and ideas beside it if you wish, but you will also have ideas of your own. Pay close attention to what the assignment asks you to write. <u>Make sure that you have chosen only ONE assignment, then plan and prepare ONE piece of writing</u>.

You may re-draft your first version if you wish. If you do, cancel it by drawing a line through it.

Read and check your work before you hand it in.

Write in the margin the number of the ONE assignment you have chosen. You may also supply a title if you wish.

ESSAY LENGTH AND TIMING

You are often given some guidance about how much to write in written examinations. For instance, in their specimen paper for GCSE the Northern Examining Association say:

> Write approximately two sides on one of the following subjects. If, however, your handwriting is unusually large or unusually small, you should make some adjustment in the amount you write. It is assumed that average handwriting produces about eight words per line.

Their answer books have 30 to 32 lines to the page, so they are asking for about 500 words. It is a good idea to know beforehand what 100 words of your normal handwriting looks like on an average examination page. There is no point in wasting valuable examination time counting words.

This book has given you plenty of opportunities for you to time yourself in answering examination-type questions. If you have worked through them, it will stand you in good stead now. Reserve 10 minutes for reading through and revision at the end; then divide your time according to the mark scheme, or any special instructions there may be. It is not sensible to spend an hour on a question which carries only 10 per cent of the marks and then have to race through another which carries 30 per cent.

INDIVIDUAL QUESTIONS

Plan your answer to essay questions by jotting down ideas and important details. You will not have time to write out a full rough version, even though you may have been doing this in your preparation for the examination.

Answer the question actually set and not the one you hoped for or (worse still!) prepared a set answer for. Do not try to twist the wording. Keep to the number of words or length you are asked for. In particular, do not write too much; this is guaranteed to annoy the marker, who may have 50 or 100 scripts to mark after yours. The marking of your paper will be fair and possibly generous, so do not spoil things by long-windedness or irrelevance, or by failing to take notice of the exact wording of a question.

It is quite likely that your essay in the GCSE written paper will be based on a picture, a poem or some other piece of writing; such questions are favoured by several examining groups. If so, the way you write it should refer clearly to the stimulus material – picture, poem, play extract, whatever it may be. In units 1 to 4 of Writing and Reading we have given you plenty of guidance in planning essays. It is sometimes a good idea to make your essay plan in your actual answer book, to show the examiner how carefully you have thought out your subject. Do remember to rule a line through all such rough work before handing in your paper.

WRITING AND PRESENTATION

If your writing is poor you should by now have done something about it. If you haven't, at least space your words evenly (fairly widely if your writing is small) and neatly on the lines, starting close to the left-hand margin. Try to form each individual letter fully; finish off 'o's and 'a's. All English examiners welcome good clear handwriting, because so much of the paper involves continuous writing. Writing that is difficult or slow to read makes it hard to follow a story or an argument in an essay.

Normally start on the second line of each fresh page. Start fresh paragraphs about one inch in from the margin (this is called 'indenting'). Fill each line, so that when the page is full your work is surrounded by a white space. Good spacing and presentation can do much to make up for not-so-good writing. Mistakes are bound to occur when one is writing under pressure, or against a clock. When you need to cross out, do it with a single line, and preferably with a ruler.

READING THROUGH; THE FINAL CHECK

You have kept 10 minutes for this valuable part of the examination – remember? If you use the time well it may earn you more than 10 extra marks.

First, sort out your answer sheets and get them into the right order for handing in. As you do so, re-check the numbering and lettering of each question, especially those in several parts. Enter your name and examination number where necessary – possibly on each page or on the front of each answer book.

Next, start your final read-through. It is often a good idea to lay a blank sheet of paper across the page, moving it down line by line so that you can give all your attention to each line of writing in turn. Look for the mistakes you *know* you make (e.g. double letters in spelling, *to* for *too* or *two, the* for *they*, small letters where capitals are needed, punctuation left out, or written indistinctly). If in this re-reading you come across a word you are not sure about, replace it by one you know you understand.

Finally, skim through each page with your eye on the whole page. Does it look clear, or messy? Is there anything on it that could confuse or irritate another reader? Are the crossings-out clear and neat? It is surprising how this final check at-a-glance can sometimes pick up a misspelling that a closer look has missed. As each page is checked, lay it with the others in the right order for handing in. If you need to do so, tie or clip all pages together.

Heave a sigh of relief; you have done your best.

Summary of advice

1 Get into the right frame of mind—keen but not tense; refreshed; hopefully determined.

2 Think of the convenience of your examiner: write legibly in dark (blue or black) ink; make clear alterations; number your answers carefully. Come to the examination room with the proper equipment.

3 Read and follow the instructions on the paper. Answer the right number of questions. Never leave a blank.

4 If there is a choice, decide which are the best questions for you.

5 Plan your time carefully so that most is given to the questions carrying the most marks.

6 The examiner does not demand miracles. He does demand a reasonable competence. Rely on yourself to get rid of all the unnecessary mistakes which may squander your marks; for this purpose leave yourself time for a close, critical reading of your script before handing it in.

A NOTE ON COURSEWORK

The writing in your folder represents your *best* work; let it cover the whole range of what you have achieved in written English during the course. However good you are at one kind of writing, don't serve it up every time, like the boy who always wrote Sci-Fi (Science Fiction), whether he was asked for personal experience, a factual account or even a letter to a future employer!

Coursework can have no last-minute advice, but it is worth making a few points about the final version of your pieces of writing for the folder.

Here is a question. You will gain by answering it honestly:

Have you kept up the highest standard you are capable of in *accuracy* and *presentation* in every one of the items in your folder, and in the folder itself?

People usually take a lot of trouble over the first piece, improving it through many drafts, being meticulously accurate in checking spelling, punctuation and layout, and taking a pride in the clear handwriting. Were you as conscientious over the *fifth* piece—or over the *eighth*? Did you rush the last pieces to make up the number? We hope you are reading this in time to recover your first standard and good intentions. You should have left yourself time to re-write a messy or inadequate piece and to put the whole folder in order. Check carefully the instructions your examining board gives for arranging and presenting coursework folders.

Some sample questions

As we have explained, there are no past papers for GCSE from which to draw sample questions. Nevertheless, we think it may be helpful to you to think about the written examination in terms of questions to be answered. So we have set out below a few typical ones for you to consider or practise answering. They were set, or are modelled on ones set for the combined GCE and CSE '16+' examinations. These were forerunners of GCSE and the experience gained from them has been used in planning the new examinations system. Apart from question 3 we have not prepared full answers; there is plenty of writing practice with answers elsewhere in the book. Some comments and hints on answering follow the questions themselves (p. 165).

1 Read the extract below, which consists of a series of notes taken from a discussion of visiting times in the Children's Ward of Wallham Hospital. Use it as a basis for your answer to ONE of the questions which follow. You may add extra detail if you wish.

Your writing should take up about 25 lines of your answer book, which is about 150 words.

Write appropriately and organize your material well.

> **Mrs Wilson** (mother of Andrew, at present a patient in the Children's Ward)
> 'Sick children need us when they're ill . . . it's upsetting to be ill without separation from your parents as well . . . we like to be with our children when they are ill or upset . . . two short visiting sessions a day is ridiculous . . . we should be allowed to visit whenever we like.'

Nurse Harris (who works in the Children's Ward)
'Children need quiet . . . parents make the child feel worried because they communicate their anxiety . . . hospital routine is upset by parents coming in when they feel like it . . . children are upset when parents have to leave.'

Doctor Turner (a doctor who visits the Ward)
'Nursing staff are already overworked . . . hospital is overcrowded . . . some parents might visit more than others, leaving some children feeling deprived. . . . two hours visiting a day is plenty . . . mothers can come in the afternoon, fathers in the evening.'

Mrs Alexander (visiting social worker)
'The children are most important and their needs come first . . . hospitals could be more flexible . . . parents might help nurses with chores . . . children get bored easily during recovery . . . perhaps unemployed fathers could help as well.'

Now write ONE of the following

(a) A letter, from Mrs Wilson to the Editor of the *Wallham Echo*, expressing her views in a fuller form.

(b) A record of the discussion explaining in detail the reasons given for opposing longer visiting hours.

(c) A letter from a patient in the Children's Ward expressing his or her opinions on visiting times.

(d) A report, from Nurse Harris to the Hospital's Senior Medical Officer, stating her views in more detail.

(e) A letter, to the Chairman of Wallham Area Health Authority, using some of these points in order to give your own views on visiting times.

2 You have just given a party for a group of six- and seven-year-olds. The party is now over; all the guests have gone and you have been left to clear up – completely alone! Describe the scene and your feelings as you think about what has gone before.

3 *The Tollund Man* The discovery of this 2000-year-old Iron Age man in a Danish peat bog is described in unit W1 (p. 22). Here are some details of the research that followed. Read them, then answer the questions.

An autopsy showed that the inner organs such as the heart, lungs and liver were very well preserved. So was the alimentary canal, which was removed by Dr Hans Helbaek, with the object of determining the nature of the dead man's last meal. This was still contained in the stomach and in the larger and smaller intestines which, though somewhat flattened by the weight of the overlying peat, were otherwise intact.

These organs were carefully rinsed externally, to remove contamination from the surrounding peat. Their contents were then washed out and proved to consist of a blend of finely reduced plant remains and particles of seeds. The contents of the stomach and the smaller intestine were inconsiderable, occupying in volume barely 0.5 and 10 cubic centimetres respectively. The contents of the larger intestine, on the other hand, amounted to 260 cubic centimetres. All was of the same character. It was not possible to establish with certainty the proportions of the different ingredients because the plants had varied in their resistance to the digestive juices which had acted on them from the time the meal was eaten and for some while after death.

By the time it has been crushed in a handmill and between the teeth, a meal of this kind, consisting largely of grains and seeds, is reduced to myriads of small particles. The basis of the investigation was a sample of 50 cubic centimetres taken from the larger intestine . . .

. . . a point of great interest was established. Investigation showed that although the contents of the stomach consisted of vegetable remains of a gruel prepared from barley, linseed . . . and knotweed, with many different sorts of weeds that grow on ploughed land, it could not have contained any meat at the time of death, since recognizable traces of bone, sinew or muscular tissue would certainly have remained.

It was further established, from the degree of digestion of the remains of the meal in the alimentary canal, that the Tollund Man had lived for between 12 and 24 hours after eating his last meal.

QUESTIONS

[As this is a useful short exercise to do as practice, we have given 'model answers' below. Don't look at them until you have tried writing your own.]

(a) What is the alimentary canal and why did Dr Helbaek remove it?

(b) Which part of the body contained the most food?

(c) Explain in your own words why it was impossible to decide how much of each item of food was left in the body.

(d) How was the length of time between the man's last meal and his death established?

(e) Could vegetarians claim the Tollund Man as 'one of us'? Give a reason for your answer.

4 This country is notorious for its weather. Describe your general attitude to weather, how it affects you, e.g. at school: PE, fieldwork, dinner hour; at home: at weekends, holidays etc.

5 Make up a story from the ideas and feelings suggested to you by these lines of poetry:

> There were strange riders once, came gusting down
> Cloaked in dark furs, with faces grave and sweet,
> And white as air.

Kenneth Slessor

6 Below is a table showing the number of books issued by a public library at different times of the year. The Library Committee has decided (a) to try keeping the library open for one hour longer during May, June, July and August; (b) to increase the stock of biographies; (c) to reduce the number of new books on sport. As Librarian, explain the changes in a brief news item for the local newspaper, using the information given in the table.

Classes of books	Numbers of books issued			
	Men readers		Women readers	
	April-Sept.	October-March	April-Sept.	October-March
Fiction	1000	1600	1200	2000
Biography	2000	2200	1000	1150
Do-it-yourself	450	700	200	500
Gardening	650	800	1250	900
Politics	520	560	900	1400
Sport	200	650	200	225
Outdoor pursuits	500	850	400	550
Travel	1000	1700	800	950

7 Read the passage below carefully, then answer the question which follows it.

Other Pests

At the age of about eight years I developed an enthusiasm for entomology and for creepy-crawlies of all kinds which has survived to this day.

My first study consisted of a detailed research project into the lifestyle of the common garden spider and was accomplished by the collection of these charming arachnids in empty 'Swan Vesta' matchboxes. My investigations were proceeding nicely until Grandmother, making one of her infrequent visits but endeavouring to light one of her all too frequent cigarettes, opened one of the boxes. Apart from the shriek which followed, the consequences were an unconscious relative on the living-room carpet, only to be revived with a stiff gin, and a spider collection which was promptly despatched by mother, together with some unpleasant popping and crackling sounds, into the solid-fuel boiler in the kitchen.

It was shortly after this that I inherited 'Fred', the stick insect; actually I won him at marbles. He presented no difficulties but his pin-like offspring emerged in their thousands to swarm through the airholes in his box on to carpets, clothes and curtains. A plague of biblical proportions was avoided by the ingenuity of my father who discovered that the Hoover, fitted with a bizarre attachment called a crevice cleaner, could be adapted to suck countless hordes of these tiny pests to a dusty death in the bowels of its dust bag.

Caterpillars came next with cinnebar larvae, gaudily hooped in Wolverhampton

Wanderers' old gold and black, strung across the living-room in futile quests for ragwort, their only food source, under the television and bookcase. Few survived this odyssey and the vast majority were colourfully mangled by tag-playing infants into the pink needlecord carpet.

Those that did, of course, turned into moths, beautiful and graceful over summer fields at dusk but demented and lunatic in the house. Insanely, they crashed from room to room, eventually to plunge dramatically into light bulbs and an incandescent self-incineration.

Finally, there were crane-flies, 'ginny-spinners' or 'daddy-long-legs' to the uninitiated, droning like lost bombers through open windows in autumn, their long articulated legs swaying below their tiny bodies to settle untidily wherever there was space. Unfortunately, my young brother found it an interesting challenge to discover how many limbs were required for mobility and at what point the entire flimsy structure collapsed into a twitching decline.

Numbering your answers from one to five describe the problems associated with each of the pests mentioned, and briefly outline the ways in which they died.

QUESTIONS ON READING

The last two questions are related to reading you have done during the GCSE course. Examinations syllabuses (e.g. NISEC, see syllabus summary p. 10) sometimes include a list of recommended reading. As we have explained in unit W3 in Writing and Reading, it is normal for work related to such reading to be included in your coursework folder. However, you may find a general question on similar lines to these two in a written paper; and in any case it is helpful to practise thinking of your reading in such terms.

8 Choose a difficult or unsatisfactory relationship that is important in a book you have studied.
  (a) Describe briefly that relationship and the people involved.
  (b) Suggest why the relationship does not work and what might have made it work.
  (c) Say how typical of real life you found this relationship to be.

Always mention the title and author of the book you are writing about. The word 'book' may be taken to include 'short story'. Credit will be given for a detailed knowledge of books and you should give suitable quotations and make frequent references to incidents and characters.

9 (a) Name a theme you have been studying this year, e.g. love, loyalty, poverty, prejudice, relationships.

(b) Show how your understanding of this theme has been made wider and deeper by the ways it has been dealt with by *any two* writers of prose, poetry or drama. (You could, for example, choose writers who hold different, even opposing views; or writers who give a full picture, the one by writing the facts, the other by writing novels about the facts; or writers from other times or places who show you how attitudes towards your chosen theme vary.)

Comuments and Hints on Answering

1 It is common for examination questions to be based on a piece of writing. Do read the *whole* extract carefully; it will help you, whichever question you choose and will also give guidance about what 'extra detail' to add. Questions (b) and (d) will be helped if you include some reported speech. See unit W5 in Writing and Reading for help with this.

2 If you are not too resentful at having to clear up, your description could be humorous. You could bring out some of the differences between six- and sixteen-year-olds.

3 (a) The alimentary canal is the passage through which food passes down the body. You are expected to be able to answer questions like this on matters accepted as general knowledge. Dr Helbaek removed it to find out what the man had eaten for his last meal.
  (b) The larger intestine contained the most food.
  (c) The process of digestion had reduced some items of food more than others.
  (d) By noting the different rates at which the vegetable contents were digested.
  (e) The Tollund Man might have eaten meat in meals before his last one.

4 You would not choose to answer a question like this unless you were sensitive to changes of weather. The way the question is worded makes it possible for you to concentrate either on weather you *like* – sunbathing, snow fights, etc. – or *dislike*. An unusual approach might be to describe your love of walking in rain, strong winds etc. Think whether your views of people and places are affected by the weather.

5 Let your mind reflect on the questions raised by the quotation before you begin your story, i.e. who were the 'strange riders'? Where had they come from? Are their 'sweet faces' a clue?

6 You need to be prepared for questions like this, based on drawing inferences (see unit W2) from statistical information. You need a clear head for this one in order to extract and present in an easily understandable way the three pieces of information asked for. Think also about the readers of the paper you are writing for.

7 Don't be put off by particular words in the passage you may find hard to understand. Even if you don't know 'entomology', 'bizarre' or 'odyssey', you should be able to make enough sense to get two marks from each of the five paragraphs. The structure of the passage should help you: para 1 'My first study . . .', para 2 '. . . shortly after this . . .', para 3 'Caterpillars came next . . .' etc. You get one mark for describing each of five 'problems' and one for a 'brief' outline or summary of the five causes of death. Be brief; use your own words, don't copy direct from the passage. Here is an example: 3 The caterpillars died when they were trodden into the carpet during children's games.

8 & 9 Questions like these are not asking for the close textual knowledge expected of you for works set for English Literature examinations. You can draw on what you remember of your favourite spare time reading, as long as it was well chosen. Decide which form of literature you feel most confident about – fiction or non-fiction, long stories or short ones, plays (including those seen on stage or screen if they were worth while), poetry – and try to shape your answer accordingly.
Important Always name the book(s) or pieces you are talking about, giving title, author etc. The note included in question 9 is worth applying generally to questions of this kind.

9 You need to think carefully about the wording of this question. Relate it to a book read recently, either fictional or based on real life (biography, travel, adventure etc.). The 'relationship' you choose, between two or more people – this might be stretched to include one between person and animal – has to be (i) difficult or unsatisfactory, (ii) important in the book.

12 ANSWERS

Unit 1.1

THE TOLLUND MAN (p. 23)

1 Non-scientific opinions:

had been deposited as a sacrifice
forehead and mouth seemed to take on a look of affliction
last sentence of the extract

2 For the record

Position: lying as if he were asleep
head and legs pointing west/east; face to south
body had been below 8/9 ft. of peat, lying about 50 yards away from firm ground.
Clothing and appearance; naked except for pointed skin cap fastened with hide/thong under chin
smooth hide belt round waist
hair very short, almost covered by cap
clean-shaven, short stubble on chin and upper lip
noose of two twisted leather thongs round neck pulled tight into throat. Ends of noose over shoulder and down across back.

3 A Life for a Life?

Museum Man Shock

The heavy work of transporting the 'bog man' to the National Museum in Copenhagen brought death to Mr Arne Jensen, 54, at 11.10 a.m. today. Mr Jensen was one of a group of helpers engaged in hoisting the peat-packed body in its wooden crate, 10 feet up from soft ground where lifting-gear was useless.

Mr Jensen had been apparently in good health on the site the previous day when plans and tests were made preparatory to the lift. But today, without warning, as the group bent to take up their positions, Mr Jensen crumpled silently on the soft earth. His horrified workmates attempted mouth to mouth resuscitation but death had been instantaneous.

The horse and cart waiting to take the 2000-year-old body found itself taking a 2-hour-old-body as well. Did the bog resent man's intrusion and claim a life for a life? (150 words approx)

MARY COE (p. 23)

1 (a) The paragraph has only a few details about the Forester's Parade (*not* the Hospital Parade) so use your imagination and decide exactly where you stood to watch and how long you had to wait before the men appeared. You could say who you were with, what you wore, how you passed the waiting time. But be sure to make the throwing of the sweets the most important part of the description. Decide whether to make the climax delight and sticky fingers or disappointment and crushed ones.

1 (b) Sharp senses make for good description. Try to see the colours, hear the sounds, feel the heat, the rain, the crush of the crowds. Are there smells and tastes as well? Find words for the ones that suit your occasion best, and remember they are to be listened to, not read.

2 Mary Coe had lived in a group of cottages and houses called the Pits all her life; she lived in her own cottage for fifty-four years. There was no water from the mains and no inside sanitation. Washing had to be dried on the roadside hedges. Her father was a labourer for the Coatesworths, big farmers. He earned ten, later twelve shillings a week for working on the land and feeding the animals twice on Sundays.

From his ten shillings, he kept one and his wife had nine on which to keep the house and the family of four girls. He could buy a pint of beer for twopence and if he could earn anything extra, he could buy tobacco, but if not he went without. The girls used to divide a pennyworth of sweets a week between them; they never had them every day as we do now.

They played hopscotch, and had wooden hoops and skipping ropes. At Christmas they were satisfied with a very cheap toy and an orange or apple. Neither they nor their parents had known anything better and so they were satisfied.

HOW TO KEEP DRY (p. 25)

1 'Find out some facts' – a walk down your street or in a built-up area will quickly provide you with facts and ideas. Lots of people have had new front doors – different shapes and different fittings; your eye may be caught by the variety of coloured paint displayed on woodwork. Facts are easily come by; how to make them interesting? Here your likes and dislikes can liven up your description; try to find more appealing words than 'beautiful' and 'horrible' to express them.

The man writing about roofs keeps producing some unexpected aspects of his subject: thatch which only lasts two years seems pretty useless, but he ends the paragraph, 'As it only takes a day to thatch a cabin this does not matter'. Then he seems to rule out another kind of thatch as too expensive but the surprise here is the many uses of the old thatch even after it has been taken off the roof.

These 'mini' shocks keep the reader alert. Although we may be scarcely conscious of them as we read, the writer has placed them to good effect. If you are describing neat front gardens with immaculate lawns, let there be one, not shaggy with weeds, just bright white with daisies. If you have had a newspaper round, you could relate the position of the letterboxes to your back muscles and the difficulty of keeping a bend/stretch rhythm going because of the absurd positions at numbers 76 and 88.

The facts must come first; they are the data for your experiment in conveying information. Then your imaginative understanding of what makes good reading takes over to decide how best to present those facts, to make the experiment work.

Now good luck with your paragraphs on floors, chimneys or whatever you choose.

2 You may have strong views for or against some types of housing but this question invites you to show good and bad in all types. If you express opinions, keep them cool.

YOGHURT (p. 26)

'A helpful account for a friend' could be written in the first person: 'I clean my bicycle on Fridays after school, . . .' or simply give instructions like the yoghurt account: 'Take 3lbs strong flour . . .'

Take care over the sequence of your instructions. Try to pass on some special methods that you have discovered or been shown; make the account personal and helpful.

Unit 1.2

'CARE AND FEEDING OF MOTHERS' (p. 29)

Light-hearted touches: The title is the first one, referring to 'mothers' as though they were a species of pet animal. The author's self-criticism shows when she interposes 'I have *nothing* if not strong opinions . . .' etc.

Further hints: The length you are asked for here means that you probably cannot simply write 'I think that . . .' and spend all the time giving personal views. Like Helen Brown you will need one or more examples to bring your argument to life. For (a) it could be a clear case known to you where a mother let her concern to earn money override her care for her child(ren). Perhaps he/she/they had to come home from school every day to an empty house, or did not get proper meals. For (b) you may be able to draw on your own experience. Have you ever argued this case with your parents? Remember that to persuade your audience you will need to show that you understand the point of view of those who oppose you, but still think yours is the better case.

THE USE OF CHEMICALS IN AGRICULTURE (pp. 34)

Our method was first to skim through the passage for the general ideas, which are not difficult and then to make a list of points for each of the two questions. Here is our list, which we then used to write our answers.

1 (a) Belief that plants need nothing but chemicals
Results:
big industry to discover and sell chemicals
money before food
factory farming
pollution
destruction of fertility
farmer obliged to use poisons, possibly dangerous
waste of energy in producing chemicals
quantity not quality – mistaken research

(b) *Alternative:*
let soil itself grow things instead of acting as a medium for chemicals
do this by returning organic waste to soil and building up its fertility
organic farming produces yields as high as those of factory farming and sometimes greater profits
possibilities if organic farming backed by research

This is how we wrote up the points in our summary:

(a) The belief that plants need nothing but chemicals and that the soil can be neglected has had undesirable results. Agriculture became a big industry, concerned with inventing and selling artificial products. The farm itself became a factory, manufacturing plants and animals to make money rather than produce food.

Further results were pollution and the destruction of the soil's fertility, as farmers were obliged to use more pesticides. Moreover there is a waste of energy in making these chemicals; and what counts is quantity not quality. (85 words. Are any savings possible?)

(b) The soil itself should be allowed to grow things, instead of acting as a medium for chemicals. This is achieved by returning all organic waste to the soil, thus building up its fertility. The method is productive, profitable and has great possibilities. (42 words)

(Note that the important parts of the original for this answer are found in para. 4, second half, and para. 5.)

2 Six possible topics are suggested. Remember they are only examples; if none of them appeals to you, choose one of your own that you feel strongly about. You need to make clear what form of publication your piece is intended for, then make sure that you know enough about the facts of the situation to present a strong case. Philippa Pullar makes it evident that she has the necessary scientific and statistical knowledge to support her case for more organic farming. The best way to test whether your piece is a good one is to ask someone to read and comment on it whom you know is *not* in sympathy with your view. Thus, if you have written an article for your peace group newsletter about police brutality at demonstrations, ask a supporter of the police or the government to give you their views on it.

HERBAL REMEDIES (p. 36)

1 *ridicule*

old crones . . . potions
whimsical superstitions
quaint remedies . . . past
interwoven with . . . magic
very poetic . . . science
myths and legends

defence

herbal medicine still flourishing
in Third World . . . care herbal . . .
experience . . . a practical art
some . . . faster effect . . . system
Once it was realized . . . revered

2 Dear Fran,

I was very sorry to hear that your dad had another 'turn' during your holiday in the Hebrides. It must have cast a shadow over your stay there.

I know you think I'm a herb crank, but has he ever tried foxglove leaves as a remedy? Before you have a good laugh, just read on a bit! Have you heard of *digitalis* as a medicine for heart disease? It is well known to doctors—ask one if you don't believe me. Well, that is simply the Latin name for foxgloves. And it has been proved that an infusion of foxglove leaves, picked when the flowers are out, can have a direct effect in stimulating the heart muscles. So before you call me 'Ferdie the flower freak' again, just get your dad to try it!

Yours ever,
Ferdie

SAHARA JOURNEY (p. 38)

1 Mixed feelings—Moorhouse is first aware of the perfection of the snake's camouflage. Although he knows it is dangerous, he seems to regret its death and the brutality involved. He sees beauty and danger in the scorpion too, with its colour and the threat of its sting.

2 The journey was physically too exhausting for Moorhouse to give the ancient quern the attention it deserved. Old Mohamed's only interest in the flint tool was as a light for his pipe.

3 Moorhouse recognizes the beauty of the creatures where the Arabs only see them as

dangerous. Their eyesight is much sharper than his, but he is more thoughtful about the discoveries than they are.

4 (No single answer to this question.)

Unit 1.3

THE OLD PATAGONIAN EXPRESS (p. 47)

1 (a) 'I don't think I can stand much more of this,' said Theroux to his neighbour. 'Where's the next stop?'

The sallow-faced Peruvian next to him shrugged his shoulders. 'Matucana – but you'll be no better off there than in the train. I know the place and it's a dead-and-alive hole if ever there was one.' He turned away and just got to the window in time.

Theroux muttered to himself. 'Anything would be better than this. I can't stand the smell of vomit.'

The Peruvian smiled wanly. 'Why not throw up yourself? You'll feel better.'

1 (b) 'How much for a fill, please?'

The old oxygen-seller, who looked as if nothing would ever make him ill, eyed Theroux closely. 'Two dollars to you, sir.'

'Two dollars!' exclaimed Theroux. 'That's disgraceful! Two dollars for an empty balloon? You are selling it far cheaper to these people.'

The old man looked crafty. 'Ah, but they are poor, sir. You are rich Americano. Two dollars! Take it or leave it.'

Theroux suddenly felt a bigger qualm, so fighting back his nausea he grumbled, 'Looks as if I have no choice. OK, but fill it properly!'

2 This is a very personal question and answer so here are a few hints about one possible situation – at the dentist's:

in the waiting room – posters of outsize teeth intensify anxiety; tooth not now aching; why do other people look so calm? forced smile as receptionist comes for you; dentist chatty – good: agony postponed; bad: longer to wait for relief.
sights and sounds – gentle running water, metallic click of instruments picked up and put down; drill accelerates to high pitched sound, smell of friction as tooth is ground; can stand it no longer – . . . rinse; relax for filling; any discomfort now tolerable.

IN THE AMAZON HOTEL (p. 49)

1 From the colour of the make-up kit
2 This is the reason for their stay in New York.
3 The hotel was for women only.
4 She refers to 'being all right again'.
5 She gave the sun-glasses case to the baby to play with.

DIRECT AND OBLIQUE WRITING (p. 52)

2 More descriptive words:
1 The brass face of our old grandfather clock stared dimly out of its shadowy corner; but age had not diminished the clarity of its chime – we counted eight slow strokes.

2 The complete silence in the empty house, which had seemed so reassuring, was suddenly broken by a distant but unmistakable sound – the noise of hammering.

3 I was pleased to see the postman, and delighted when he handed me a little parcel. As I took it, my first thought was – how can such a little box be so surprisingly heavy?

4 There are many people who have, to a greater or lesser extent, a weight problem. The most obvious way of controlling overweight is to limit the calorie intake.

3 Obliquely, linking the fact to something else:
1 We were happily managing to eat, drink and talk all at the same time. A noisy, carefree, laughing group – until from the clock in the corner a wheezy whirring followed by eight resonant strokes brought a sudden silence – we needed to get moving.

2 Our new house was nearing completion. The roof was on, windows were glazed and plaster was drying. Picking my way from one empty room to another, over rubble barely visible in the late evening half-light, I suddenly heard, from upstairs, the sound of hammering.

3 I suppose I am lucky to have a job at all. But being secretary to a peevish old professor, typing and re-typing his boring notes, listening to his complaints, making his endless cups of coffee and filing his mountains of mail is not my idea of fun. But one morning, with letters in one hand, the postman held out in the other a little parcel. Addressed to me, and surprisingly heavy.

4 The street was almost exactly as I had remembered it. I angled my camera, wanting a shot of the elegant half-timbered facades and the stone Market Hall; then I noticed a trendy new snack bar called 'The Calorie Counter'–good for weight watchers, I thought, bad for my picture–I moved, trying for a different slant.

4 *More obliquely, rendering the original item of seemingly casual importance*
1 The TV set was new–large and black, with hoops of aerial angled on the top, and chrome and plastic legs firmly astride the Wilton. Beside its volume of sound and rainbow of colours, the dim face and dimmer chime of the old grandfather clock, striking eight, seemed to belong to a forgotten world.

2 Desperately, he shoved at the door; unbelievably, it opened. Just inside, panting from his flight, he stood slumped against the wall and listened for the chasing footsteps getting fainter down the lane and away. Then silence, and he assumed the house to be empty–till he heard the sound of someone hammering. Strangely, this did not scare him.

3 A person needs to live in Northern Ireland to know what it is to be scared of ordinary things–a knock at the door by a man you don't know, an army jeep turning into your road, a phone call late at night. One day the postman handed me a small, heavy parcel–I would not open it, but all it was, was a box of golf balls from my brother. My mum opened it, she recognized his writing.

4 I got mad at my mother. She was grumbling at me about what she called my extravagance–she said I should be able to control my urge to spend every single penny I had in my purse every week. I retorted that she should be able to control her urge to eat–I said 'with your calorie intake you'll be fifteen stone by Christmas!' Unfortunately my father just walked in then and he got mad at me for speaking rudely. As you can imagine we had a really cheerful evening.

I KNOW WHY THE CAGED BIRD SINGS (p. 56)

Brobdingnag was the name Jonathan Swift gave to the country of giants in his *Gulliver's Travels*. Maya Angelou feels small and defenceless as she wakes in the car to see apparently huge faces peering in at her.

1 In the book Maya Angelou goes on to describe how she makes friends with the other homeless children who use the junkyard as their base. They had worked out for themselves rules of behaviour and sharing which she recognized to be morally good, hence the reference to 'the brotherhood of man'.

2 The best source for this would be a true episode–perhaps when you or your family moved to a new neighbourhood, or when you travelled overseas. If you were born or grew up outside Britain a suitable subject might well be your first impressions of this country, or a particular incident when you knew little or nothing about school or home life here.

Unit W2

ADVERTISING (p. 61)

This question concentrates on the language of advertising. (See unit 2.6, Persuasive Writing.) Because there is less substance to the three extracts than to some comprehension passages there are no questions asking simply for observation (Type 1). Questions (*b*)(5) and (6) involve *summarizing*. We have helped you with questions (*a*)(5) and (*b*)(2).

(*a*)(1)	Types 2 and 3
(*a*)(2),(*a*)(5), (*b*)(1)	all Type 4. The answer to (*a*)(5) is on lines 11 and 12,
(*b*)(2), (*b*)(3), (*b*)(6)	and to (*b*)(2) on lines 3 and 4
(*a*)(3), (*d*)	Type 5
(*a*)(4), k(*c*)	Type 3
(*a*)(6), (*b*)(4)	Types 3 and 5.

PLAYING LISZT (p. 62)

Notice that although this passage involves plenty of dialogue and describes an encounter between people rather than simply stating facts or opinions, we use just the same techniques in studying its meaning, i.e. in *comprehending* it.

1, 5(*c*)	Type 1

2	Types 4 and 3
3, 4, 5,(*c*)	Type 5
5(*a*) and (*b*)	Type 3
6	Type 2

THE FOOTBALL GAME (p. 64)

When you begin to look at the passage to find material for (1), train your eye to look for capital S's. Not all will be 'Sugden' (there are some 'Sir' and 'Spurs'), but intelligent scanning saves time.

'Mr Sugden' appears in the first line and 'Sugden (teacher)' a few lines further down. The next time 'Sugden' appears, it is preceded by 'Mr' and followed by '(referee)' so your brain registers that you have now found two of Mr Sugden's parts; simultaneously your eye drops down a few lines to the next 'Sugden' and there's the third part: '(player)'.

It is not obligatory to describe the parts in the order in which they are mentioned provided that you make clear which one you are describing. After reading the extract, you probably remember most about Mr Sugden (player) so start with that, beginning your answer:

(1) Mr Sugden plays three parts: teacher, referee, player.

As *player*, Mr Sugden is not very good . . .

Keeping your eyes open for capital S's, collect information from the passage, e.g.

    fails to stop ball – 'rolled under studs'

    couldn't dribble – 'too far ahead each time'

    his pass to wing 'shot out of play a good ten yards in front of him'

    Tibbut can outjump S

    gets out of breath – 'S started to chase . . . ball crossed line before he could reach it'

Such notes can quickly be written into a good paragraph to show Sugden's standard of play.

As *teacher* . . .

    too keen on his appearance and on winning himself – childish

    (Do you think this is the main point against Sugden as teacher?)

    blames others for his own faults – winger didn't run fast enough

    stands on his dignity – 'Don't argue with me, lad!'

    expects the impossible – Billy to save a goal headed into the top right-hand corner of the net

    no sympathy for the mud-covered Billy – S largely responsible for this

Do you think Sugden's criticism of Sparrow, the right back, is justified? If you answer no, you could add it to these points, all of which add up to a pretty poor report on Sugden as a teacher.

As *referee* . . .

Information on this role is given only at the beginning of the game and the end of the extract. Sugden starts the game efficiently, perhaps too efficiently, waiting for the exact second? At the end, his team, Manchester United, is one goal down. The referee (Sugden) awards a penalty. A player (Sugden) scores. The author makes no comment but leaves the reader to draw his own conclusions. What are yours? Does Sugden take unfair advantage of his position?

(2) The snatches of the boys' conversation are the best places to look for this answer. They are prepared to defend themselves (give examples) but are remarkably polite in the circumstances. Private mutterings though are more outspoken – 'chuffing carthorse', 'hopeless'.

Have the boys got Sugden weighed up? Do they humour him out of habit? Look at Tibbut's wink and his readiness to go along with Sugden's refusal to allow him to choose Liverpool as his team.

If you know a teacher like Sugden, do resist the temptation to get carried away and write pages of criticism! Keep to Sugden and the information about him in the passage; that will be enough to give you full marks for (2).

(3) The right back stood looking at Billy.

    'I can't see tha shirt for mud.'

Billy continued to pick at the hardening layer on his sleeve.

    'It weren't fair. He only did it for spite.'

    'If tha hadn't dropped down when tha did, he could've winded yer, or worse.'

    'I saw the look in his eyes; I knew I were going to get something.'

    'It's a rotten shame. He's always picking on you. Why doesn't he try someone his own size?'

    'D'you think he'd notice if we bunked off? It's nearly dinner time.'

    'He'd notice all right but come on, he's pulling out his whistle to blow for time.'

Sympathy (commiseration) for Billy and antipathy (the opposite) for Mr Sugden would be a proper theme for this conversation. If you get that and the layout right – full marks.

PACKAGING (p. 68)

Although this passage presents plenty of straight information for you to select from, it is a trickier test than the previous one, because the writer's method is less clearcut. He moves back and forth from arguments in favour of packaging to its disadvantages, without committing himself to either. A careful set of preliminary notes is essential here. You should head two columns 'advantages' and 'problems', then work through the passage, jotting down the points as they occur. We shall not do this for you, but the following key will help you to check your list of completeness before writing your paragraph:

> advantages – lines 11-20, 21-3, 27-31, 31-5, 47;
> problems   – lines 2-10, 24-7, 36-46, 47-51.

As you can see, more space is devoted to problems than to advantages, so this should be reflected in the respective length of your two paragraphs.

THE ART OF THE CAVE-DWELLERS (p. 70)

At first it is not easy to connect the two quoted statements; yet until we understand them we can't start the article. The best way to deal with something apparently obscure like this is to tackle it bit by bit. 'Art and science . . .' What examples have we been given? 'Art' is easy – the cave-paintings; but 'science'? The nearest we can get to this seems to be the tool-making skill of early man.

Now, if we start thinking about it, these *do* both show man 'visualizing the future' – preparing for the hunt the next day, or month. Once this is clear to us we can soon see what is meant by the other quotation: a telescope is an instrument for looking into the distance. The cave paintings and the tools and weapons were ways of 'looking' into the future. After this preliminary thinking we are in a position to set to work:

When a caveman painted hunting scenes on cave walls he was imagining the dangers of hunting. By making pictures of these dangers he could prepare himself to face them, just as he could make tools and weapons for future hunting. He also used his imagination – as we do – to convert the two-dimensional pictures into three-dimensional reality. By making paintings he used his imagination to anticipate dangers; we use ours, when *we* see the paintings, to re-create the culture of the cave-dwellers. These basic ideas can be expanded into the article.

INTERPRETING STATISTICS (p. 72)

1 No. The bar chart shows that home-drinkers form one of the smallest groups. For instance, more than six times as many women office workers drink.
2 A factory worker – but factories also have a higher proportion of non-drinking women than the other two occupations.
3 Yes. Whatever their drinking habits, wine accounts for more than a quarter of all alcohol consumed by women, on the evidence of the bottom chart. However, it would appear that heavy drinkers prefer spirits to wine, while the reverse is true for light drinkers.
4 The mother could point to the fact that of the heaviest women drinkers (drinking how much per week?) over half are unmarried, while married women make up three-quarters of moderate-drinking women. To clinch the matter she might also say that 80 per cent of those who take no alcohol at all are likely to be married.
5 The biggest contrast is amongst the heavier drinkers: only 1 per cent of the women sampled in the survey illustrated (top right) are heavy drinkers, whereas 21 per cent of men come into that category. The small proportion of women is reflected in the comparative sample numbers in the bottom diagram, 31 to 296.

Most women (95 per cent) are light drinkers or teetotal; significantly higher numbers of men drink moderately or heavily (35 per cent to 5 per cent).

PERSUASIVE WRITING

Advertisement – 'Pit Flit' (p. 74)

1 Because people like being one of a crowd.
2 The freshness of the countryside in spring – 'country-fresh', 'sparkle of spring', 'flowers'.
3 Because it removes fears of smelling unwashed and the user can face the world without risk of being criticized.
4 Either of 'sparkle of spring' and 'fragrance as fresh as the flowers of the field'. Alliteration helps to imprint words and the ideas behind them in the mind and feelings of the reader or hearer.
5 It is scented.

FILLING IN FORMS (p. 75)

Please write in CAPITAL LETTERS and in ink

1 TO BE FILLED IN BY ALL APPLICANTS

Tick correct box — Mr **Mrs** Miss Ms or title (Mrs ticked)

Your surname — CLARKE

Christian names or forenames — ROSE BERNICE

Maiden surname (if applicable) — BROWN

Tick correct box — **Married** Single Widowed Divorced Separated (Married ticked)

Age last birthday — 36 — Country of birth JAMAICA

Present address — 22 LONG ST. WIGAN LANCS — Postcode PR3 4QT

Daytime telephone no. (We may need to get in touch with you urgently) —

Job/occupation — NURSING

Town of birth — KINGSTON

Date of birth — 25·5·51

Country of residence — ENGLAND

Height (in metres) — 1·63 ✳ See note 1 for a conversion chart

Visible distinguishing marks — SCAR ON RIGHT WRIST

Have you changed your name other than by marriage or adoption? Yes / **No** (No ticked)

What was your previous name? —

Go to section 2a

6a TO BE FILLED IN BY ALL APPLICANTS ✳ Read note 6

Have you had any sort of passport before or applied for any passport? **Yes** / No (Yes ticked)

Is your last passport attached? Yes / **No** (No ticked)

Previous passport number — L1 123456

Please complete **section 11**

Is your husband/wife to be included on your passport? Yes / **No** (No ticked)

Have they had any sort of passport before? Yes / No

Is their previous passport attached? Yes / No

Previous passport number —

Please complete **section 11**

CAUTION
You are warned that the making of an untrue statement for the purpose of procuring a passport is a criminal offence. Passport Office procedures include a check on the authenticity of countersignatories. The application should not be countersigned until the form has been completed, signed and dated by the applicant.

Please write in CAPITAL LETTERS and in ink

➜ 6b Declaration To be signed by all applicants
And by husband/wife if they are to be included on your passport
I the undersigned, declare that
1 I have made no other application for a passport, other than that stated above.
2 (delete if not appropriate) If the passport mentioned in section 11 comes again into my possession, I will return it immediately to a British Passport issuing authority.
3 No one included on this application owes money to Her Majesty's Government for repatriation or similar relief.
4 I am a British citizen or
   British Dependent Territories citizen or
   British Overseas citizen or
   British subject or
   British protected person.
   And I have not lost or renounced this status.
5 I (and any children shown in section 3) am/are today in the United Kingdom.
6 The information given in this application is correct to the best of my knowledge and belief.

Sign Rose B. Clarke Date 16·10·86

Your husband's/wife's signature (if he/she is to be included in your passport)

10 TO BE COMPLETED BY ALL APPLICANTS ✳ Read note 10

Countries to be visited — JAMAICA, U.S.A.

Purpose of journey — VISIT RELATIVES

Please give the names of two relatives or friends who can be contacted if you meet with an accident. This information will only be used in an emergency.

Name — J. CLARKE
Address — 12 ROYAL CRESCENT, BRADFORD, W.YORKS.
Telephone number — Relationship (if any) UNCLE

Name —
Address —
Telephone number — Relationship (if any) —

Space below is for Passport Office use only
MISC 314

Unit W3

'MASTER HAROLD' . . . AND THE BOYS (p. 78)

1 (a) This is an easy question because the way it is worded almost gives you the answer, i.e. that the black servant Sam is teaching Hally, relating the dancing contest to the life he has experienced in racist South Africa. A proper answer would need to make it clear that you understand this.

(b) It is about politics, both within South Africa and in the world generally.

2 We cannot answer this question for you. It is a good opportunity to practise writing a play-script (see also Test 24). Notice how the passage is set out, with the stage directions in brackets, e.g. (The telephone rings, SAM answers it.) Earlier in the play Hally has been telling Sam the meanings of some long words new to him, like 'magnitude'. They also talk about history and famous men, in particular Alexander Fleming who discovered penicillin.

CATHEDRAL BUILDERS (poem p. 81, questions pp. 82-3)

1 (a) The structure and syntax of the first three stanzas emphasize the repetitiveness of the work: 'They climbed . . .', 'And came down . . .', 'Every night slept . . .', 'And every day . . .'. Stanza two in particular, with its list of humdrum activities – 'quarrelled', 'lied', 'spat', 'sang' – separated by commas, portrays their lives as routine and ordinary.

(b) Their home circumstances are just like those of people living today or in any age, e.g. (1) after work they 'came down to their suppers and small beer'; (2) when they grew older they 'became less inclined to fix a neighbour's roof' (an authentic touch, because neighbours would naturally rely on them to do such jobs).

(c) 'Heaven' is a more appropriate word than 'sky', for instance, because it reminds us of the building's purpose, reinforcing the idea of 'towards God' in line 1. Also the *h* follows the alliterative pattern: *h*oisted, *h*ewn, in*h*abited, *h*ammers, which suggests hard breathing from sustained physical effort.

(**d**) Migrating birds have habitual and instinctive flight paths. The official sounding phrase 'impeded the rights of way' suggests, ironically, that the swallows have established a legal right to that part of the sky. The idea helps us to imagine the great bulk of the cathedral as it must have seemed when first completed, and at the same time places it in a natural environment.

2 On the day the bishop came to consecrate our cathedral a little gang of us builders stood in the crowd. Most people shoved to get near the front to see his lordship in his fine robes, but we didn't. We stopped near the back to get the best view of the building. My mate who I've worked with all my life stood by me. He nudged me and pointed to the arch above the west door.

'Remember that day up there when I was crawling about and you were on the ladder end? Remember the wind?'

I surely did. I've been up in some weathers but that day was the roughest. All weathers, all seasons – icy winter dawns, blazing summer noondays; our whole lives were spent in raising the stones of that massive building they were all staring at now. I could hear the bishop's voice:

'. . . this wonderful work of God given its form through the hand of man –' My mate nudged me again.

'Never been up a ladder in his life, doesn't know sandstone from granite!'

I felt sorry for the bishop. He could only ever walk on the floor of our building, in the shadow cast by it, inside or out; he could never feel the satisfaction we had known in our lifelong work.

'I'd rather my lad grew up to be a builder than a bishop,' I said to my mate.

GLASS (p. 83)

1 The title 'Glass' fits the poem because the quotation gives two characteristics of glass, 'cuts and reflects' which the poet uses in two senses. The 'chandelier', the stained glass and the rear view mirror literally reflect light and images but then the poet changes the sense to show that poverty reflects an even clearer picture than glass. What it cuts is our conscience. (62 words)

2 The poem gives you plenty to work on here. Your remarks to your friend should include some comment on the contrast between the 'glittering ceremony' of the official papal visit and the squalor of the poor in their shantytown surroundings. You will need to decide whether to adopt Rajendra's critical standpoint or to write approvingly of the cancellation. A good answer might run to 150-200 words.

RIVER AFTERNOON (pp. 40-4, questions pp. 84-5)

2 The girl feels antagonistic to Peter, and therefore sides with the fish. She tries to shame him into throwing the little fish back, first by implying he is not a proper fisherman, secondly by promising to respect his skill in spite of 'hating' it.

4 The first opening is the better one, because it pays attention to the context of the paragraph. This is asked for in the question in the words '. . . at this point in the story'.

5 The two phrases which add nothing to the changed atmosphere are 'lain so still' and 'began to reel in'. All the others help to express the excitement both children are feeling.

6 Their ages must be between 10 and 13. The boy seems a little older than the girl. Neither wants to be thought 'a kid' or 'a baby', but both behave childishly in some ways – the boy teasing the girl by holding on to the fish, the girl 'sobbing', then quickly forgetting all about her distress.

They have obviously known one another well for some time; they could be related – cousins perhaps. (They are not likely to be brother and sister, because she refers to 'your father'.) They are good friends, but take their closeness for granted. Each depends on the other, the girl looking to the boy for leadership, he to her for support and encouragement.

CANE IS BITTER (p. 85)

1 This question is not as easy as it sounds. You can argue in favour of either, because the behaviour of Romesh and his family is so closely connected with the setting of the Trinidad sugar-cane harvest. Even Romesh's decision to leave is described in terms of his actions – fetching his own cutlass – kept sharp for him by his father, 'hacking savagely' at the canes; even his final decision to defy his father's wishes and leave home.

2 Cleaning teeth, his sister's wish to be taught by Romesh, Hari's hostility towards his 'lazy' brother, his defiance of his father and the family's marriage plans for him.

3 Your answer will depend on how well you have answered questions **1** and **2**. It will refer to the new ideas, opportunities and habits that Romesh's education (at college or university presumably) away from home has given him.

4 & 5 We cannot prescribe particular answers to these questions.

MOORINGS (p. 88)

1 The main image concerns the moored dinghy, which is seen as a tethered horse. In the opening stanza the dinghy's movement on the water is described as 'pawing' and 'nodding'; then in the final verse the poet returns to the image, referring to 'his stable' and to the movements of the 'restless steeplechaser' who, when released, can be seen leaping over hurdles (i.e. waves).

We cannot answer the question of suitability to subject matter for you. In an open-ended question like this an examiner will accept whatever view you state, as long as it is supported from the poem. Thus you could argue that the 'horse' image fails to add to the meaning because it is a land creature; or, conversely, that it *does* help because it suggests, in words like 'pawing', the restless movement of the boat. After our answer given above we would have 40 or so words left for this part of the question.

2 The poet is using *alliteration* in each of the lines referred to, in order to enhance the *visual* impression with a suitable *aural* one. In line 2 it emphasizes the bobbing movement; in lines 7 and 8 there is a contrast in sound between the 'gr-' on land and the watery 'w's. In lines 17-18 the word 'harsh' is made real by the hard 'k' sounds in the following line.

3 We cannot answer this for you. Try to use some of the details in the poem in your account, e.g. the chain, the oars wet with dew, the seaweed.

SWORD OF HONOUR (p. 89)

(Use the mark scheme as a guide to how long you should spend on each question. As a rough guide, think of *a mark a minute*. This gives you 10 minutes to look through your answers.)

1 Look through the passage closely. The first reference to Guy is his discomfort at the cold and peat smoke (l. 30-1). This is followed by the comically exaggerated description of Guy's 'probable destiny' (l. 37-9). Later we have to *infer* Guy's feelings from what happens, e.g. Hector Campbell's mistaking him for the invited guest (l. 54-9) and his suspicion that Guy has been lying to him (l. 95). Look also at his feelings about Kate Carmichael and their conversation, and his views on the food.

2 This question earns few marks, so need not take long. An adequate answer would be:

Tommy demonstrates this by pacifying the dogs (l. 39-43). He also is able to engage Mrs Campbell in conversation at table (l. 68), while Guy simply answers her husband's rather hostile questions.

3 Many of the descriptive details seem comically exaggerated, e.g. the bagpipe music is excessively loud (l. 14), the size of the rooms and the dining table are far bigger than might be expected. It is funny that the smallest dog makes the biggest noise ('in inverse proportion to their size'). The smoke seems also to be exaggerated, as though the owner of the voice (l. 27) couldn't be seen through it, nor his actual treatment of the dogs. Soon their hosts 'emerged through the smoke'. (Other potentially comic features you might refer to in your answer are the antler furniture, Tommy's amusing way of treating the dogs (l. 40), Guy's fanciful idea of how he might end up (l. 37-9), the host's manner of conversation and Guy's response, and the odd greatniece with her obsession over her ancestry, amusingly reflected in Guy's imagination (l. 140-3). His description of the food is also comic. As the question is only worth 10 marks not all these need be given.

4 We cannot provide an answer to this. Note that the question expects you to write in the first person, i.e. to use 'I' and 'me'. If you can base it on a recent incident – perhaps a visit to or from a little-known relative or older person – your account will be more vivid.

Unit W4 Letters, reports, practical writing and notes

WRITING LETTERS

Here is our answer to the practice question on p. 96.

Walcot Dene,
Shooter's Lane,
Kempton,
BROWSHILL,
Herefordshire BL4 5SL.

14th May 1987

Miss Pamela Johnson, M.B.E.,
Shotton Park,
Kempton,
BROWSHILL,
Herefordshire.

Dear Miss Johnson,

As secretary of the Kempton Over-60s Club I have been responsible for organizing a very successful sponsored 'slim' in aid of the Kempton Home for the Disabled. As you know, the Home has recently moved into larger premises at Kempton Hurst, and is in need of funds to develop and extend its facilities there. Our Club has raised £550 towards this valuable work.

Knowing your concern for disabled people, I am writing to ask whether you would be prepared to be Guest of Honour at a tree-planting ceremony in the grounds of Kempton Hurst on the afternoon of Wednesday 22nd May, when we shall formally hand over the cheque to Lord Mount, patron of the Home. We hope this will be an important occasion, that will attract publicity to the work of Kempton Hurst in particular, and to the need for further support for the disabled in   this   area. our name, and your fame as an international ballet star, would ensure the success of the occasion.

The actual planting ceremony will be quite short. You will be asked to use a specially inscribed silver trowel, and to make a short speech. Proceedings will begin at about 2 p.m., and should be over by 4.15 p.m., when tea will be served in the Hurst to all invited guests. These will include the Lord President of the County and local dignitaries and officials, probably about forty in all.

Our Club, and the staff at Kempton Hurst, would greatly appreciate it if you could help us in this worthy cause. Please let me know if you need any further information. I look forward to hearing from you.

Yours sincerely,

(Mrs) Eva Blöm,
Hon. Secretary, Kempton Over-60s Club,
Organizing Secretary, The Friends of Kempton Home.

2

23 Uptown Rd
Oldcastle
Lancs.
24th October 1987

Dear Mrs Blank,

I am very sorry that we woke you up when we were leaving my friend's house last night. My parents say that we were very thoughtless and I suppose we were. We were laughing so much when Jamie fell over a flowerpot that we never thought about disturbing anyone.

I know I cannot give you back your sleep, but if you would like me to weed the garden or go shopping for you next weekend, please ask me.

Yours with apologies

Karen.

3

Frodham Manor
Frodham
Sussex.

12th May 1987

Dear Charles,

No doubt you receive begging letters from charities almost as often as I do. I am writing about two particularly insistent ones I had the other day. As the two charities are situated near us both you have probably had them as well. One is for the Frodham Strays' Hospital, which was set up a couple of years ago by a group of animal lovers. It was well funded then, and has since had a large legacy, so I would urge you, if you are thinking of supporting a local effort (and I know your generous nature!), to join me in contributing to the 'Friends of Frodham' Old People's Home. This, you may remember, was set up nearly forty years ago. Rising costs have hit it hard and I know there is now quite a long waiting list, because Ellen, our old housemaid, has been on it for a year already. They are trying to raise £40 000 for a new wing and for modernizing the place. Why don't we make them a joint endowment, Charles? It would mark their 'ruby' anniversary.

Yours ever,

Humphrey.

4 (a)

2 Good Street
Grantham
Lincs

2nd April 1987

The Editor
Grantham Gossip
Talk Street
Grantham

Dear Sir,

What is the world coming to when a person cannot even take a short bus ride without being subjected to filthy language and insolent abuse from badly dressed young people?

Bring back National Service and flogging I say, to make up for the discipline that is so lacking at home and at school.

Yours etc.
(Mrs.) Queenie Quiet

4 (b)

2 Ruby Street
Grantham
Lincs

4th April 1987

The Editor
Grantham Gossip
Talk Street
Grantham

Dear Sir,

As a grandmother I feel very sad about the hostility of your correspondent Mrs Quiet to our young people. Has she forgotten her own childhood? Personally I welcome the cheerfulness and high spirits of the children I share my daily bus ride with; and I think the rudeness she says she had from them was probably prompted by her own unfriendly attitude. It will be a sad day when children stay glum and silent on the buses.

Yours truly,

(Mrs) Gwen Stallard
(Grandmother to ten)

THREE LETTERS TO A SPROCKET MANUFACTURER (p. 97)

1 The engineer concerned found this letter adequate for its purpose and enjoyed the wit of the conclusion. We agree, but would prefer:

(a) a date (useful in a business letter for filing purposes);

(b) accurate punctuation and spelling (two question marks, two full stops, and at least three commas missing; *original* misspelt);

(c) more courtesy – 'How much' seems curt as a request for price;

(d) less clumsy sentence construction; it should be easy to avoid the 'but' . . . 'but' and repetition of 'as'.

An examiner would also object to the unconventional way of signing off.

2 This was less satisfactory to the manufacturer, because the machine is a rare model and the information is incomplete (no bore dimension, not known whether flat or dished sprocket required). We note also:

(a) no year given in date;

(b) no punctuation in address, no question mark for first sentence;

(c) sloppy use of *etc.* (and full stop omitted after the abbreviation); what does he want besides the price?

(d) 'forward . . . on' ('on' is superfluous);

(e) rather sprawling final sentence (containing another question) 'If you . . . would you . . . so I . . . to you . . . as I'm . . . as I . . .';

(f) irrelevant information (the reference to college);

(g) misspelling of *college*.

3 The engineer found this letter the least satisfactory of the three. The information about the chain 'slightly larger' is hopelessly vague; it is not even clear whether the Suzuki mentioned is the motorcycle in question. The engineer had to ask, among other things, for the ratio (gearbox: rear sprocket).

We find the layout and phrasing adequate, apart from the confusion of meaning referred to. The final sentence is particularly muddled – 'either sprocket . . . *it* . . .' (which sprocket?). This sentence in fact adds no useful information and could be omitted. Note also:

(a) comma missing at end of first line of address;

(b) 'Bank' and 'Yours' should have capital letters;

(c) At the end 'Hope . . .' should read either 'Hoping . . .' or 'I hope . . .'.

SHARKS (p. 103)

1 Sharks can appear in most waters warm enough to produce the food they like. They also like sewage and garbage and this brings them inshore. There are reports of sharks attacking men and boats in the English Channel, North Sea, Irish Sea, and Scottish waters. They have also appeared in fresh water – the Fowey River in Cornwall, Lake Nicaragua and Zambesi. So it is not surprising that most of the unpleasant stories about sharks are founded on fact. (79 words).

2 Dear Sir,

A shark has been seen almost within sight of Budmouth. As all types of shark are extremely dangerous to man, bathing from our beaches should be forbidden until a patrol boat armed with a gun is on duty throughout the hours of daylight. Moreover sharks feed avidly on human refuse, so it is very likely that the one already observed will venture further inshore.

Yours faithfully,

Clarissa James

Dear Sir,

The very name 'shark' is naturally alarming. But no one should be deterred from bathing by the news that a shark has been sighted fifteen miles away. The beaches of Budmouth slope very gradually, and there can be no danger provided that bathers keep within 100 yards of the shore. Visitors should know that the watch tower, manned to look out for bathers in difficulty, will be able to sight a shark well before it gets anywhere near the 100 yard limit. The rescue launch will shortly be equipped with a wide-bore, high-velocity gun capable of killing a shark with one shot.

Yours faithfully,

Humphrey Harris.

IMPROVING NOTICES/SEEING THROUGH ADVERTISEMENTS (pp. 104-5)

1

NOTICE

Will all visitors please report

at the guard room for permission

to enter.

(This is both politer and shorter.)

2

No parking on this road.

Use the park in Avon Street,

next turning on the right.

3 The Education Officer must be informed as soon as possible if bad weather makes it necessary to end school earlier than usual.

Advertisements

1 tries to make the reader feel that he or she should join the great majority, by using expressions like '2 000 000', 'most popular', 'don't miss out'.

2 aims at making the reader afraid of (i) other people's opinion, and (ii) the danger of dirt, by words like 'ashamed', 'harmful', 'expose . . . to risk'.

3 seeks to make the reader envy and imitate the rich who can afford to have things specially made for them. All the words contribute to this.

4 To be offered the reputation for 'good taste' as well as shiny hair is attractive. The assumption that Ascot is a possibility when not at the office appeals to the snob in us and the 'guarantee' to transform *any* hair reassures the most lacklustre heads.

5 Clever double meaning in 'good taste': you are a connoisseur in beer as well as having high standards of appreciation. You can be relied on to respond to the 'poetry' of 'diamond' and 'velvet'; in fact your standards are so high that the extra cost of Bluff's beer is assumed to be beneath your notice.

6 Here there is some flattery ('the top'), some appeal to fear ('under par' etc.) and an attempt to make Nervax seem both different and the only scientific remedy.

 Unit W4 Further Practice

THE DOMESTIC WATER SUPPLY (p. 106)

(a) Turn off the water at the main; the stop-cock for this is just inside the house, low down to the right of the kitchen sink. Then run the cold tap in the kitchen till it stops flowing.

(b) The *rising main* is the pipe which brings the supply from the main pipe in the road into the house.

The *stop-cock* turns off the main supply, usually just inside the house. In older houses it is often in the garden.

The *storage tank* will be found in the loft or attic. It supplies w.c. cisterns, the cold taps in bath and basins, and the hot-water system.

ADDITIVES BAN IN CHILDREN'S FOOD URGED (p. 106)

To All Parents

> This letter is being sent because a number of parents are worried about additives in children's food.
>
> They are concerned mainly about Tartrazine, an artificial yellow colour, originally derived from coal tar.
>
> Some of the dyes in the same group are suspected of causing cancer, and Tartrazine itself is linked with hyperactivity and illness in young children.
>
> The big supermarkets like Sainsbury and Tesco have removed Tartrazine from their own-label lines, and it has been banned from food in Birmingham schools.
>
> Further action is needed. Many MPs believe that the Government should (i) forbid it in all foods liable to be eaten by young children, and (ii) start more research.

WRITING DETECTIVE STORIES (p. 107)

1 The writer's aim is to baffle the reader; almost any method may be adopted to achieve this end. Important clues must not be concealed, but otherwise the writer is not obliged to reveal everything that goes on in the characters' minds. The good writer will try to bluff and double bluff the reader, but misleading trails should not be introduced simply to deceive the reader. They should have some relation to the natural development of the story and the characters.

If this advice is followed the reader will not feel cheated at the end of the story, but will be surprised when the identity of the murderer is revealed. If the reader is past caring who 'did it', the writer has failed to provide enough suspense.

Sometimes every character is a suspect, so that the reader is constantly guessing while the choice is narrowed down. The reader should have enough information to enable him to eliminate suspects on both psychological and factual grounds.

Real life is not a good basis for detective stories. The writer must accept the necessity for fantasy but try to work out the development of the story in logical steps. (194 words)

2 How writers work

The answer above contains much of the material needed for this question. The main difference is that here the emphasis is on *method*, (*How . . .*) rather than *advice*, and, of course, the presentation must be in note form.

You could start this question by fixing the word 'method' or 'how' firmly in your mind, and then running your eye over the passage to find the relevant points, e.g.:

para. 1 don't conceal material clues
        avoid red herrings

para. 2 how to place clues – genuine or false
        how to be too clever for readers but not for characters

para. 3 presentation of murderer

para. 4 maintaining suspense

These notes will be too brief for a final intelligible version but they help to extract the relevant points quickly and can easily be expanded.

COMPENSATION FOR VICTIMS OF ROAD ACCIDENTS (p. 109)

1 The injured person is obliged to put his or her case in a court of law. Here the victim has to prove that the accident was caused by the negligence of some person.

2 In all cases there will be automatic compensation, paid promptly and regularly as long as the victim needs it.

3 Very serious loss – deaths in the family, physical and emotional injury – can be suffered by someone who is entirely blameless.

4 Either through insurance by motorists or by a new tax on petrol.

5 The Government prefers the petrol tax, because this would fit in with its energy saving policy, by discouraging the unnecessary use of petrol.

6 I write to record the strongest possible objections to the proposed scheme for compensating those injured in road accidents. It will impose a fresh financial burden on a section of the community that is already seriously overtaxed . . .

7 The cost of looking after people injured in road accidents is already over £400m a year. If motorists pay for some of this it will take a load off the health service.

DIAGRAM: GEO-THERMAL UNIT (p. 110)

This is slightly different from earlier exercises. Instead of a piece of writing you have a diagram to interpret. This is a very simple one. Here are our suggested answers:

(a) a method of extracting heat from the centre of the earth, by means of pumped water

(b) two bore holes on the same site are drilled to the hot rocks three or four miles down. Into one of these water is pumped at 25°C; it is then extracted from the other, heated to 180°C.

M25 NEWS ITEM (p. 110)

1 To ease the flow of traffic round London.

2 (a) On reaching M25 turn right and continue to the junction for M11 turning right here. There may be delay at the Dartford Tunnel, where there are four lanes instead of six.

(b) On reaching M25 turn left and continue to M20; there may be delay at the Dartford Tunnel. If there have been warnings of hold-ups here, turn right at M25 and take the southern route to M26; here the Staines to Wisley section might be very crowded.

3 Inaccurate forecasts of the growth in the amount of traffic resulting from the construction of the M25.

HOW VISION IS AFFECTED BY SPEED (p. 111)

1 Pedestrians move so slowly that they can easily avoid colliding.

2 When moving at speed a driver focuses his sight far ahead, so that the foreground becomes blurred. Under these conditions he will fail to see any dangerous situation developing near him, and may well have an accident unless he slows down. (Note that this point comes from para. 8). This focusing of the eyes according to speed makes it dangerous to drive fast in the wrong places.

3 (a) Comparison with pedestrians; slow speed = no collision
     Normally no need to look far ahead

  (b) (i) The faster a motorist moves, the further he must look ahead; thus risk neglecting foreground. If he does, he won't see danger developing.

      (ii) Foreground must be watched, speed reduced for effective action.

  (c) Danger of driving when tired: concentration difficult, less awareness of possible dangers.

Unit W5

GRAMMAR AND USAGE

Indirect speech (practice question, p. 122)

'You ought to hold it . . .Everyone knows that.'

She said that he ought to hold it still. He retorted that he knew what he was doing; that the fish were used to things moving; they were all fed already; they had had plenty. The girl said there were not many mayfly, to which he rejoined that that was the reason for their not jumping. She contradicted him by saying that fish did not jump for mayfly; they waited till they got waterlogged. He asked sharply why fish jumped in that case, and the girl's answer was that they jumped for joy. He accused her of talking nonsense, but she insisted, saying that she had read it. He angrily disagreed, reiterating that fish jumped for mayfly and that everyone knew that.

USING A DICTIONARY

Prepositions (practice, p. 126)

complimented *on*	different *from**	immune *from, to, against*
contrary *to*	exempt *from*	liable to *(for)*
deficient *in*	identical *with, to*	persevere *in, at, with*

* Purists (people who insist on absolutely correct English) allow only *from* as correct, but *to* is so frequently used nowadays as to be acceptable. Some dictionaries also recognize *than*, but it is less confusing to use *than* only after a comparative, e.g. sooner than, more accurate than.

Answers – Self-Test Unit

TEST 1 ACCURACY (p. 141)   *(Total 32 marks)*

1 Two commas; *In a mixed class the girls, who are cleverer, soon get bored.* This has the effect of making the meaning '. . . the girls, who anyway are cleverer than boys, soon get bored.'   *2*

2 The marksmanship of the company is highly satisfactory; that of the sergeant-major is especially praiseworthy.   *3*

3 *(a), (b), (a)*   *4 if all correct*
1 each for 1 or 2 correct

4 colon, or colon and dash together (:–) *2*

5 lain (*lay* is the past tense – *he lay there; laid* is the past of *to lay* – *she laid the table*) *1*

6 etc. = and other things (Latin: *et cetera*)
   cf. = compare (Latin: *conferre*)
   e.g. = for example (Latin: *exempli gratia* ('for the sake of example'))
   i.e. = that is (Latin: *id est*)
   n.b. = note well (Latin: *nota bene*)   *4 if all correct*
1 for each if 3 or less correct

7 (e) Yours sincerely. (a), (b), (f) and (g) are incorrect, (d) and (h) are suitable for a business letter. (c) is less conventional, but acceptable *2*

8 'You know I can't.' 'Do I?' 'Of course you do!' she said scornfully. *10*

9 'You know I can't.'
   'Do I?'
   'Of course you do!' she said scornfully. *3*

10 (a) implied (b) passed (c) uninterested *1*

TEST 2 SPELLING (p. 142)

1 When the syllable is pronounced 'ee', place -i- before -e- except after -c. *3*

2 contemporary – 5; responsibility – 6; occasionally – 5;
   originally – 5;   criticism – 3;   similar – 3 *6*

3 disease separate argument business temporary disappointed *6*

4 When the syllable is pronounced 'ee', place -i- before -e- except after -c-. *3*

5 The *u* after the *g* indicates that the sound is hard (as in *got*). The *u* is silent. Other words: disguise, guilt, intrigue, rogue *5*

6 rose *and* risen, submitted, preferred, remembered, dispelled, occurred *6*

7 When the syllable is pronounced 'ee' place -i- before -e- except after -c-. *3*

8 The *ea* sounds like -e- (as in *pet*).
   Other words: feather, head, realm, wealth *5*

9 The silent *g* *3*

TEST 3 MAKING NOTES (p. 143)

(a) *advantages*
– saves irreplaceable fossil fuels (e.g. coal, oil)
– clean, non-polluting
– space-saving
– could provide employment in windy areas (compensate for agriculture losses)
– could already produce one fifth of energy requirements (more than nuclear power)   *10 marks*

(b) *achievements so far*
general: reliable and cost-effective wind turbines already made worldwide
UK: mainly small (3 ft. diameter), but generating boards erecting big wind turbines, e.g. Carmarthen 200 kW, Orkneys 3 MW.
Denmark: farmers using them, up to 100 kW, surplus energy sold locally.
USA: 'wind farmers' – very big e.g. California over 1000 MW in past four years   *12 marks*

TEST 4 VOCABULARY (p. 144)

1 *lenient*   tolerant
   incentive   motive/spur
   redundant   unnecessary/superfluous
   relinquish   give up
   grotesque   absurd/odd
   synthetic   man-made/artificial compound

2 *impudent*   respectful
   opaque   clear/transparent
   tranquil   lively
   destitute   well off

deciduous   evergreen
acquiesce   disagree   *1 mark each*

TEST 5 W2 (p. 144)

Chairman's Statement

(a) Marks and Spencer expects its policy to purchase British-made goods to continue. The policy in store development is to open new stores, to modernize existing ones and to extend their stores, or where this is not possible, to open additional premises nearby. A new venture is to build on out-of-town sites and to cooperate with other firms in this development. Plans take into account customers' comfort and the use of cars for shopping. Experience of increased sales in modernized stores and hopes of additional sales in new ones are grounds for making large capital investment. (98 words)   *14*

(b) There is no right answer to this question. Perhaps a counter-question: What does their market research show? Or: If the policy of good quality and value for money, attractive materials and style, awareness of public tastes, applies to the furniture department, sales should be satisfactory.   *6*

TEST 6 ACCURACY (p. 144)

Drivers of the *next generation* of trains will not have to sit *in* the front *cab, potentially* the most *dangerous* place, because they will be *travelling* too fast.

At more than 190 *mph* it would be *impossible* for a driver to *stop* a train within the *range* of vision.   *1 mark each*

TEST 7 W4 (p. 145)

9 Spring Gardens
Ellertine
Suffolk IP7 8CW

10 January 1987

Your Ref. OO/MM
Messrs. Maylow
Fishpond Lane
Middlefield, Yorks.

Dear Sirs,

I am returning the dress that I bought from you on December 21st in reply to your advertisement in *The Post* on December 15th.

It is not fit to wear, as two buttonholes are missing and a side seam above the waist is not sewn up.

Would you please replace it as soon as possible?

Yours faithfully,
Mary Aston   *10 marks*

TEST 8 W3 (p. 146)

1 The poet's description of the sound of the bells through the trees in a village suggests he is being ironic when he says they are 'too many' and that the trees ('timber') should be cut down.   *4 marks*

2 Cottages are to become 'workers' flats'; the church service ('Evensong') is to be replaced by 'the Challenge' broadcast to millions; the traditional trees and gardens are to become 'fields of soya beans'.   *6 marks*

3 (This question gives you a chance to express your own ideas. You are given the choice of describing it 'straight' i.e. without criticizing it, or 'ironically'. Betjeman is deeply ironical; he pretends to be welcoming the 'chummy' vision of the future, but is really saying how horrible it would be.)   *10 marks*

TEST 9 (p. 146)

for the high jump   slang
got down to the nitty-gritty   cliché ⎫ the use of both these in the same sentence
beat about the bush   cliché ⎭ is tautological
got it coming to me   colloquialism
no messing about   colloquialism

all over and done with   cliché
no hard feelings   cliché   *7 marks*

If I am to be punished I prefer the headmaster to come straight to the point.
If I am in the wrong and I know I must be punished, I prefer a caning, which is soon over; it would not be resented by me.   *3 marks*

TEST 10 (p. 146)

1	absence	2	were
3	give	4	the
5	refused	6	gives
7	book	8	Mary
9	wants	10	can't
11	Joe	12	saying
13	to	14	go
15	as	16	toy

1 mark each

TEST 11 (p. 147)

1	are	2	been
3	introduce	4	would
5	one	6	happened
7	for	8	and
9	did	10	they
11	both	12	accustoming
13	their	14	like
15	the		

1 mark each

TEST 12 UNDERSTANDING AND MAKING NOTES (p. 147)

1 hunger and cold
the rate at which deaths occur
variations
ten years
cause loss of life   *5*

2   (i) para. 4 climatic fluctuations . . . species
   (ii) para. 7 The species . . . strategies
   (iii) para. 9 first sentence So . . . misplaced   *6*

3 The process in nature whereby stronger forms of life survive.   *5*

4 moving south   changing their breeding habits   *4*

5 Despite great losses in bad weather, the bird population, including even the smallest species, reaches its former level and remains steady.
Bad weather weeds out weaker stocks; the fittest survive.   *5*

TEST 13 SPELLING AND USAGE (p. 148)

                (*Score: each answer earns three marks; total 30*)

1 recesses   spoonfuls   tomatoes
2 indefinite   illegal   dissatisfied
3 He began.   She did very well.   I always chose nylon bearings.
4 The message was transmitted. The words were spoken clearly. Her bag was laid on the counter.
5 engage   occur   reason
6 anything   can   ever
7 argument   family   omit   athletic   mischievous   similar
8 accommodate   February   immediately   except   government   surprise
9 mathematics   definitely   repetition
10 business   introduce   fuel

TEST 14 (p. 149)   *10 marks*

Mary Coe points to contrasts between the quantity of sweets and Christmas presents then and now; the simple pleasure of watching shearing compared with today's 'ready-made' entertainment; unwrapped sweets and hygiene, and the brass band killed by radio and television.

TEST 16 (p. 150)   *9 marks*

1 The deadliest drug of all   3
2 The delay in publishing a report on the drinking habits of the young   3
3 Indirect; it causes so many deaths on the road   3

TEST 18 (p. 150)   *12 marks*

(a) 'I know this town! That's where those jolly children live – usually something worth picking out in these dustbins. I'll take these newspapers – they help to keep me warm in the junk-yard. And this can will do to get drinks in.'

'What's this? A clockwork mouse – no, two mice joined together. Wonder if I can make them work again. Let's see . . .' It was cold, but I didn't have anything else to do, so I took the toy to pieces. Scamp, my only friend, sat watching. I gave him some of the snap I had saved – it was a bit mucky but he didn't mind. 'I'll be really pleased if I can get this fiddly little thing to work,' I thought as I tinkered away at it. There were bits broken, and one or two missing, but I pieced it together somehow and got the clockwork motor moving.

'Let's try it out.' When I wound them up the mouse could only walk forward. 'Well, that's better than nothing. At least he keeps his child out of the muck, holding it up like that.'

I had a sudden idea. Why not make them tramps, like me? I took them on to the highway outside town, wound up the mouse and set him on his way. 'Be tramps', I said.

(b) We cannot write your answer for you to this question. Remember the mouse walks, carrying his child in the air. The child can only see backwards. Before you start writing decide what or who they might meet on the road – human or animal, car or bike – and what the consequence might be.

TEST 19 BBC APPOINTMENTS (p. 152)   *33 marks*

1 Two highest salaries:

Deputy Editor: £20 747 + £971 = £21 718   4
Producer: £18 205 + £971 = £19 176

2 Six places: Belfast, Milton Keynes, Central London, Cambridgeshire, Leeds, Central and West London   3

3 Knowledge of Africa to be gained by living or travelling in the country   4

4 (i) Information technology means conveying information by computers, word processors and other electronic means.   3

(ii) 'Unsocial hours' are times when other working people are free or asleep.   3

5 The Deputy Editor and the Radio Cambridgeshire Reporter advertisements use an informal tone, addressing questions directly to the reader. A 'self-starter' and 'You'll need to know a lot about Ireland' suggest a friendly but efficient working atmosphere. Perhaps if you can answer 'Yes' to the initial question, you will be more likely to read on and send for the application form.   4

6 A secretary with no initiative is not a 'self-starter' and is likely to sit around waiting to be told what to do. Lack of discretion means repeating information in the office or elsewhere which is not top secret but is not intended for general consumption. Such a secretary would disrupt the efficiency and harmony of the firm.   4

7 'We are equal opportunities employers' implies that the job is open to anyone, disregarding sex, race, colour, height, weight etc.   3

8 The formal letter layout is needed here and you must quote the reference number (given at the end of each advertisement) as requested. The last sentence could read: I enclose a stamped, addressed envelope for your reply. (This is the s.a.e. asked for.)   5

TEST 20 VOCABULARY (p. 153)   *40 marks*

1 false
2 legible
3 (a) serrated   (b) indelible   (c) moribund   (d) arrogant   (e) ambiguous
4 not
5 (a) in to   (b) into
6 (a) up on   (b) upon

 7 crossroads
 8 dancing-teacher
 9 corpse
10 (a) the second 'from' (b) pair of (c) absolutely (d) back (e) up with
11 medium
12 neuroses
13 (a) imaginative (b) illusion (c) have (d) effect/affected (e) principle
14 etymology
15 innocent
16 occasional

17
True	*False*
frank	perjury
candour	forgery
verity	fallacious
paragon	fraud
sincere	duplicity
guileless	deceive
honest	spurious
unfeigned	lie
fidelity	distortion
irreproachable	sham

−½ each mistake

18
Speaking	*Writing*
drawl	signature
mute	stationery
discourse	shorthand
raucous	manuscript
intonation	hieroglyphic
eloquence	inscribe
utter	brochure
audible	index
orator	essay
recite	journal

−½ each mistake

Mark scheme: 1 each for questions 1, 2, 7-9, 11, 12, 14-16
2 each for questions 4-6
5 each for questions 3, 10, 13, 17, 18

TEST 21 COMPREHENSION (p. 154)

16 marks

1 offices	2 into	3 town	4 a
5 by	6 town	7 peaceful	8 on
9 and	10 to	11 with	12 ill-at-ease
13 contentment			

1 mark each

TEST 22 LETTERWRITING (p. 154)

Western Engineering
Long Lane
Cleverton B9 3KO
10 July 1987

Ref. JL/MO/392

Dear Sir,

We have not received the seventh instalment of £8 due to us on 1st July as part payment on the Waverley bicycle. This sum must be paid by the end of July in order to keep the deferred payment agreement in force.
We should appreciate an immediate reply.

Yours faithfully,

J. Lynn
Sales Manager

J. Smith Esq.
12 Manor Road
Winbridge GV2 5ZK

12 Manor Road
Winbridge
GV2 5ZK
12 July 1987

Your Ref. JL/MO/392

Dear Sir,

   With reference to your letter of July 10, I sent you a cheque for £8 on
June 30 by first-class post. The cheque was signed by my father, Robert
Smith.

   My father says that the cheque has not been cashed. He is therefore
notifying the local branch of Southern Bank Ltd. that it may have been lost.
   Would you please take the matter up with the Post Office, as I shall?

Yours faithfully,

J. Smith

Western Engineering
Long Lane,
Cleverton B9 3KO

12 Manor Road
Winbridge
GV2 5ZK
12 July 1987

Dear Sir,

   On June 30 I posted a first-class letter at the Manor Road sub-Post
Office to Western Engineering, Cleverton B9 3KO. It contained a Southern
Bank Ltd. cheque for £8, signed by my father, Robert Smith.
   Western Engineering tell me that they have not received the cheque.
   Would you please investigate this matter?

Yours faithfully,

J. Smith

The Manager
The Head Post Office
Winbridge   *10 marks each*

TEST 24 (p. 155)

Much of the dialogue is already there, but you will need to adapt and omit parts and add others
and to put in 'stage directions' – saying what the characters do, where they move, etc. Below we
have given you a sample opening:

CAST (in order of appearance)
   Colonel Tommy Blackhouse, aged 47, short grey hair and neat moustache, tallish (5ft 10ins)
                    and slim.
   Lieut. Guy Crouchback,   aged 35, medium height, dark hair, clean-shaven,
                       stocky build. He speaks quietly and with some diffidence.
. . . etc. [Include also the butler, the piper, Colonel and Mrs Hector Campbell and their great-
niece Katie.]

     (*Tommy and Guy are standing at the doorway of the Castle.*)
     Tommy: Don't be put off by the old boy, Guy. He's not as fierce as he seems – and
     he's deaf too, so won't hear you unless you shout.
     Guy: Well, sir, I must say, you've let me in for it this time. But I'll do my best.
     (*Door opens to a skirl of bagpipe music. As it dies down, they hear the last words of*
     welcome from the butler.)
     Butler: . . . expecting you sooner, sir! Come this way, please.
     (*He leads the way to the dining-hall. The piper brings up the rear. Camera cuts to*
     dining room. It is cold and smoky. As they approach, dogs bark and snarl. Close-up
     of Colonel Campbell: 'Silence, you infernal brutes . . .' etc.
     [You will probably need to omit the conversation between Tommy and Mrs
     Campbell – not given here but referred to (l. 68) – and shorten the one between Col.
     Campbell and Guy, so as to get to the entry of Katie and her exchange with Guy.]

TEST 25 DICTIONARY WORK (p. 155)

1 BOOKworm   NEWSprint   floating RIB   FLOATING kidney
BENCH-mark   GOODwill   good TASTE   POLAR bear

2 (a) cocky (b) cocoa (c) cocoon (d) codicil (e) coelacanth (f) coerce
(g) co-exist (h) coffin (i) cogent (j) cognition (k) cognoscente (l) coherence

−1 each mistake

TEST 26 (p. 155)

40 marks

1 It is clear that Timothy did understand Phillip and wanted to make him feel more useful by teaching him a skill. He gives a good reason for doing this, his recollection of the blind mat-maker in Frenchtown.   *6*

2 Phillip lost his temper first, because he didn't want to try and the old man was insisting on it. Timothy lost his temper when Phillip insulted him about his colour and his ignorance. Timothy was more justified, because Phillip's words must really have hurt him; Phillip's bad temper was due to selfishness.   *10*

3 The rope was to act as a guideline so that Phillip could light the bonfire if rescue seemed likely. Phillip got tired helping to make it and this led to his bad temper. But it also reminded him that Timothy was trying to help him. 'The rope, I thought. It wasn't for him. It was for me.' So it helped to make them friends.   *10*

4 (We cannot answer this for you. Try to be as honest with yourself as Phillip is in this extract. Ask a friend to read your piece and to award you a mark out of 14 for it.)

GLOSSARY

Abbreviation A shortened form of a much used word: Mr (Mister), etc. (*et cetera* – and other things).

Accent The stress or emphasis put on part of a word in saying it: pro*fess*or, *disc*otheque. Note the difference between *per*mit, per*mit*.

Accusative The name of something on which action is taken is called the *object*; this is sometimes said to be in the *accusative* case.

Active The form of a verb which shows that a person or thing performs an action. *See* Passive.

Adjective A words that tells us more about a noun: *blue* sky, the *National* Trust.

Adverb A word that adds to the meaning of a verb or adjective: She writes *quickly*; you'll *soon* see; *well* done.

Agreement The rule by which a word form decides the form of words following it: *That girl is* running well. *Those girls are* running well.

Alliteration The repetition of a letter at the beginning of words: *c*old *c*omfort: *P*rofessor *P*ink *p*refers *p*lums.

Apostrophe (') Used to show possession: Jean*'s* book; or to show omission of a letter or letters: I'll come.

Appreciation The full understanding of a piece of writing.

Appropriateness The 'fitness' of a style of expression to the circumstances in which it is being used.

Argument The reasons given to explain or prove; hence the thread of thought holding a piece of writing together.

Articulate To pronounce words clearly.

Assessment Judgment, weighing up the value of something.

Association The linking of ideas and meaning: Spring is *associated* with joy and renewal.

Aural Connected with hearing, intelligible to the ear.

Board In this case, a number of people appointed to manage an examination or business.

Brackets The punctuation marks ( ) used to separate a group of words: Bill passed in English (as we expected) but failed in French.

Brevity A short or *brief* form of expression: She spoke with admirable *brevity*; her speech was over in five minutes.

Cliché An expression which has lost force through being over-used: He is *exploring every avenue* to find a solution.

Colloquialism An expression used in everyday conversation, rather than in writing.

Colon A stop (:) used to introduce a list or quotation, or to separate two sentences.

Comma A stop (,) used when a very brief pause would be made in reading aloud.

Comparative The form of an adjective or adverb used to compare two things or people or actions: Being old*er*, he works *more* slowly.

Composition A piece of writing made up by the writer and not just copied.

Comprehension The understanding of a piece of writing.Conjunction A linking word: *and, but, because.*

Consonant Any letter of the alphabet except *a, e, i, o, u* and sometimes *y*.

Context In this case, the writing which surrounds a word or phrase.

Dash A stop (–) used to indicate a break in thought, to act as a bracket or to introduce an explanation.

Deduce To reach a conclusion by arguing from something known: She *deduced* from the slime that a snail had passed.

Dialogue The use of direct speech to add life to narrative or description.

Direct speech The actual words of a speaker, shown by quotation marks.

Evaluation Deciding on the worth or *value*, e.g. of an argument.

Exclamation mark A stop (!) used to mark surprise or strong emphasis: Get out!

Fiction A piece of writing made up from the writer's own imagination, such as a novel or short story (as opposed to non-fiction, biography etc.).

'Formula' writing Writing according to a set scheme, without real freshness or originality.

Full stop Used at the end of sentences and after abbreviations, this (.) is the most important of all stops.

Future The part of a verb used to indicate 'time to come' is said to be in the *future*: I *will* go; they *won't* stop me.

Gist The essential part of a statement, book, etc.: The reporter noted the *gist* of the speech.

Grammar The study of words and the ways in which they are used.

Imagery The use of images—mental pictures—in speech or writing: As strong as a horse; You're the cream in my coffee.

Imaginative writing Creative writing that draws up from the imagination.

Imply To suggest in an indirect way: So you're *implying* that I took your umbrella?

Inappropriate (Here) unsuitable in style to the occasion: His 'cheerio' to the chairman of the interviewing panel was *inappropriate*.

Indirect speech The style into which direct speech is turned when reported: 'I'm going,' he said becomes: I heard that *he was going*.

Infer To reach a conclusion by reasoning from facts: I inferred from Sheila's lack of enthusiasm that she didn't like the idea.

Inference See *Infer above*: the conclusion reached.

Inflection (Inflexion) The change made in a word to show its relationship with other words: he, him; they, them, etc. *See* Agreement.

Interjection A single word or phrase, such as 'Rubbish!' etc., interrupting someone.

Intransitive The term applied to verbs which have no object: They *were hurrying;* she *slept* well. *See* transitive.

Inverted commas Also known as quotation marks, their main use is to enclose words actually spoken: 'Anyone in?' he shouted.

Italics sloping letters used for titles of books, etc. and sometimes for emphasis: *This is italicized, that is, printed in italics.*

Journalese The style of writing used in popular newspapers, often using monosyllables, especially in headlines, and a special vocabulary: Show Biz Pay Slash Shock.

Layout Arrangement of material on the printed page; 'plan'.

Lucid Clear and readily intelligible.

Main verb The essential word in a sentence, without which there can be no complete meaning: The train *arrives* at 2.00 p.m.

Metaphor A way of concentrating and adding meaning in which one thing is identified with another: Gwilym was a tall young man aged nearly twenty, with a thin stick of a body and spade-shaped face. You could dig the garden with him. (Dylan Thomas)

Moderator A person appointed to visit schools and ensure that school-based examinations are set and marked at the same level.

Narrative The telling of a story, an experience or an event.

Nominative The subject of a verb is sometimes said to be in the nominative: *Cars* menace our peace; *they*'re a nuisance.

Noun Any word which names something or someone: frog, Jean, bicycle.

Object In grammar, the word or words for the person or thing acted upon by a verb: Jill wrote *pages*, but Jim could find *little* to say.

Objective (adj.) Regarding things from a calm and detached point of view.

Open-ended Planned so as to allow for various different results or conclusions.

Oral Spoken; an *oral* examination tests a candidate's ability to speak.

Paragraph Part of a piece of writing, dealing with one aspect of the main subject.

Passive The form of a verb changed to show that a person or thing is acted on: She *was chosen*, though her wrist *had been sprained* a week before.

Past The form of a verb used to show that the action etc. has already happened: I *went* early, because I *had done* all I could.

Pedantic Fussily careful over details: The language of advertisements enraged him; he was pedantic over such matters.

Phonetic Use of forms of spelling that indicate the actual sounds of words.

Phrase A group of words without a main verb, forming a unit within a sentence: *Travelling light, we reached the top in five hours—quite a reasonable performance.*

Plural The form of a word that expresses more than one: cats, dogs, children.

Possessive A noun in a possessive form tells us that the person or thing referred to owns or is connected with something: *Jane's* bike needs a new tyre.

Prefix An addition at the beginning of a word to alter its meaning: *Pre* added to *arranged* gives the meaning *arranged beforehand*.

Preposition A word that shows the relationship of a noun or pronoun with another word: Nowadays one is free *from* pain *at* the dentist's.

Present The form of a verb indicating that something is going on at the moment is said to be in the present: I work *or* I am working.

Pronoun A word used in place of a noun: *They* were waiting; *which* is right? *I* can't tell *him* from *her*.

Prose Continuous writing without the patterns of rhyme and metre used in poetry.

Quote To repeat part of a passage of writing. (The noun is *quotation*.)

Register In this case, the choice of vocabulary and speech forms for particular circumstances. Children use different *registers* in playground and classroom.

Relevant Connected with the matter being discussed.

Reported speech The style used for recording something said: 'Jill said, "Are you coming, Sue?"' becomes in *reported speech* 'Jill asked Sue if she was coming'.

Root The part of a word on which all variations are based: the root *ject* is found in: abject, dejected, inject, interjection, object, project, reject.

Semicolon The stop (;) between two sentences (about the same subject) that make sense on their own, but are joined to give a long 'two part' sentence. Also to mark off groups of items in a list.

Sentence A group of words that makes complete sense on its own.

Simile A comparison between two things or two actions, connected by 'like', 'as' or 'as if'.

Singular Expressing only one. *See plural.*

Slang A new and lively expression used in conversation, but not normally used in writing, except in letters to friends.

Stanza A verse with two or more lines in poetry.

Stress *See* Accent.

Subject The word or words in a sentence indicating the topic about which something is said: *The castle* was built 800 years ago.

Subjective Regarding things from a personal point of view.

Suffix An addition at the end of a word: weak, weak*ness.*

Superlative *Best, tallest, most expensive* are the superlative forms of adjectives. *See* Comparative.

Syllable The smallest unit of speech. I, you, film are words of one *syllable.* Begin has two; dictionary has four.

Synonym Two or more words with nearly the same meaning are *synonyms:* odour, smell; aged, old, elderly.

Syntax The arrangement of words in phrases and sentences.

Tautology Unnecessary repetition: The floor was wet with water.

Transitive The term applied to verbs which have an object: He *flogged* the boy without mercy. It *fills* the jug right up.

Usage The way in which words are used in a language; forms of language which have become accepted through use. *It's me* is now accepted as correct, though at one time it was not.

Verb A word expressing an action or a state: She *caught* a bus because she *was* in a hurry. All sentences must have a verb.

Verse Poetry; a group of lines in a poem.

Visual Seen with the eye, or in the imagination.

Visualize To see in the mind: *Visualize* the scene!

Vocabulary The range of words used by an individual or group: He has a good *vocabulary;* most occupations have a *vocabulary* of their own.

INDEX